FLAK DODGER

A Story of the 457th Bombardment Group
1943-1945
8th AAF

Lt Col Roland O. Byers
USAFR (RET.)

Roland O. Byers

Pawpaw Press
P.O. Box 9191
Moscow, Idaho 83843

This Book Is Dedicated

To those men of the 457th Bombardment Group
who made the supreme sacrifice by giving
their lives for their country

457th

Lt Col William F. Smith Jr., C.O. 750th Bomb. Sqdn. Air Medal presentation to T/Sgt Radford (Lt Charles Newmeyer assisting) 8 August 1944.

Air Medal

Distinguished Flying Cross

The two medals which most of the combat crew members of the 457th Bomb Group were awarded were the Distinguished Flying Cross and the Air Medal.

Crew members were usually awarded the DFC at the completion of their tour or for displaying exceptional performance or bravery under fire.

The Air Medal was usually awarded to combat crew members for completing five combat missions.

The combat crew member could be awarded an Air Medal and three Clusters (a Cluster was symbolic of a second award of the same medal) and a DFC if he completed a tour of 25 (30 or 35) missions.

 Published in the United States by Pawpaw Press, P.O. Box 9191, Moscow, Idaho 83843

Library of Congress, Card Number 85-60155

ISBN 0-9614563-0-2

Manufactured in the United States of America

Cover and book design by A.K.B. Cathcart
Printed by McNaughton and Gunn

A STORY OF THE 457th BOMB GROUP (H) DURING WORLD WAR II

457th

Long fingers of feathery condensation "con" trails stream revealingly out behind the formation of invading bombers

Acknowledgements

Few events occur during a person's life which leave an imprint on the mind and psyche as indelibly as does a war. As a young boy I sat on the wooden bench in front of the mercantile store in Somerton, Ohio, and intently listened to veterans of World War I tell of their experiences in France. Although at the time only between ten and fifteen years had elapsed since World War I, to me it seemed to have occurred many years before. However, now I have here attempted to recall and document what happened to me and others, 40 years ago.

Time does dim specific events which occurred many years ago. However, with the aid of diaries, newspaper clippings, and help from the 201 files and recollections of many people, events are here recalled and documented. Although while stationed in England we were not permitted to write home about the missions we flew, I did cut from the Armed Forces newspaper, *Stars and Stripes,* news stories about most of the missions on which I flew. My father and later my wife saved all the news clippings and letters which I had written home during World War II.

I also kept a diary of the daily events of the time I spent in the service during World War II. Possibly because I had read from the diary and looked at the many pictures I had saved, I had not forgotten the events that had occurred 40 years ago, some of which I have documented here.

There are included in this book events provided by many other members of the 457th Bombardment Group, men to whom I am deeply indebted for their help in making this book a story about more than just my own experiences. To Clayton E. Bejot, Thomas A. Goff, Clarence E. Schuchmann, William J.P. Meng, J. "Mac" Dickinson, Harold W. Wiseman, Jerome Silverman, Marshall Sumner, Clyde B. Knipfer, Charles E. Newmeyer, Charles R. Blackwell, William J. Morrow, Ralph E. Windell, Oscar Stauff, and Duane Zemper, I wish to extend my appreciation for their contributions to this book.

While I did not originally set out to write a history of the 457th Bomb. Group, the book did turn out to be more a history than a single story.

Contents

8th AAF shoulder insignia

Prologue

It is the suddenness that characterizes the air war five miles above mother earth. Life seems almost serene there in the frosty sunlight, your senses lulled into false security by the synchronous beat of the four whirling yellow-tipped propeller blades.

Long fingers of feathery condensation trails stream revealingly out behind the formation of invading bombers—marking the intruders' trail across the sky to the Luftwaffe pilots if today they choose to defend their homeland. For far beneath the layer of fluffy white clouds lurk echelons of deadly enemy fighters as well as phalanxes of anti-aircraft "flak" guns.

High above the bombers against the azure blue sky are contrails formed by "little friends"—hundreds of United States VIII Fighter Command escort fighters—shuttling in and out along the bomber stream, S'ing to slow their progress along the parade of bombers. The fighters are waiting to "pounce on" from the "high ground" any attempt by the Luftwaffe to attack their charges. It is almost as if the bombers were serving as bait to attract the Luftwaffe into an air battle—and so it was!

For over the interphone comes the scratchy high-pitched voice of the tail gunner—"Bandits at seven o'clock low!" Suddenly your senses are shocked back to reality—the lump that was your stomach hardens—if you are fortunate and have a gun to fire, you grab the cold handles and search out in the immense space the silhouette you would recognize to be that of an Me 109 or a FW 190.

Over the VHF radio frequency can be heard pleas by an unfortunate bomber crew which has been shot up and is calling for aid from escort fighters to shepherd them back to friendly environs.

Will your turn be next? Will the swarm of fighters decide your formation is loose, that you cannot defend yourself effectively? Then comes the answer to your question as the vibration of the guns in a turret travels through the structure of the airplane. The tail gunner calls out—enemy bandits attacking in waves from seven o'clock low. The ball turret gunner calls out—fighters from five o'clock low. All guns that will bear are swung toward the rear of the plane. Where are the "little friends"? Why aren't they protecting the bombers? In fact they are, but the Luftwaffe is up to its old tricks of concentrating a large number of fighters in one area, more than the thinly distributed fighter cover can counter in a short time.

The "snowball" bursts of 20mm cannon fire explode within and around the formation of bombers. Three B-17s drop back out of the protective environs of the formation, victims of cannonfire. A fire flares around the outboard engine of your wingman. The beleaguered airplane slowly drops back. You watch and wonder—Will the crew bail out? Will the airplane explode? The airplane now peels up and away and dives—under control—the pilot attempting to blow out the fire. You wonder as to the fate of the crew.

And then as suddenly as it began the enemy "bandits" are gone, chased away by friendly escorting fighters, but not before they—the Luftwaffe—had collected their toll for the intrusion into their homeland.

The pilot calls on interphone—check in—all crew members answer the call. You and those on "your" crew will continue to the target, drop your load of bombs, and return to base to fight again another day.

The impersonal news release would say: April 9, 1944—Today 399 heavy bombers of the 8th Army Air Force made the deepest penetration of the war into the German Reich.... Our bombs plastered the primary target, an air field in Gdynia, Poland.... Thirty-two of our bombers did not return to base....

But to you the results of this mission were more than a set of statistics. The crews of three of those thirty-two lost bombers were friends of yours, friends with whom you have bunked for what seems like an eternity of time in this unreal artificial environment. Friendships were kindled by a common purpose in only a relatively short calendar time, to a depth which in your lifetime would never again be attained. That purpose: to pursue and satisfy your personal obligation to your country but yet to survive to complete the tour of twenty-five missions to return to the United States where you could once again call your life your own and not be called upon each day to fly through a hail of 88mm anti-aircraft flak and 20mm cannon fire. Some of the 320 men alluded to by the news release were made prisoners of war, if they were fortunate enough to parachute to earth, while others were killed in the air battle and made the ultimate sacrifice by giving their lives for their country.

Prelude I

As first conceived in January 1942 the 8th Army Air force was created to support a planning version of the invasion of North Africa.

The 8th Army Air Force as then constituted included the VIII Bomber Command, VIII Fighter Command, VIII Air Force Base Command, Headquarters Squadron and was formed on 19 January 1942 at Langley Field, Virginia.

The Combat units assigned to the 8th AAF included the 17th Bombardment Group (M), the 48th Bombardment Group (L), the 20th and 52nd Pursuit Groups, the 68th Observation Group, and the 7th Photo Squadron.

By the end of March 1942 the specific North Africa invasion plan for which the 8th AAF was created had been abandoned and all the Combat units assigned to the 8th AAF were transferred to the Third Air Force.

Major General Carl A. (Tooey) Spaatz, Commanding General of the Army Air Force in Great Britain (AAFIB), requested that the 8th AAF, now a taskless Air Force, be assigned to AAFIB. The War Department agreed to the request by General Spaatz and the 8th AAF was transferred to the AAFIB and given the task of the strategic bombing of Germany.

The 8th AAF was officially activated in England on 18 June 1942 with Headquarters located at Bushey Park, Teddington, southwest of London. It was assigned the code name "Widewing."

Brigadier General Ira C. Eaker was selected as Commander of the VIII Bomber Command with Headquarters in Buckinghamshire, thirty miles northwest of London. The VIII Bomber Command was assigned the code name "Pinetree."

By April 1942, a number of Combat units had been assigned to the 8th AAF. These included 23 heavy bomber groups, four medium bomber groups, five light bomber groups, four dive bomber groups, and thirteen pursuit groups. Many of these groups would subsequently be reassigned to other budding Air Forces around the world and would never be transferred to England as part of the 8th AAF.

In anticipation of the United States establishing an Air Force in England, Brigadier General Ira C. Eaker was assigned to England to observe the functions of the Royal Air Force (RAF). He was charged by General Henry (Hap) Arnold, Commanding General of the United States Army Air Force, to prepare for the eventual arrival of the 8th AAF in England.

The time span between conception and arrival of elements of the 8th AAF in England came painfully slow. General Arnold and the War Department planners projected the build-up of United States aircraft and personnel to be in the order of fifteen heavy bomber groups by July 1942, thirty-five groups by November 1942 and sixty-six groups by March 1943. The actual strength of the 8th AAF in England by June 1942 was 1871 personnel and zero bombers and fighters.

Much of the failure to achieve the projected numbers of men and aircraft was due in part to the needs of other Air Forces throughout the world where demand was deemed more critical at that time than were the needs of the 8th AAF.

The British criticized this diversion of equipment and men to other theaters of war and were concerned about the United States' commitment to the European war in which the German Air Force was devastating the cities and industrial machine of the United Kingdom.

In May 1942, 39 officers and 348 enlisted men reached England to join the hollow shell command of the 8th AAF. These officers and men were the first of the many thousands which would ultimately compose the greatest strategic bombing force ever assembled. Before the European war was terminated the 8th AAF would consist of over 2000 heavy bombers and 1000 fighters.

As would be the pattern, the ground echelons of each unit were transported to England by ship and the flying personnel flew their aircraft to their bases in England. The ground echelons of the 97th Bombardment Group (Heavy), the 1st and 31st Fighter Groups, the 60th Transport Group, and the supporting 5th Air Depot Group boarded the British luxury vessel (now converted to troop transport) the Queen Elizabeth at New York on 4 June 1942 and arrived in England six days later. The 1st and 31st Fighter Groups, which, while in the United States, had been equipped with P-38s and P-39s respectively, were transferred without their aircraft and were equipped with English Spitfires when they arrived in England.

Meanwhile the flying echelon of the 97th Bombardment Group

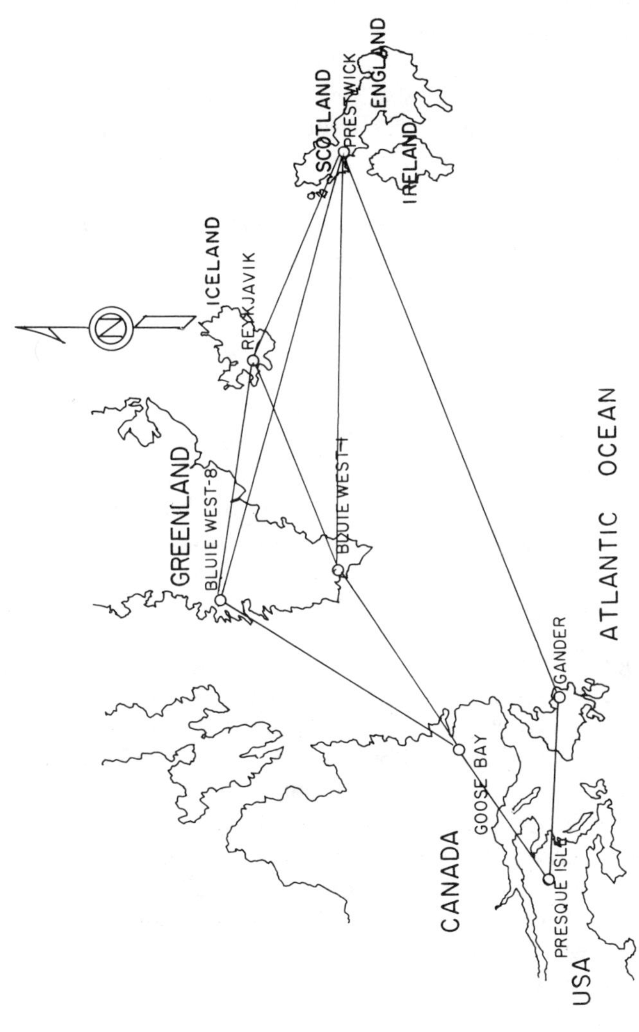
ICELAND
REYKJAVIK
SCOTLAND
PRESTWICK
ENGLAND
IRELAND
GREENLAND
BLUIE WEST-8
BLUIE WEST-1
ATLANTIC OCEAN
GANDER
GOOSE BAY
CANADA
PRESQUE ISLE
USA
NORTH ATLANTIC FERRY ROUTE
ROLAND O. BYERS 1984

(H) equipped with B-17-E four-engine aircraft made preparations at Presque Isle, Maine, to fly the North Atlantic to England. The B-17s, along with the P-38s being flown to England, formed into elements of one B-17 and four P-38s, the B-17s providing the navigation and escort for the fighter planes. Eighteen B-17s departed Presque Isle on 23 June 1942 and flew the 569 statute miles to Goose Bay, Newfoundland. Three days later all departed Goose Bay and flew the 1002 statute miles to Bluie West 8, or the 776 statute miles to Bluie West 1, Greenland. Nine reached their destination safely. Six, however, were forced by weather to return to Goose Bay, while three crash-landed along the coast of Greenland (the crews were all later rescued). The B-17s and P-38s which had reached Bluie 1 and Bluie 8 continued the flight and the first aircraft arrived in Prestwick, Scotland, on 1 July 1942.

Such was the beginning of what would become almost daily flights of long range bombers from the United States to England during the next three years.

By the end of August 1942, 119 B-17s, 164 P-38s, and 103 C-47s had crossed the Atlantic Ocean to England by the North Atlantic Ferry Route. The planes had been flown for the most part by their own combat crews. The loss rate of 5.2% over the difficult route was much lower than had been previously estimated.

* * * * *

Providing the bases from which the combat units would operate, the British would eventually build and turn over to the United States to use, seventy-seven stations with sixty-six A/Fs and eighty-two operational and Hq. groups, most of which were located in East Anglia, an area north and east of London.

Support for the Combat Units was as critical as were the bases. Modification and maintenance Depots were established at Langford Lodge, Ireland, and Wharton, England. Temporary use of Burtonwood, an RAF Depot, was made until the two Depots were completed in October 1942 and January 1943 respectively. Eventually Burtonwood itself would be transferred to United States' exclusive use. Other support bases would be established throughout England as the 8th AAF grew in size.

The initial elements of the 8th AAF arrived in England ill-equipped and relatively untrained for the demanding high altitude bombing missions in which they proposed to engage. General Spaatz considered, however, the advisability of having the show of commitment of combat units to the European war more important than their ability to function effectively.

The air crews of the 97th Bombardment Group (H) were not adequately trained to fly combat missions into enemy territory when the group arrived in England. The pilots had received very little instruction and training in high altitude formation flying; the gunners were inadequately trained to operate the turrets on the B-17E; the radio men had not been trained to send or receive Morse Code and were unaware of British radio prodecures; and the navigators were not trained in the use of electronic forms of navigation such as Gee and H_2X, aids used by the British.

The premise on which the 8th AAF would perform the daylight high altitude strategic precision bombing was based upon the need for a compact formation of bombers. This compact formation would provide concentrated firepower for mutual protection against enemy

Bains

British "Spitfire" in foreground. "Handley-Page" British bomber in rear.
Photograph taken at Wittering RAF base near Glatton, 1944.

fighters, as well as forming a compact bomb pattern on selected targets as all bombardiers in the formation dropped their bombs simultaneously with those dropped from the lead ship.

General Eaker, VIII Bomber Command, Commander, learned of these shortcomings and established a training program to overcome the deficiencies. With the help of the British and with American observation of British procedures and techniques, a training program was developed. Pilots, navigators, radio men, gunners, and bombardiers were included in the training program. Support personnel: intelligence, maintenance, ordinance, chemical, and medical were also included in the training program. Pilots spent many hours practicing high altitude formation flying; radio men learned the Morse Code; navigators were instructed in the use of Gee, and selected navigators were instructed in the operation of H_2X (the radar used for bombing through a layer of clouds which obscured a target); gunners were instructed on how to identify and fire on an enemy fighter as it attacked on a pursuit curve. This training was achieved within a relatively short period of time in spite of inclement weather and primitive maintenance conditions.

The VIII fighter groups also had their problems, as did the bomber groups. The change in equipment, trading P-39s for Spitfires, compounded the problems. But they too overcame their deficiencies by a concentrated training program and by flying combat missions as wing men with experienced RAF British and Canadian pilots.

Although other fighter groups had arrived in Britain, by the middle of August 1942 the 31st Group was the only United States fighter group combat ready. The small number of fighters from the 31st Fighter Group was inadequate to fly cover for the bombers of the VIII Bomber Command, for to operate over enemy territory without adequate fighter escort would surely result in unacceptable losses.

By mid-August the crews of the VIII Bomber Command were declared "combat ready." They had received training in high altitude formation flying, navigation, bombing, radio, and gunnery essential to successful high altitude aerial warfare.

The flying crews had learned how to survive in the foreign, high altitude environment in which they must operate. They learned to use life sustaining oxygen without which for even 30 seconds a person could lapse into unconsciousness. To prevent the loss of life of any crew member due to failure of his oxygen system, a regimen of periodic crew member oxygen checks was established. On many

Barr

P-39
Airplane in which many of the pilots of the VIII Fighter Command trained

crews the co-pilot called for an oxygen check on the interphone at regular intervals. They learned to guard against frost bite in temperatures that would reach 50° and 60° below zero. They also learned how to evade enemy fighter attacks by taking evasive action, by changing altitude, side slipping, and, if alone, even turning toward the attacking fighter, to alter the pursuit curve the fighter must follow to shoot down a bomber with gunfire. They also learned about the anti-aircraft "flak" the enemy shot at the invading bombers.

The 97th Bombardment Group (H) based at Polebrook was declared "combat ready" and, after the usual dry runs and "scrubbed" missions due to weather, an alert was called on the night of 16 August 1942 and a field order was received for a mission on the following day.

Major General Carl A. (Tooey) Spaatz, the 8th AAF Commanding General, was at Grafton-Underwood to watch this historical first 8th AAF heavy bomber mission. Selected as the primary target was the railroad marshalling yard in Rouen-

Sotteville, France. Eighteen B-17E bombers were launched at 1539 hours on 17 August 1942 and assembled in formation for the mission. Twelve of the airplanes would attack the marshalling yard and six airplanes would fly a diversion mission along the French coast. General Eaker flew in the airplane named "Yankee Doodle" and led the second flight of six bombers.

The bombing results of the mission were considered good, with bombs striking in the immediate vicinity of the aiming points. There were no losses of aircraft and the flak was ineffective. RAF fighters escorted the bombers to the target and others met the formation as they withdrew. Three enemy fighters, ME-109s, attacked the bombers but did little damage. All aircraft returned to Base.

The first 8th AAF mission did little damage to the enemy war effort but did incite confidence in the American air crews and did quell a rising doubt by the British as to the suitability of the B-17 for daylight bombing and also its ability to penetrate enemy territory without prohibitive losses of aircraft and crews.

Whereas the British bombed targets at night, and flew individually both in and out of enemy territory, much doubt had been cast by both official British government circles and by the British press as to the suitability of the B-17 for the job the Americans had envisioned. The British would, by jove, relegate the B-17 to ocean patrol duties rather than strategic bombing.

Strategic precision bombing of enemy targets could, as proposed by American planners, be more effective if performed during daylight hours when individual targets could be seen and bombs be dropped by the effective Norden bomb sight on a specific small target. This concept was different than the bombing method utilized by the British, who used night, pattern bombing. British Pathfinder airplanes dropped flares in the selected target area and the following bombers dropped bombs in the vicinity of the flares, or on explosions and fires in the area, depending on the large numbers—a pattern—of bombs to strike the selected target.

The heavy bombers, the B-17s and B-24s, in the 8th AAF would fly 512 missions between the first mission into enemy-held territory on 17 August 1942 and the last combat mission on 25 April 1945.

The 8th AAF launched 1000 heavy bombers on a single mission for the first time on 20 February 1944 and launched 2000 heavy bombers on a single mission on 24 December 1944.

The bombardiers would drop nearly 1,000,000 (640,000 by

B-17s) tons of bombs on targets in Germany and occupied territory; 4,750 B-17s in all theatres of war during WWII would be lost to enemy action, weather, collisions, mechanical failure, and being interned in the neutral countries, Sweden and Switzerland. Heavy bomber gunners would claim 11,481 German aircraft destroyed.

The development of the long-range fighter, the P-51 "Mustang," made it possible for the heavy bombers to penetrate any corner of the German homeland without suffering prohibitive losses to aircraft and flying personnel.

At the end of the war, it was the decision of the "United States Strategic Bombing Survey": The victory in the air was complete and allied air power had been decisive in the war in Western Europe.

457th

Wendover Field, Utah 1943. Note the almost sterile desert landscape

Prelude II

The 457th Bombardment Group (H) came into existence under General Order number 78, Headquarters, Second Air Force, Fort George Wright, Washington, section number 1, paragraph number 1, per the following action:

> Pursuant to instruction contained in restricted War Department letter AC-322 dated May 18, 1943, OB-1-AFRPG-M; 19 May 1943, Subject, Constitution and activation of certain Army Air Force units, the following units having been constituted and assigned to the Second Air Force are activated as indicated.

Hq. 457th Bombardment Group (H) and the 748th, 479th, 750th, and 751st Squadrons. The home station to be Geiger Field, Spokane, Washington, on this date 1 July 1943.

Part of General Order number 78 was by command of Major General Johnson by Aubry N. Moore, Col. U.S.C. Chief of Staff.

To implement the order, a cadre of officers and enlisted men was formed from personnel of the 395th Bombardment Group (H) located at Ephrata Army Air Base, Ephrata, Washington. Col. Herbert E. Rice was designated as commanding officer of the group.

The 457th Cadre was transferred to Camp Rapid Army Air Base, Rapid City, South Dakota, and reported to the 17th Bombardment Training Wing for combat training.

Although Geiger Field, Spokane, Washington, had been designated as home base for the 457th Bomb. Group (H), the group would never be stationed there.

The base at Ephrata, in 1943, was a miserable place to live. The Army Air Force lived up to its reputation of assigning combat crews to bases located where the weather was miserable and having as few distractions as possible. The base was located in what was known as the Columbia River Basin. The land was covered with sagebrush, the annual rainfall being a scant 6" annually, as the soaring Cascade Mountains rose up to the west of the basin with peaks rising to 14,410 feet (Mt. Rainier) blocking the moisture-laden Pacific Ocean winds. The dry sandy soil was punctuated with outcrops of black basalt rock, which reflected the hot July sun, while the continuous wind drifted the dry sandy soil across the runways and taxi strips.

In later years after dams were built in the nearby Columbia River and the water pumped into the maze of irrigation canals, the once almost useless land would sprout bumper crops of potatoes, corn, alfalfa hay, and wheat. The transition would seem unbelievable to those who in 1943 had faced the blowing sand on the taxi strips as they hurriedly climbed into the hatches of the B-17s to escape the eye-smarting sand.

Making sure the troops were not distracted in their training program, the 457th Cadre was transferred to Camp Rapid AAB, Rapid City, South Dakota. Here the troops saw, as they flew east, the beautiful ponderosa pine covered Black Hills and on one of the prominent peaks, Mount Rushmore, Gutzon Borglum had carved the likenesses of four of the United States' greatest presidents, George Washington, Abraham Lincoln, Thomas Jefferson, and Theodore Roosevelt from the grey granite of the precipitous mountain.

Nestled in the foothills of the Black Hills was the beautiful town of Rapid City, built along a clear sparkling trout stream which cascaded down from the hills. The panorama there before the members of the 457th was however deceiving for 10 miles to the east of the verdant pine covered "hills" the troops found a tent city—Camp Rapid AAB. Amenities in July 1943 were nil—the Army Air Force had not relented. The troops would plead for combat to get out of the miserable conditions under which they would live.

The continuous wind, averaging thirteen miles an hour, blew the tumbleweeds over the countryside first to the north and the next day to the south. In July and August the temperature in South Dakota is fierce, climbing above the 100 degree mark day after day. Even though the wind is debilitating, when it ceased to blow the heat is unbearable.

Jackrabbits on the runways were a menance, distracting the pilots in landings and takeoffs. Rattlesnakes made an unwary step disastrous.

One had to admit that the climate tended to make the residents a hardy folk, for those of us who departed Rapid City AAB in December found that, even though the summers were unbearably hot, the winters were worse, with temperatures dropping to 30 degrees below zero not uncommon. One would literally get lost in a blizzard between the airplane on the taxi strip and the operations office.

The 457th B.G. Cadre which set up shop at Camp Rapid on 9 July 1943 was composed principally of administrative personnel and was a hollow shell of what an operational Combat Bombing Group would eventually be.

One hundred and thirty officers and enlisted men on the 457th B.G. Cadre were ordered under provisions of Special Order Number 28, Paragraph 2 and 3, Headquarters 17th Bombardment Wing, AAB Camp Rapid, Rapid City, South Dakota, 29 July 1943 to temporary duty at Orlando, Florida, to attend the Army Air Force's school of applied tactics. The troops departed Camp Rapid and arrived at their destination on 5 August 1943. During the temporary duty the flying personnel participated in seven over-water flights from Brooksville Field, Florida.

Just prior to the temporary duty in Orlando, Florida, Lt. Col. Hugh Wallace replaced Col. Rice as commanding officer of the 457th B.G.

On 29 August 1943, upon completion of the course the troops departed Orlando, Florida, and returned to Camp Rapid AAB, the flight echelon traveling by air and the ground echelon traveling by rail.

The 457th B.G. Cadre continued training for only a short period after returning to Camp Rapid AAB from Orlando, Florida. On 23 October 1943 the Cadre was transferred back to Ephrata AAB, Ephrata, Washington, per Special Order 291, paragraph 13, dated 23 October 1943, Headquarters, Camp Rapid AAB, Rapid City, South Dakota, the change of station to participate in combat training Phases I and II.

In October before the 457th B.G. Cadre departed for Ephrata AAB, the personnel strength of the Cadre was 98 officers and 694 enlisted men. This strength constituted only 26% of the authorized officer strength 98/370 and 42% of the authorized enlisted strength 694/1638. The composition of the Cadre was for the most part not flying personnel but rather administrative officers and enlisted men. The 72 (approximately) combat crews which would join the group at Ephrata AAB and at Wendover AAB were at this time training at other bases.

When the 457th Cadre arrived at Ephrata AAB on 28 October they were met there by the first of two groups of combat crews that would eventually fill the authorized strength of the 457th B.G. The crews are listed in the appendix.

The training program in Phase I and Phase II were intended to weld the 10 man combat crew into a fighting unit, each man to become as familiar with the equipment he would operate in combat as possible. The pilots were trained to be able to fly the airplane under all conditions, an ability much of which came from long hours of flying, many take-offs and landings, both day and night, and flying on instruments both in the airplane and instrument flying practice in the link trainer. The two pilots were to establish a routine—one to help the other. To work in concert with the bombardier on "bomb runs," it was essential for the pilots to be as familiar with the B-17 under conditions as nearly like those they would encounter in combat as possible. The pilots must learn to fly formation with other B-17s, to tuck the wing of the airplane into the space behind and just above or below the wing of the leader of an element (flight) of six airplanes. Tight formation flying was the means of protection, of providing a concentrated defense of multiple .50-calibre machine guns squirting hot lead at attacking German Luftwaffe fighters—single engine Messerschmitt (Me) 109s, Focke Wulf (FW) 190s, and twin-engined Me-110s and Junkers (JU) 88s.

A tight formation also provided the platform from which the tight pattern of bombs could be dropped on the selected target. Strategic daylight bombing was a synchronized system as all aircraft in a formation—a group, combat box (18 aircraft), a squadron (12 aircraft), or a flight (6 aircraft)—bombed at the same time, usually at the moment the lead bombardier in the lead ship dropped his bombs. The bombardiers in the other aircraft in the formation would "toggle" or salvo their bombs. To toggle is to string out individual bombs and to salvo is to drop them all at once.

The navigator is responsible for plotting the course the airplane must follow to any required destination. This could be accomplished by the pilot, merely by flying the predetermined compass course to the intended destination were it not for the wind. The wind causes the airplane to drift either to the left or right of course depending on the direction it is blowing from at any one time. The ground speed at which the airplane will travel to its destination is determined by adding or subtracting the speed vector of the wind from the indicated air speed. Altitude and temperature are factors which change the speed of an airplane and must be included in the calculation to determine the estimated time of arrival (ETA) of the airplane at its destination.

The direction and force of the wind can be determined by following a plotted compass course for a period of time and at the end of that time measuring the distance traveled away from the intended course. This resultant will provide the navigator with a correction factor – the speed and direction of the wind – which he can apply to the next "leg" of his course and thus arrive at the prescribed destination.

The unknown factor – wind, direction, and velocity – must be calculated by determining where the airplane is located relative to the desired destination at the end of a given unit of time. This can be determined by pilotage, placing the airplane at a given point relative to a position on a map showing geographical features representing those on the ground. To accomplish this – pilotage – the earth must be visible. While flying over water pilotage is useless, for the position must then be determined either by electronic means (radio beams) or by celestial navigation.

Radio beams are useful in a non-combat area but are essentially useless in combat, as are many other electronic navigation systems. Gee, Loran, and Shoran can all be altered or jammed by the enemy and are unreliable and of little use.

Locating one's position on the earth (latitude and longitude) by celestial navigation is possible by determining the elevation of a star, the sun, or the moon above the horizon from a given location (line of position) at a given instant of time. Combining the line(s) of position of two or more stars adjusted to a common time will determine for the navigator a "fix" – a position. With a series of positions – fixes – the track or course an airplane is flying will determine wind direction and speed and thus the ground speed and course to a destination can be determined and an ETA specified.

The navigator becomes more proficient as do the pilots of a heavy bomber by practice. Phase I and Phase II combat training provided cross country missions during which time the navigator gained this expertise.

Phase training also provided other members of the crew – the bombardier, the engineer, the radio man, and the gunners – with practice and experience. Knowledge of their equipment through practice and use provided all crew members with the confidence to perform their jobs efficiently.

The accurate placement of the bombs on the selected target was the responsibility of the bombardier and the ability to perform that function effectively demanded a "cool head" and considerable dexterity on his part.

The bombsight, either a Norden or Sperry, was a precision instrument which computed the bomb release point along the bomb run, between the IP (initial point) and the target. As with all computers, however, the bombsight would only function correctly if the data entered into the sight were correct for the given situation, i.e., wind drift, temperature, altitude, and the ballistics of the specific type of bomb considered for programming the bomb. With the information entered into the sight, the bombardier could set the cross hairs of the telescope (bombsight) on the target and proceed to "kill" course and rate (maintain the cross hairs on the target while the aircraft was traveling through the air). When actuated through the automatic pilot of the aircraft, the bombsight guided the aircraft toward the target.

As with all crew functions, a steady hand, whether flying through "flak" or being attacked by enemy fighters, was necessary to perform the job effectively.

The bombardier, possibly more so than any other crew member, knew he would be performing his job during what was the most fearsome part of the mission. Targets were usually located in large population areas and were defended with many flak batteries.

Although weather conditions were poor for flying during the months of October and November, the combat crews at Ephrata AAB satisfied the requirement of Phase I and II. Certainly they were thoroughly trained in the ground school portions of the phases. The inclement weather did contribute to the loss and resultant death of six officers and one enlisted crew member who chose to crash-land in their disabled airplane. Four enlisted crewmen parachuted to safety.

Married members of the Group had difficulty finding places for wives and families to live during the two-month stay at Ephrata. However, some found apartments for family members in nearby Wenatchee, Washington (53 miles away). Troop morale was maintained by weekend passes. Some of the troops traveled by train to cities as far away as Seattle (168 miles) and Spokane (114 miles), Washington, for recreation and to sow a few wild oats before their imminent departure for overseas and combat.

On 2 December 1943 the 457th Bombardment Group (H) departed Ephrata AAB for Wendover Field, Utah, per the following authority: Special Order 330, Paragraph 1, Headquarters Ephrata AAB, Ephrata, Washington, dated 26 November 1943.

The arrival of the 457th B.G. at Wendover Field, Utah, for Phase III Training on 4 December 1943 coincided with the arrival of the 36 combat crews of the Hutchison Provisional Group (H.P.G.), which were assigned to the 457th to fill the T.O. and bring the group up to authorized strength (listed in the appendix). Before arriving at Wendover Field, the Hutchison Provisional Group had traveled a route exactly opposite that of the 457th B.G. – created at Ephrata AAB on 14 October 1943 per S.O. 287, Hq. Ephrata AAB, Ephrata, Washington, 395th Bomb. Group. The 36 crews of the Provisional Group were transferred to Rapid City AAB, Rapid City, South Dakota (name changed from Camp Rapid), and arrived there on 17 October 1943, eleven days before the 457th departed the same base for Ephrata AAB. The 36 crews of the H.P.G. completed Phase I and II combat training at Rapid City AAF during the next six weeks.

Weather at Rapid City AAB was relenting, albeit cold during the period and the crews completed phase training in propitious time.

Many of the crew members of the Provisional Group found Rapid City to be an excellent military town with treatment by the residents to be very hospitable. Some, including the author, met young women who eventually became their wives. The author married Elaine Maxine Hohenberger a year later while on R and R in the United States between tours of combat.

The officers club in the Alex Johnson Hotel became the local watering hole and is remembered by many with fond memories.

Crew number 21 – Robert M. Krumm's crew of which the author was navigator – developed during the few short weeks while at Rapid City AAB into an excellent crew with considerable expertise and were soon well prepared for combat as they envisioned it.

Orders were received on 30 November 1943 for the Hutchison Provisional Group to proceed to Wendover Field, Wendover, Utah, and join the 457th Bombardment Group (H). This order: S.O. 329; Paragraph 24; Hq. Rapid City AAB, Rapid City, South Dakota.

The 36 combat crews arrived at Wendover Field on 2 December 1943 by rail. Some of the crews who had been transported in the same railroad car as had a crew member diagnosed to have contracted meningitis were quarantined at the gunnery range on the mountain above the air base. Those not quarantined joined their assigned units of the 457th and started their Phase III combat training.

Phase III training was accomplished in good time, due in part to the relatively good weather which prevailed during the stay at Wendover Field. This expertise resulted in a timely decision to ship the group overseas.

The training program was disrupted at 23 December 1943 when two aircraft collided in mid-air and one crew—four officers and four enlisted men—fell to their death. The pilot of the other crew managed to bring his aircraft back to base and land without loss to any of the crew.

Combat aircraft were assigned to crews and orders were issued for the 457th B.G. to proceed to Grand Island AAB for POM (Preparations, overseas movement), per S.O. 363 dtd 29 December 1943, Par. 4, Headquarters AAB Wendover Field, Utah.

Not all crews were assigned aircraft as not enough new B-17G aircraft were available to equip all crews at the time the orders were issued and some crews traveled to Grand Island AAB by rail. One of these crews was that of 2nd Lt. Robert M. Krumm and the author.

Those traveling by rail departed Wendover Field, Utah, at 1730 26 December 1943. The memories of Wendover Field would be similar to those of Ephrata AAB and Moses Lake AAB. The Army Air Force had placed the base in a location where there were few distractions—in a desert—and the urge to get on to the war was welcomed.

The Air Echelon remained at Wendover Field until 4 January 1944, forced to remain there because of inclement weather. The new olive drab B-17G aircraft manned by crews eager to try their new wings departed individually from Wendover Field, their destination Grand Island AAB, on the 4th of January. Weather caused all but six aircraft to land at air bases throughout the Midwest, and not at Grand Island AAB, their intended destination. On the flight one of the original model crews, that of Lt. Hugh R. Ashby, crashed; six of the crew were killed and five bailed out and parachuted to safety.

On 4 January 1943 Lt. Col. James R. Luper, Jr., assumed command of the 457th Bombardment Group (H), replacing Lt. Col. Hugh O. Wallace who had commanded the 457th during Phase Training.

Lt. Col. Luper was a 1938 graduate of the United States Military

Academy at West Point and had selected the Army Air Force as the service in which he chose to serve. Previous military experience before appointment as commander of a combat unit had been in the Training Command.

Luper adhered to the tenets which he had learned in the Military Academy and administered the 457th Group as a disciplinarian.

These tenets were not always accepted carte blanche by the converted civilian soldiers: the farmers, the businessmen, the college students, the salesmen, the policemen, the mechanics, and the teachers who made up the combat crews and ground echelon of the group. There were few who would count him as an effective commander. Better had he led the group by example and not bullied the men by disciplinary action.

Luper was not a commander who would consider any reason valid for a man not to perform a given order. In his book, there were no excuses. Empathy for his fellow man was not part of the woof in his cloth. He was aloof and unapproachable to most of the men in his command.

By 12 January 1944 the 457th Bombardment Group had passed POM (Preparation overseas movement) with flying colors and was cleared by the 21st Bombardment Wing to proceed to the European Theatre of Operations (ETO) to join the 8th Army Air Force in its assault on Adolf Hitler's "Festung Europa."

On 17 January 1944 the flying echelon manned their B17G combat aircraft and flew northeast toward the North Atlantic ferry route, some aircraft landing at Presque Isle, Maine, and others at Grenier Field, Manchester, New Hampshire. Gander Lake, Newfoundland, was the next step and from there across the formidable North Atlantic ferry route. The route tested the ability and training of both the pilots and the navigators. The navigators now utilized the training they had received in celestial navigation, navigating by the stars, to arrive at their destination.

All the aircraft succeeded in crossing the Atlantic and landed in Europe, some at Prestwick, Scotland, others at Nutts Corner, Northern Ireland, and yet others at Valley Airdrome in Wales. However, two aircraft crash-landed at Nutts Corners, those piloted by Lt. Donald G. Karr and Lt. Tracy E. Geiger. None of the members of either crew were seriously injured in the landings and the crews eventually arrived at Glatton, albeit minus a couple of B-17G aircraft.

The combat crews had all arrived at Station 130—Glatton AAB—by 1 February 1944 except that piloted by Major Henry B.

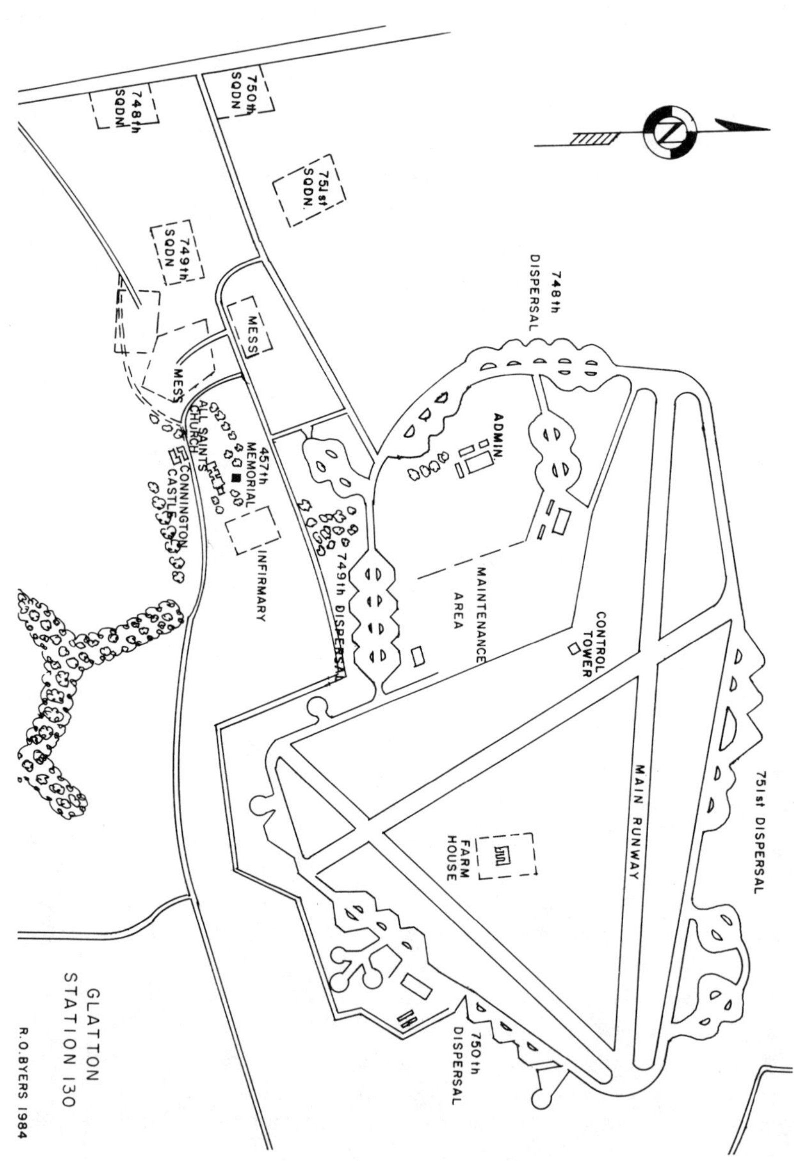
748th SQDN
750th SQDN
751st SQDN.
749th SQDN
MESS
MESS
ALL SAINTS CHURCH
CONNINGTON CASTLE
457th MEMORIAL
INFIRMARY
749th DISPERSAL
ADMIN
748th DISPERSAL
MAINTENANCE AREA
CONTROL TOWER
MAIN RUNWAY
FARM HOUSE
751st DISPERSAL
750th DISPERSAL
N
GLATTON
STATION 130
R.O.BYERS 1984

Wilson, which arrived three weeks later. Station 130 – APO 557 – Glatton AAB would be home for more than a year and one-half for the permanent party – the ground echelon and a few of the flying personnel.

Glatton AAB was located in the County of Huntingdonshire in what is known as East Anglia, England. The elevation of the country is low – 20 feet above sea level – and is flat. The "Fens" are a good farming country and where well drained raises excellent crops.

At 52° 27′ 53″ N latitude, 00° 15′ 00″ W longitude, the base was about 60 miles north of London. Connington was the nearest village but the name conflicted with the name of another air base so Glatton, another small nearby village, was selected as the name for the base.

The base had been built as an Royal Air Force (RAF) airdrome but was turned over to the United States as one of the 66 the 8th Air

457th (Zemper)

USAAF Glatton Air Base 1944-45

457th
View of Glatton AAF Base from Connington Tower

457th (Dickinson)
Col. James R. Luper, Commanding Officer 457th Bomb. Group

457th (Bains)

Signal square, located in front of the control tower at Glatton AAF Base

457th (Dickinson)

Connington Castle (Has been demolished since World War II)

Force would eventually occupy with combat organizations.

Almost a mile square, the base is bounded on the east by the L.N.E.R. Railroad. The old Roman Road to Peterborough—Highway A-1—bounds the west side of the base. To the north is Glatton Lane and Holme Brook. To the south is Connington Lane and there too trickles Connington Brook. At the southeast corner is the small hamlet of Connington, Connington Castle, and Holy Cross Church.

Difficult to locate from the air because of the large number of airfields in the vicinity, land marks used by aircrews were the canals which ran northeast into "The Wash" and the tall chimneys of the brick factory about 7 miles to the north. The main L.N.E.R. Railroad was of some use, but the country is criss-crossed by many railroads and railroads all look alike from the air—only their direction appears different. Electronic devices— "Gee"—were useful when the visibility was low, an atmospheric condition which existed a large percentage of the time. The navigator could set the coordinates of "electronic pulses" of the end of the runway on the Gee set and, upon return to the base, he could "home in" on a line of position—LOP—and thereby locate the field precisely. Wooded areas were printed on the pilotage maps and were shaped exactly as they existed. Holme Woods, for example, located just north of the air base, was of some help in locating the base on clear days.

The living quarters, places of work, hospital, and latrines were all Quonset huts—quickly erected metal buildings, poorly insulated and poorly heated, the heater being either a 10" diameter brick lined coke burner or a sheetmetal stove. The ration of coke or coal was not adequate to take the bite out of the cold. The troops cut down the King's trees, burned packing boxes—any means to generate a little heat. The English took a dim view of the troops cutting down their trees and the troops faced severe disciplinary action if caught doing so.

Beds were metal bunk beds with "saggy" springs, almost like a hammock. The biscuit mattress and wool blankets provided only a place to lie down, sleep coming to the occupant only after almost utter exhaustion.

The living quarters were dispersed around the air field to prevent Germans from easily killing the occupants by bombing or from strafing. This dispersion and the lack of motor vehicle transportation made "getting" from the living quarters to the flight line or place of work, difficult. An attempt to alleviate this problem was made by the government issue of bicycles. On 6 February

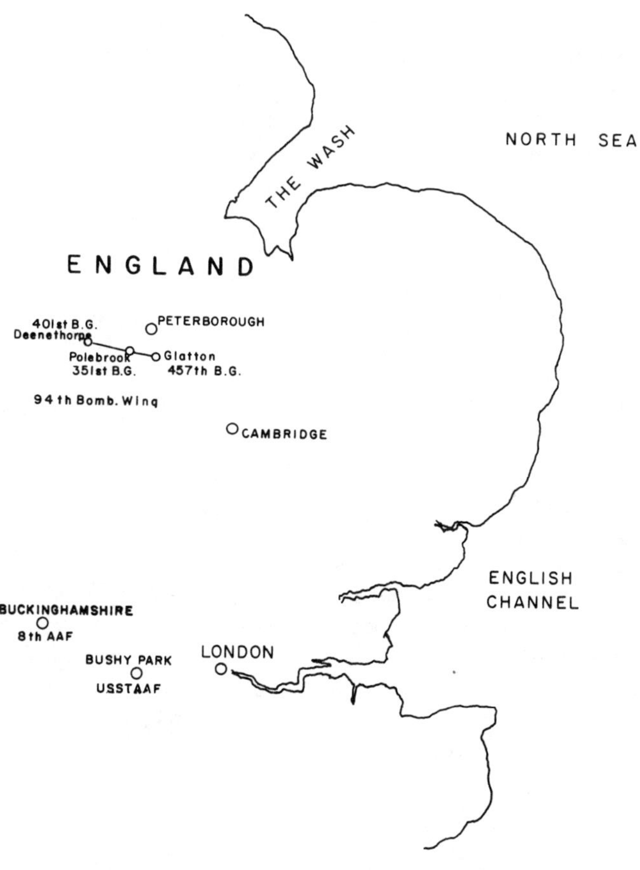

457 BOMBARDMENT GROUP (H)

ROLAND O. BYERS 1984

1944, 100 bicycles were issued in each Squadron.

Mud on a newly constructed base was a constant problem and many cries of anguish were heard on the fens. The base commanding officer used mud as a means of discipline. Motor vehicles, airplanes, equipment of all kinds, living quarters, and places of work were the target of a "mud campaign." Needless to say, there was much grumbling against the commanding officer by the ground echelon.

The flight crews were not much affected by this "mud campaign" and so that they too would be aware that military discipline was the realm of the commanding officer. Leather "A-2" flight jackets became the point of a campaign—flight jackets were issued for flying purposes only and would be worn only while the crew members were either flying or on the flight line. For a period of time the troops were ordered to carry the jackets under their arms to the flight line before wearing them.

The 457th Bombardment Group (H) was assigned to the 94th Wing, joining two groups: the 351st Group, located at Polebrook, and the 401st Group at Denethorpe. Of the two groups, the 351st had been operational since early in the war. Brigadier General Williams was the commander of the 94th Wing.

The 94th Wing was in turn assigned to the 1st Division of the 8th AAF. The 8th AAF was made up of three heavy bomber divisions: First, Second, and Third. The First and Third Divisions were equipped with B-17s and the Second Division was equipped with B-24s.

The troops survived the cold damp climate, the mud, the miserable living conditions, the military discipline, the terrible meals, but many of the combat crews would not survive the aerial war over Germany. The green spot at Glatton with a farm in the middle of the airbase would be the last home of many of the young men who arrived at Station 130 in early 1944.

Standing left to right: Hrubos, Walsh, Tozzi, Barrett, Hightower, Vitalie. Kneeling left to right: Horn, Byers, Green, Krumm.

Rapid City AAFB
Crew Flak Dodger

P	2nd Lt	Robert M. Krumm	0-864464
CP	2nd Lt	Leo R. Green	0-687295
N	2nd Lt	Roland O. Byers	0-675976
B	2nd Lt	Robert G. Horn	0-749635
AEG	S/Sgt	Lawrence J. Walsh	12145200
ROG	Cpl	Billy E. Hightower	18217598
AAEG	Sgt	Charles J. Hrubos	36279812
AROG	Cpl	Anthony W. Vitale	32357125
AG	Sgt	John D. Barrett	16078398
AAG	Pvt	Anthony J. Tozzi	33365664

457th (Zemper)

Flak Dodger "Bombs Away"

Trial by Fire

The instant he saw the bombs drop from the bomb bay of the lead "Flying Fortress," the bombardier of the "Flak Dodger," salvoed the six 500-pound G.P. (general purpose) bombs toward the T/O target of opportunity: Roye Army Airdrome in France. (The primary target had been a V-1 Buzz bomb launching site, however, the 10/10 cloud cover prevented bombing the ski-shaped site and a target of opportunity had been selected.) He flipped the switch that closed the bomb bay doors, as I entered the time of bombs away of 10:22 in the navigator's log. The formation of 18 B-17G "Flying Fortresses" of the 457th Bombardment Group (H) swung away from the target area to escape the pinpoint accuracy of the "flak" that was exploding around the "fortresses" in the formation.

The "bomb run" from the I.P. (initial point) to the target was "sphincter puckerin' time" for the formation of heavy bombers did not take evasive action during the run. The straight and level flying was necessary to permit the bombardier to synchronize the Norden bomb sight, "to kill rate and course," which if performed correctly would drop the bombs on the selected target. The anti-aircraft "flak" gunners on the ground also "zeroed in" their 88 millimeter guns on the bombers during the run, the result of which was flak damage to twelve of the eighteen bombers in the group and injury to two of the crewmen.

Moments after the bomb release, I heard, above the roar of the four Wright-Cyclone (R-1820-97) engines, the explosion of a "burst of flak" and felt the tug on my pants leg as a piece of "flak" tore through my heated suit, just missing my leg. I glanced down to see a hole I could stick my finger through in the metal just above the bootlegged flak suits with which I had lined the bottom of the navigator's compartment in the "nose of the fortress."

Then I heard, on the interphone, 1st Lt. Robert M. Krumm, the 1st pilot, call Staff Sergeant Tony Tozzi the right waist gunner, "Pilot to right waist gunner." Tozzi answered right back, "Go ahead, sir, this is Tozzi." "Sgt. Tozzi, can you see any flame coming out of number three engine?" "The flame is streaming back under the wing almost to the waist window, sir." Then I heard Krumm tell the co-pilot, 2nd Lt. Leo R. Green, "'Feather the prop' and cut off the fuel to engine number three." Green answered, "Roger," and I could see through the 16" square windows in the right side of the "nose" and just to the rear of the navigator's hand-held .50-calibre machine gun, the whirling propeller stop revolving and the blades turn edgewise into the airstream.

Every second was important now as Krumm peeled the burning fortress away from the protective group formation and dove it steeply but steadily downward. Krumm calculated that the only hope to save the airplane was to blow the fire out—with the 100 octane gasoline cut off to the engine, possibly ... just possibly ... he could blow out the fire by increasing the speed of the airplane. The speed of the bomber increased as we quickly lost altitude: 150... 160... 170... 180... 190... 200... 210... 220... 230. As the needle on the airspeed indicator moved steadily clockwise around the dial and the whine of the engines increased, Krumm again called Sgt. Tozzi, "Pilot to waist gunner...." "Go ahead, sir...." "Do you see any flame coming out around number three now?" "Not much flame—mostly just smoke," Sgt. Tozzi answered. Then I felt the downward pressure as Krumm pulled back on the control column and leveled out the fortress at about 20,000 feet. The dive from 25,000 feet down to 20,000 feet and by also cutting off the source of fuel had apparently extinguished most of the fire. Krumm did not want to lose too much altitude because of the "flak" guns we would need to evade as we flew from our position inland, westward to the English Channel.

It was decision time for Lt. Robert M. Krumm—should he give the command for the crew to bail out or take the chance that the fire would go out? If the airplane continued to burn, the fire would sooner or later burn through the aluminum nacelle to the fuel tanks in the wing and the gasoline would explode. The airplane was still over enemy territory and an order to bail out would mean the crew would probably be taken prisoner—that as well as losing a perfectly good airplane of which he had come to be very fond. However, the alternative of living, even as a prisoner, would be far better than that of losing ten lives if the airplane blew up.

Krumm thought back to the second mission on which the crew had been scheduled to fly—a mission to Berlin—on 7 March 1944. When Sgt. Charlie Hrubos, the ball turret gunner, had reached into the small opening through which he must crawl to man the ball turret, he somehow turned the handles which operated the turret such that the turret opening closed and caught his arm. As the turret squeezed Hrubos's arm, the force also turned the turret, pulling his body around the top of the turret, the sharp metal tearing huge chunks of flesh from his face and severely wrenching his arm.

The electrically driven turret could have literally torn him apart except for the quick action of S/Sgt Tony Tozzi and S/Sgt Tony Vitalie. The two waist gunners by sheer strength burned out the electric motor which powered the turret by holding the vertical members which supported the turret in the aircraft.

When Krumm learned of Sgt. Hrubos' condition, he aborted the mission and returned to base.

Lt. Col. James Luper called Lt. Robert Krumm "on the carpet" and asked for an explanation as to why aircraft 42-97075 had aborted the mission.

Lt. Krumm explained the situation of Sgt. Hrubos and his need for immediate medical treatment.

Lt. Col. Luper severely reprimanded Lt. Robert Krumm for aborting the mission and told Krumm that he was derelict in his action and should have dropped Sgt. Hrubos out of the aircraft by parachute over one of the many air bases in the area and continued on the mission. One injured man was not an excuse for aborting the mission.

This episode flashed through Krumm's mind and the threat of losing an aircraft forced him to think again whether to push the bail-out button.

Krumm called the ball turret operator, Staff Sergeant Charlie Hrubos, "Pilot to ball turret." Sgt. Hrubos answered, "Go ahead, sir." "Do you see any flame coming out of engine number three?" Krumm asked.

Of all the crew positions on a B-17G the ball turret, located under the belly of the airplane, was the least desirable in which to fly. A four-foot diameter sphere, the turret was operated by a small person who fired the twin .50-calibre machine guns from a fetus position. Because of the difficulty of getting in and out of the ball turret, the operator had almost no chance to survive if the airplane blew up. To remain in the ball turret when the airplane was burning took lots of just plain "guts." He knew, however, that his turret was the only one on the airplane the guns of which could bear on an enemy fighter attacking from below the airplane. Sgt.

Hrubos had been watching the flames that had been streaming out of the engine nacelle and had noticed that the intensity of the fire had been steadily diminishing as the fuel was cut off from the engine and the speed of the airplane had increased. Sgt. Hrubos answered Krumm's call, "The flame is mostly gone now, sir, but it is still smoking badly."

An airplane on fire scared the hell out of everyone on the crew, more so than did any other aspect of fighting a war five miles above the earth where just the loss of life sustaining oxygen for a minute could mean losing consciousness and probable death from anoxia. Enemy fighters you could shoot back at. Flak that you could see didn't usually hit you or seriously damage an airplane. But fire in the airplane often caused whole crews to bail out without even waiting for the pilot to press the "bail-out" bell. More than one airplane had returned to base after a fire had been extinguished with only part of the crew aboard.

Then to add to the tension, the tail gunner, Staff Sergeant William Barrett, called out on the interphone, "Fighters approaching from five o'clock high." The fighters were still too far away to identify. He couldn't determine whether they were friendly or enemy fighters. The Luftwaffe never passed up a chance to attack a damaged bomber which had been knocked out of the friendly environs of a group formation. The gunners on the crew all forgot about the fire for a moment and swung their .50-calibre machine guns toward the rear of the airplane.

All of this activity had happened in the short span of only about five minutes and now for a few moments the crew were all strangely quiet. Krumm was still debating as to what would be the most prudent course of action. Technical Sergeant Lawrence Walsh, the flight engineer operating the top turret, was intently watching the fighters which Sgt. Barrett had called out, ready to fire his twin .50-calibre machine guns if the approaching planes were identified as German Air Force Luftwaffe fighters. The top turret was located between the pilot's compartment and the bomb bay and was the most effective defense against fighters attacking from any direction above the airplane. The fighters were, however, still too far away to be certain of their identity. The front profile of a German Messerschmitt (M.E.) 109 and an American P-51 Mustang were very similar as was the front profile of a German Focke-Wulf (F.W.) 190 and an American P-47 Thunderbolt. If the nose of a fighter is pointed your way and appears to be on a pursuit curve, gunners often shot first and asked questions later.

Sgt. Hrubos, in the ball turret, could not see the approaching fighters but kept his guns trained toward the rear of the airplane. However, he kept watching the smoke coming out of the engine nacelle and thankfully noticed that it was diminishing.

Sgt. Barrett relieved the tension somewhat when he identified the fighters to be "Little Friends," American P-51 Mustangs, which were now flying parallel to the course of the "Flak Dodger." It was good to have the "Little Friends" in the vicinity just in case the Luftwaffe decided to take advantage of a "wounded duck."

Sgt. Hrubos called on the interphone, "Ball turret to pilot." "Go ahead," Krumm answered. "Sir, there is very little smoke coming out of the engine now." "Thanks, Sgt. Hrubos," Krumm answered.

Krumm now made his decision and called the crew on interphone. "Apparently the fire is going out and I'm going to take the 'Flak Dodger' home." The whole crew had heard what Sgt. Hrubos had said and to a man cheered the decision and were considerably relieved.

Krumm then called on the interphone, "Pilot to navigator." I said, "Go ahead." "Give me a compass heading home," Krumm said. I answered back, "Hold the heading you are on and give me a minute or so."

Long hours of training, six months as an instructor, and fifteen combat missions and innumerable practice missions had made an indelible impression on me and despite all that had been happening during the past few minutes I had almost subconsciously watched the readings on the altimeter, the magnetic compass, and the airspeed indicator. There hadn't been a whole lot for me to do anyway, other than snap the chest pack parachute on my harness just in case Krumm hit the bail-out button or—God forbid—the airplane blew up. However, more than one person had survived an airplane explosion and lived to tell about it. I had looked out the navigator's celestial astrodome on top of the airplane trying to "pick up" the fighters which Sgt. Barrett had called out but could not see them.

When Krumm had called on the interphone, I looked at my A-11 "Hack" watch and noted in the log the time of 10:29. Between six and seven minutes had elapsed since Krumm had "peeled off" and dived the "Flak Dodger" out of group formation. I recalled the direction of the dive to be generally northwest at 300° magnetic. Our indicated airspeed averaged 200 MPH. The temperature was -30° centigrade. Our average altitude was 22,500 feet. All this data converted to a true airspeed of 285 knots. We had, in that seven minutes, traveled an estimated 25 miles, I calculated on my E6B computer.

I placed my Weems plotter on my pilotage map and drew a course of 315° from our calculated position to our air base at Glatton, England. To achieve the true compass course I added +10° magnetic variation and +14° of drift correction for the 340°/70 knot briefed wind — a wind I had confirmed as we flew toward the target — giving a compass course of 339°. The course would avoid the flak areas around Dunkerque, France, indicated by large red circles drawn around the towns by S-2 intelligence personnel who had prepared our flight information during the wee hours of the night prior to the mission.

Then I called Krumm on the interphone. "Navigator to pilot," "Go ahead," Krumm answered. "Turn to a course of 339°." Krumm answered, "Roger." I then felt the airplane turning and watched my compass needle turn to the 339° reading.

We had bombed the target of opportunity Royce Army Airfield, a German fighter base not far from the coast of occupied France in the Pas de Calais area and from our position four miles above the earth I could easily see the English Channel ahead.

I "picked up" our position in relation to the pilotage map as a coastline with its harbors and landforms provides a navigator with excellent position determing features. I was certain we could avoid the flak areas indicated by the red circles on the map.

After we had flown for about ten minutes and were approaching the coastline of the English Channel, I could see four bursts of flak appearing just to the left of our course at our altitude. Lt. Green, the co-pilot, called on interphone, "Co-pilot to navigator." I answered, "This is the navigator, go ahead." "Byers, I think your heading (course) will take us over the flak at Dunkerque! We are turning to the right about ten degrees!" I quickly looked again at the red circles on the map both to the left and to the right of our course. I determined that a ten-degree correction to the right would take us over a flak area now to the right of our course. I called the co-pilot back and told him, "Hold the heading I gave you — 339° magnetic." I looked out the plexiglas nose of the airplane and could see just ahead four more bursts of flak just to the left of our course, coming up from Dunkerque. Then I felt the airplane turn to the right. I looked at the compass and saw that the needle had turned ten degrees right — to 349°. I immediately called on the interphone, "Navigator to pilot." Krumm answered back, "Go ahead." "My instructions were to fly a heading of 339°. If you hold the heading you are on we will be over the flak area northeast of Dunkerque." Then I felt the airplane turn back left again to the 339° heading, about which time four bursts of flak tracking our course burst just off the end of our right wing, where we would have been had we continued on the 349° course.

The remainder of the mission was uneventful. We continued on to Station 130 Glatton, our base, where we landed without difficulty and taxied to our hardstand where Sgt. Sumner Marshall, the crew chief, and others of the ground crew were anxiously awaiting our return. The other seventeen aircraft had arrived at the base about fifteen minutes before we had and there was some concern about our whereabouts.

When we climbed down out of the airplane we walked around and counted 88 holes made by the flak which had almost been our undoing! In spite of that, not a member of the crew had been wounded—never mind the hole in my pants leg, which hadn't severed any of the electrical wiring of the heating flying suit.

Sgt. Marshall and crew took the cowling off of number three engine and found the main fuel line had indeed been neatly severed by a piece of "flak." Because of its short duration and timely action by Krumm, the fire had not seriously damaged the airplane or the surrounding accessories or the engine mounts which held the engine in place. There would be a few holes to patch, however a few pieces of aluminum, some rivets, and a rivet gun would take care of that problem in "jig time." The "Flak Dodger," which hadn't been too nimble on this mission, would be back in commission ready for another mission into Adolf Hitler's "Festung Europa" in a couple of days.

The canvas-covered personnel carrier picked up the crew and transported us to base operations where S-2 intelligence personnel debriefed us concerning the mission. They wanted to know all about the mission: What was our estimate of the bombing? Did we hit the target? Were there any enemy fighters in the area? Did any of the gunners shoot down any German fighters? Was the flak intense? Did we get hit by flak? Did we notice any new flak guns not marked on the maps? Did we see any other bombers get shot down? Were any parachutes seen? There were many more questions concerning the mission and, in our case, S-2 wanted to know the whole story concerning our "being shot out" of formation and how Krumm had managed to put out the engine fire and fly the airplane back to the base. Obviously we had been fortunate, for the odds of extinguishing an engine fire are long. Only Krumm's quick assessment of the situation and timely action had made it possible for us to avoid a probable explosion and resultant loss of an airplane and crew of ten men.

Medical personnel including the Squadron flight surgeon, if he was not needed at the base hospital to care for wounded crew members, were on hand at the debriefing to talk to crew members, particularly those who showed signs of stress after a particularly difficult mission. They also provided the crew with an ounce ration of medicinal bourbon for those who desired it, just to calm the nerves. "Clean-living'" Leo Green, co-pilot, an ex-state patrolman from New York State, never accepted his ration of bourbon which was very difficult to obtain in England. However, some of the "Flak Dodger" crew were always willing to drink two ounces of "nerve soother."

A shot of "medicinal whiskey" entered the blood stream particularly fast when swallowed into a stomach which had not had food or water ingested for the period from breakfast at 0330 hours until the end of a mission often twelve to fourteen hours later. The stress, body tiredness, and extreme cold—often as low as −50°—and sucking oxygen all day produced a tiredness that left you too tired to eat even though you knew you should eat and not succumb to the desire to go back to the "Q" hut and "crawl into the fart sack," for more often than not there would be another mission the following day.

An extreme stress situation such as the crew of the "Flak Dodger" had experienced takes its toll, as evidenced by the confrontation between co-pilot Leo R. Green and I, over what magnetic heading to follow through the "flak areas" along the French coast. This indication of lack of confidence in my ability as navigator to guide the damaged aircraft safely through the flak areas may well have been brought about by this stress. My reaction to this confrontation was to accept an offer which had been previously made by the group navigator, Capt. Norman Kriehn, of the position of lead navigator for the 750th Squadron, an offer which I had not previously accepted because it required that I transfer off of the crew with which I had flown fifteen combat missions and looked forward to only ten more to complete my combat tour.

There is a feeling of comradeship that develops among the members of a crew which engages in combat, quite unlike that of any situation in civilian life. To place ones very life in the hands of each and every member of the crew day after day, knowing that one member's failure to perform his job may cost you your life as well as the other nine members, brings about a comradeship and trust which will never be experienced by people who have not been in a similar situation. Consequently, to show a lack of confidence in the ability of any one member of a crew by another member of the crew can seriously disrupt the whole close-knit group.

After having been assigned to the crew at Ephrata AAB in November of 1943, I had trained with, argued with, drank with, bunked with, laughed with, grieved with, achieved with, failed with, whored with, suffered with, and shared confidence with the crew for the better part of a year. Time in this sense, while measured by the calendar, must be compressed for it involved memorable happenings.

The personal relationships developed within the ten-man bomber crew is at the onset divided by the fact that four members of the crew are commissioned officers and six non-commissioned officers. The pilots, the navigator, and bombardier are commissioned officers, usually 2nd Lieutenants when they were assigned to a crew. The enlisted men, flight engineer and top turret operator, ball-turret gunner, radio man, left waist gunner, right waist gunner, and tail gunner, were usually all staff sergeants. If any one was of a higher rank, technical sergeant, it was usually the flight engineer and radio operator who had more responsibility than any of the other enlisted men.

As in all military organizations, the officers live, eat, sleep, and associate socially with other officers. The military is not a democratic organization and enlisted men function at the order of their officers. The hierarchy in a bomber crew, however, becomes somewhat confused as each man, regardless of whether he is an officer or enlisted man, has a specific job to perform which is at the direction of only one officer—the 1st pilot, who is also the commander of the airplane. However, military courtesy is expected of the enlisted men for any commissioned officer and in return the officers look out for the interests of the enlisted men.

Because of their similar functions on a heavy bomber crew, the pilots normally "pair off" in off-duty activities while the navigator and bombardier tend to travel together. All four man associate socially together, however. Since there are six enlisted men they tend to select among themselves with whom they wish to associate socially during off-duty hours.

457th (Zemper)

457th at Schweinfurt, February 24, 1944

457th

Sgt. Sumner Marshall (right), "Flak Dodger" crew chief; Jack Merrill (center), Carl Gardner (left).

Flak Dodger

She was a beautiful ship, "a fine kite," the British would say, there on the tarmac hardstand. One of Boeing's finest products, A/C #42-97075. One of the 12,731 B-17s that would be built, 6,981 by Boeing Airplane Company, 3,000 by Douglas Aircraft, and 2,750 by Lockheed Aircraft Co. Four thousand seven hundred and fifty B-17s would be lost on combat missions during World War II.

She was 104 feet from wing tip to wing tip—75 feet, give or take a gun barrel, from her shiny plexiglass nose to the twin 50-calibre stingers in the tail. She carried 2,680 gallons of 100 octane gasoline to fuel the four Wright-Cyclone R-1820-97 radial engines, each of which developed 1,200 horsepower. She could carry as many as twelve 500-pound bombs for a thousand miles at a speed of 180 miles per hour. She bristled with thirteen .50-calibre machine guns with which to defend herself. She was awesome—a fighting machine that any finely tuned combat crew could fly with confidence.

A "have not" crew, Lt. Robert M. Krumm's crew had joined the 457th Bombardment Group at Wendover AAB, Utah, on 2 December 1944. The name "have not" described a combat crew which had not been assigned a B-17 while in the United States. Only two-thirds of the 72 combat crews of the 457th Bombardment Group (H) had been assigned an airplane to fly across the North Atlantic to the 8th AAF base at Glatton, England.

We as a crew had been quarantined for a week at the gunnery range at Wendover AAB because a fellow crew member had contracted spinal meningitis as we traveled from Rapid City AAB to Wendover AAB. It was during this period of time that combat crews were assigned new B-17G airplanes.

Although we completed Phase III crew training as did the other crews at Wendover AAB, when it came time to ship overseas the "have" crews flew across the North Atlantic while the "have not" crews went by ship. We wallowed across the North Atlantic Ocean during the month of January on the U.S.S. Lyons—a small freighter, converted to troop transport, operated by the Army Transport Service.

The ship was a miserable "slave ship," men stacked three high in bunks in the hold. You stood in line for the latrine, for chow, and for a sticky salt water shower. Shaving in salt water was impossible.

Recreation included watching the navy gunnery crew practice dry firing the 6" gun on the stern of the ship. Also waiting expectantly for the DEs—destroyer escorts—to bob up after a huge wave would wash over and almost completely cover the deck.

So after 14 days of dodging German submarines, practicing celestial navigation, and playing a marathon chess game, we arrived in Glasgow, Scotland, on 31 January 1944.

The "have" crews, those which had flown across the North Atlantic, had arrived at the new base on or about 21 January 1944.

What does a finely tuned combat bomber crew do without a bomber to fly? Attend a lot of ground school and occasionally fly a training mission in another crew's airplane.

Ah! but now we were no longer a "have not" crew. We had acquired an airplane of our own. Waiting for an airplane had its compensations. We had been assigned one of the first silver B-17G aircraft in the ETO. Previously all aircraft (A/C) had been painted an O.D. (olive drab) color. 075 was the first of many which the 457th Bomb. Group would be assigned. In fact, the group would be the first all-silver group in the ETO.

We wondered how the German Air Force would respond to A/C without camouflage and were at first apprehensive, but as far as we know the silver A/C formations were never attacked by fighters in preference to the painted A/C.

We had flown to Burtonwood, an RAF Depot where new A/C were modified to incorporate equipment necessary for operation of the A/C in the ETO—a GEE navigation receiver for the navigator, IFF (Information Friend or Foe) unit for the pilot, radio equipment for the radio operator and the pilot, among other modifications.

The flight back to our base in our newly acquired airplane was interrupted by weather and some close calls avoiding barrage balloons. But after being grounded for two days at an RAF bomber base—Nuneaton—we returned to Station 130.

The 457th B.G. had arrived in England just in time to participate along with the other groups of the 8th AAF in a maximum effort popularly called "Big Week" — officially known by the code name ARGUMENT.

In May 1943 at the Joint Chiefs summit conference in Washington, D.C., a directive named POINTBLANK was issued. While previously the number one priority had been given to bombing submarine construction targets, now almost equal priority but still second priority would be given to bombing targets associated with German fighter aircraft construction.

The British would continue to bomb German industry in general, while the USAAF would select targets which would presumably reduce the number of fighter aircraft, a feat to be accomplished by bombing ball bearing, airframe, aircraft engine, depots, and aircraft storage parks. A combined British and United States operational planning committee picked the individual targets which would be attacked. (The Germans, being the ingenious people that they are, were producing more aircraft near the end of the war than they were in 1942 and 1943, in spite of the intense bombing campaign carried on by the United States and England in 1944. Weaknesses which contributed to their undoing were the inadequate air crew training program and the shortage of oil with which to fuel their war machine.)

The attack on the aircraft industry — "ARGUMENT" — awaited a break in the weather and such a break was forecast on 19 February 1944 by the USSTAF weather section. There would be high barometric pressure in the Baltic and west of Ireland, conditions which foretold good weather for England and Germany.

With the promise of good weather, Major General Frederick L. Anderson, USSTAF's Deputy for Operations, decided on a commitment to ARGUMENT by the 8th AAF, thereby satisfying the directive by Gen. Spaatz that ARGUMENT must be completed by 1 March 1944.

The commitment by Gen. Anderson to ARGUMENT caught Gen. Eaker of the 15th AAF with a commitment to the army forces at Anzio, Italy, however. General Anderson decided to proceed as planned without the 15th AAF. Neither Major General James Doolittle of the 8th AAF nor Lieut. General Lewis Brerton of the 9th AAF had confidence in the forecast of a break in the weather and would provide only limited diversionary forces on the 21st of February. However, on 20 February 1944 the field order went out for units of the 8th AAF to provide 1,000 heavy bombers, 16 combat wings of A/C, to strike targets at German aircraft production centers. This was the largest effort made by the 8th AAF to date. All available fighter escort aircraft were provided, 17 groups: 13 P-47, 2 P-38, and 2-P51s from both the 8th Fighter Command and the 9th AAF. The RAF also provided 16 squadrons of fighters which included both Spitfires and Mustangs.

Targets in twelve industrial centers were selected, which included Me 109, Me 110, Ju 88, Ju 188, and FW 190 aircraft production plants. Most of these plants were in the Leipzig-Brunswick area.

Bombing was visual and the results good. Twenty-one heavy bombers were lost from a force of nearly 1,000 A/C. Compared to previous raids the loss was minimal. By comparison, 650 of the heavy bombers had been sent to Germany on 11 January 1944 to attack targets at Halberstadt, Aschersleben, and Brunswick. Sixty heavy bombers had failed to return from that mission.

The 457th Bombardment Group received its first field order to fly a combat mission on the night of 20 February 1944. (A previous mission, on 14 February 1944 had been "scrubbed"—cancelled.) The target was to be aircraft installation A/F at both Guttersloh and Lippstadt, Germany. The 457th would "put up" 36 A/C and fly the high group, with 18 A/C, in each of two 49-ship boxes of the 94th wing.

The mission was completed with undetermined results as the box which attacked Guttersloh bombed through 10/10 cloud cover with H_2X. The box which was to bomb Lippstadt bombed a T/O (target of opportunity). The group which was to bomb Lippstadt encountered accurate flak and were attacked by fighters resulting in the loss of one A/C—that flown by Lt. Lew Bredeson. In addition five other A/C, including Lt. Dozier's A/C, received extensive battle damage and had crewmen injured.

Lew Bredeson's crew was the first of 86 crews which would be lost to enemy action by the 457th Bomb. Group while flying 236 combat missions. Lt. William Thistle's crew shot down on 20 April 1945 would be the last.

The 457th B.G. would fly again the following day on 22 February 1944 to Oschersleben: stand down on 23 February, fly to Schweinfurt on 24 February, and Augsburg on the 25th of February.

One crew was lost on the Schweinfurt mission and two on the Augsburg mission.

Until 2 March 1944 the crew of "Flak Dodger" hadn't lifted a finger to win the war. Finally, after a "scrubbed" mission and flying as a spare A/C on one mission, on 2 March 1944 the crew was alerted, briefed and flew its first mission to Frankfurt. The target: a M/Y (railroad marshalling yard). This was the fifth mission for the group.

The mission was, as would occasionally occur, a "milk run" for the 457th. No fighters and very meager flak, no damage or loss of any aircraft. 10/10 clouds obscured the target and the H_2X radar equipment failed to function correctly. All in all the mission was a bust!

All the anticipation, the tension, the fears were held in abeyance for death and destruction had not ridden with a Luftwaffe Me 109 or a FW 190 fighter or on an 88mm flak shell for the neophyte crew of the "Flak Dodger."

Our bunk mates in "Q" hut #11 only four days later would not be so fortunate, however. Lt. Eugene Whelan's crew would not return from a mission to Berlin, knocked out of the sky by a collision with a Luftwaffe Me 109 which collided with their bomber and that of Lt. Roy Graves. Both crews were lost.

The "Big Week" was over, 6 days of CAVU weather. The 8th AAF and the RAF had dealt the German war machine a succession of crippling blows. Nineteen thousand tons of bombs had been dropped on the German A/C plants, 10,000 by the 8th AAF and 9,000 by the RAF. The raids would force the German high command to rethink their production methods. They changed the A/C production responsibility from Reichs Marshall Hermann Goering's Air Ministry to Albert Spier's Ministry of Armament and Munitions on 1 August 1944. The Germans would salvage what they could in machine tools from the bombed out A/C plants, disperse their A/C manufacturing plants, and by 1944 be making 1,581 A/C a month (the allies estimated 655 a month) as compared to only 851 A/C a month in 1943. Although the bombing did disrupt German aircraft production for a short period of time and did deny them many needed fighter A/C for use during the invasion in June 1944, the concerted bombing program by the allies did not particularly cause the Germans much difficulty in their production of A/C.

The crew of "Flak Dodger" continued to maintain their charmed existence through the next two months. There were missions to Berlin (4 times), Gdynia, Sorau, Bac-Queriette, Watten, Tours, Brunswick, Hamm, and Munster, twelve in all.

For those who are superstitious, and one can get that way very easily in such an environment, we were briefed to fly our 13th mission on the 13th of April, 1944, and to where? Of all places in the German Reich—Schweinfurt! It was a target to which, on 14 October 1943, "Black Thursday," the 8th AAF had lost 60 of the 230 bombers sent to bomb the ball bearing plants. Almost 25 percent A/C failed to return!

At the early morning briefing, when the "black" curtain (the color was even ominous) was drawn back and the crew of the "Flak Dodger" saw the long "black" ribbon end at Schweinfurt, hopes were low! A couple of the crew even stayed after briefing and talked to Holy Joe (chaplain). A charmed existence could not last forever. This could just be the day! One's confidence could only hold up so long. However, those of us who feared the Lord and thought little of superstitions agreed to call the mission 12B, just in case!

Well, to make a long story short, the mission was almost a "milk run" for the 457th B.G. with only five A/C receiving flak damage. Luper's "iron ass" methods, although groused about, were saving lives and A/C. The formation was as "tight as a bull's bung in fly time"! The Luftwaffe passed by a tight formation! This was not true for all groups which attacked aircraft plants that day. Thirty-eight heavy bombers failed to return to base.

The Luftwaffe had become selective as to when they would defend Hitler's 1,000 year fatherland. They had conceded overall air superiority to the U.S. Air Forces and chose to conserve their aircraft and personnel except at specific targets. They would send large numbers of fighters 4-500 at a time to intercept the bombers on some missions. On the 13th of April 1944 the 10/10 clouds completely obscured the target. Because of weather the Germans knew that bombing would be by radar—H_2X—which at best was only an approximation and seldom hit specific targets such as a ball bearing plant. H_2X also referred to as PFF.

On this date the Luftwaffe remained on the ground and the 38 8th AAF A/C lost were to flak. "Flak Dodger" once again brought back her crew unscathed.

This reluctance to fight by the Lufwaffe did not achieve the objectives of POINTBLANK—that of the destruction of the Luftwaffe. Future efforts were taken by the 8th AAF to draw the German fighters into the fray. United States escort fighters were given permission to go down and find a reluctant "Jerry."

Through the months of May and June of 1944, Lt. Krumm's crew continued to fly "Flak Dodger" on the missions the group flew—the tough missions to Berlin, Politz, Ludwigshafen,

Aschersleben, Hamburg, as well as the "milk runs," the short missions to attack V-bomb sites on the coasts of the occupied countries of France, Holland, and Belgium. There were also missions flown to support the invasion (OVERLORD) troops—the A/Fs, the M/Ys and other tactical targets. Through all of these missions, "Flak Dodger," although slightly damaged on occasion, brought the crew through unscathed.

The members of the crew were approaching the end of their tour—25 missions (30 missions after May 1944)—when, late in June, Krumm and crew were alerted to fly a mission to Berlin. (The author had been made Squadron navigator and no longer flew with the crew.) "Flak Dodger" had been damaged on an earlier mission from 20mm cannon fire and was being repaired by the Sub Depot. Since "Flak Dodger" was not available, the crew was assigned another A/C: A/C 42-107015, new engines had just been installed in #015 and they had not been adequately "slow timed" (break-in time, just as the engine on a new car must be driven slowly for a number of miles). But the requirements of a mission must be met

457th

Lt. Blackwell's A/C #42-107015 landing at Glatton AAF Base. Note farmhouse and buildings located in the middle of the airfield. Lt. Krumm flew 015 to Sweden on 21 June 1944.

and A/C #015 was assigned to fly the mission.

As the Group flew east over the Baltic Sea, Krumm began experiencing trouble with first one and then a second engine; each started losing power. The Group was approaching land fall along the northern coast of Germany, still climbing toward the target, and 015 was losing power and falling back. Krumm could not keep up with the formation. The Luftwaffe had been reported in the area just looking for stragglers such as 015. Krumm took his only option—with only two engines functioning and losing power on a third, he jettisoned the bombs, steered north, and landed in Sweden.

The crew was interned until late in WWII when it became apparent the Germans would lose the war and the crew was flown back to England—the base—and home to the U. S. of A.

The number of 8th AAF bomber crews landing in Sweden and Switzerland, ninety-four by the end of July 1944, caused some

457th

Tracking Flak! Barrage Flak over Berlin in distance.

concern in the higher Air Force command. Rumors were circulating in the combat zones as well as back in the United States that combat crews were enjoying the war comfortably ensconced with beautiful Swedish and Swiss women and good food without fear or danger to themselves for the duration of the war. This rumor was corroborated by diplomatic interrogators who reported that an unusual number of the so-called emergencies were not valid, that cowardice was the main reason the internees were flying to neutral countries.

General Spaatz took exception to these reports and asked that Air Force officers and civilian technical officers be permitted to examine the A/C and interrogate the crews. Permission to do so was given by the neutral countries. When the interrogation was completed in August 1944, the report stated that in all cases the crews were justified in making the decision to land their disabled A/C in the neutral country. There was not a single instance that a crew had landed in a neutral country to avoid further combat.

Rather, the interrogators found that the authorities had problems dissuading the internees from escaping and returning to their bases.

When Gen. Eaker reported the outcome of the investigation to General "Hap" Arnold, he stated, "Our crews like all normal human beings do not want to be killed. They look at this business very grimly and are happy when they get through what they consider is all that a man can be asked to stand, and all of them without exception are glad to return home when their time comes up for rotation. This does not mean low morale, it means they are normal human beings."

After Lt. Krumm's crew was interned in Sweden, Major Dickinson assigned A/C #075 to a new crew, that of 2nd Lt. Clayton E. Bejot. Sgt. Sumner Marshall, crew chief of A/C #075, "Flak Dodger," took particular pains to assure that the A/C was in A-1 condition when the newly assigned pilot came to look at "his" airplane. "His" meant Sgt. Marshall's airplane. He only grudgingly permitted the crews to fly the airplane on the missions for which they were alerted. Sgt. Marshall and his ground crew cared for the A/C as if it was their own. He had birthed it—so to speak—it had been his to maintain since it was assigned to the 750th Bomb. Sqdn. It had been his hands which had changed the engines, patched the holes the Germans had ungraciously shot in her, cleaned up the .50-calibre shells and shell links the gunners spread all over the A/C. He had been fortunate in one respect: he had never had to clean up blood—except for the time Hrubos had been caught in the ball turret. No one had ever been seriously injured on "Flak Dodger"! There had been no "purple hearts" for crew members who made their last flight on "Flak Dodger."

Sgt. Marshall and the ground crew had as much right to "ownership" as did the assigned flying crew. Certainly they took care of the airplane, watched it fly away in the morning and hopefully awaited its return in the afternoon. No frugal Yankee from down east—from Maine—ever cared more for a possession than did Sgt. Marshall. His dedication would be rewarded when he was later made line chief of all 750th Sqdn. A/C and Sgt. Ken Hogenson was made crew chief of A/C #075.

There was very little "glory" which came to the ground crews of the 8th AAF combat units. They received few decorations, maybe a good conduct medal now and then, and promotions were scarce. They watched flight crews arrive, finish their prescribed number of missions, and rotate back to the United States. The ground crews were stationed in England for the duration. The one difference of course was the ground crews did not face the danger each day that a flight crew did.

The motivation for doing a good job came from within these men rather than without, yet without their dedication and patriotism, fewer of us who flew the airplanes would be here today to talk about it.

Lt. Clayton E. Bejot, as were several of the pilots of the 750th Squadron, Lt. Robert Krumm, Lt. Clarence Schuchmann, and others, were farm boys. Bejot came from Ainsworth, Nebraska, Krumm from Mason City, Iowa, and Schuchmann from Hawkeye, Iowa. Seems the bread basket of the United States produced more than just bumper crops of wheat, corn, and soy beans.

Lt. Bejot and his crew arrived at Station 130—Glatton—on 18 June 1944. The crew was one of the many which would replace the original crews of the 457th B.G., original crews which had either finished their tour of 25 missions (30 after May 1944 and later 35) or had been lost in combat. In the early days of 1944 the ratio had been about one crew out of three lost, to two which finished a tour.

The four officers of Lt. Bejot's crew did not arrive at the 750th Sqdn. at a particularly auspicious time, as they were assigned, as a place to live, the bunks of a crew which had just been shot down. Neither they nor the other crews in the "Q" hut felt very good about the situation. Stuffing a missing crew's belongings into a mattress cover so you had a place to sleep wasn't the ideal way to start fighting the war.

Lt. Bejot and his crew's love affair with "Flak Dodger" was a carbon copy of the experience of Lt. Krumm's crew. In three months of flying Bejot's crew experienced little difficulty, in spite of the fact they flew missions to Munich, Merseburg, Ludwigshafen, Cologne, and other targets which were deep into Germany—a few holes in the well patched "hide" of a now aging old lady, but still a "fine kite."

Lt. Bejot likened "Flak Doger" to an F-20 Farmall tractor. She was a relatively simple machine and would respond to good treatment and bring you home if it had any chance at all. 075 was a very stable old girl—would trim up and fly hands off better than any other B-17 I ever flew. She was very stable to fly in formation as well as take-off and land.

Bejot said, "Although no crew member was ever injured in 'Flak Dodger,' our closest call was on October 7, 1944. The mission—Politz—we were flying the number three slot in the lead flight of the High Squadron of twelve ships. We were the second box of twelve ships to bomb in trail. Col. Luper was in the lead box just ahead of us. I could see the flak bursting among the ships ahead knocking them all over the sky! The flak was accurate and heavy and was breaking up the formation.

"We were next over the target and they had us zeroed in just like they had the lead box. We took three almost direct hits underneath the airplane just as we dropped our bombs. Fortunately, the damage to 'Flak Dodger' was minimal. The airplanes in the formation went all directions after 'bombs away.' It's the first and only time I ever saw that happen. Fortunately there were not any fighters in the area at the time or our goose would have been cooked!"

Col. Luper's airplane (A/C 44-38046) was shot down over Politz on the mission. Lt. William J. Morrow was the D.R. navigator in the lead ship and tells the following story.

"Our target was the oil refinery at Politz. We had quite a long run from the IP to the target. We were the lead ship over the target and the flak guns were zeroed in on our airplane. I had my hand resting on the navigator's table and a piece of flak came up through the table and through my hand, breaking the bone in my middle finger. I recall holding my wrist with my other hand and looking out the window and seeing oil spouting out of a hole in the cowling of number two engine. About that time a fire started burning in the hatchway between the flight deck and the nose and I tried to put it out with a fire extinguisher to no avail. There was another burst of flak and I could see the right wing was on fire.

"Capt. Al Fischer, the lead pilot, rang the bail-out bell and I yanked off my flak suit and oxygen mask and released the nose escape hatch. The rush of air cleared the smoke from the hatchway revealing Col. Luper who had come down from the flight deck to see what was causing the fire. Luper shook his head no and pointed for me to get back in the nose, which I did. Capt. Henry P. Loades and Major Norman A. Kriehn also backed up and did not bail out.

"Things got a little hazy about that time—probably because I had not put my oxygen mask back on.

"I recall a red flash out of the right window and the airplane went into a spin. I remember the high pitched whine of a propeller running away and then an explosion. We were flying at 29,000 feet and I came to my senses somewhere around 8,000 feet. By the time I had sense enough to open my parachute I must have been down to about 4,000 feet. I landed in Stettin Bay and luckily managed to free myself from the parachute, which quickly sank. One other person landed about 50 to 75 yards away—I do not know who it was—I yelled and asked if he was OK but got no answer. I then heard some wild thrashing in the water coming in my direction. I pulled the cords which inflated my Mae West and rolled over on my back to swim in his direction, but he had disappeared. Although I swam around looking for him I was unable to find anyone.

"I had thought the man might be the bombardier because I could recall a Mae West laying in the 'nose.' But I later found out that Capt. Henry P. Loades had been picked up by a boat but had died in a hospital a few days later.

"I tried in vain to reach a channel buoy but the current carried me away from it. After a time, however, a mine sweeper came into the bay and picked me up. They treated me well—bandaged my hands and brought me a blanket and some hot tea. They took me below deck and dried my clothes. They then took me to the Baltic port of Swinemunda. There I met Col. Luper and Major Norman A. Kriehn, the lead navigator. They had been picked up by a second boat several hundred yards from where I had been picked up.

"My hands were redressed in an infirmary at a Naval Hospital in Swinemunda. Col. Luper had cuts on his forehead and on his leg which were dressed at the hospital. Major Kriehn, who was also in the nose of the airplane, was only bruised.

'They were taken to the local jail and from there to Frankfurt the next day. They met Lt. Fredrick W. Asbell, radar navigator, and S/Sgt. John J. Derling, waist gunner, at the jail.

"All of us eventually were sent to prison camps where we were prisoners for the rest of the war.

"I do not know what happened to the others on the airplane. I can only assume they were killed in the explosion.

"We were evacuated ahead of the Russians from Luft 3 and taken to Stalag 7 near Munich, where we were liberated on April 29, 1945."

Lt. Bejot's crew flew the remainder of their 35 missions in "Flak Dodger" and on 28 October 1944, without injury to any member of the crew, completed their tour. They had flown 24 missions in 075.

Lt. Bejot's crew is as follows:

P	1st Lt	Clayton Bejot
CP	2nd Lt	Augustus J. Harris
N	F/O	Andrew Solari
CHIN	S/Sgt	Fernando P. Biancalana
AE	T/Sgt	Norman Depelteau

457th

Lt. Clayton E. Bejot and "Flak Dodger."

RO	T/Sgt	Paul C. Parker
LW	S/Sgt	Karl E. Kamer
BT	S/Sgt	Oliver F. Orris
TG	S/Sgt	Vinell L. Bush

"Flak Dodger's vertical stabilizer and rudder assembly was replaced by an OD (olive drab) color assembly from a cannibalized war weary B-17G. The original assembly was badly damaged by the flexible mounted .50-calibre gun in the radio room. An over eager radio operator failed to stop firing at an enemy fighter when the field of fire crossed the tail assembly.

"Flak Dodger" was now to be flown by many different crews. She was becoming war weary and had many patches on her "hide" to show for it. But still her reputation held true. She brought every crew that flew her back to base. But crews were getting leery of her age and even though they were aware of "Flak Dodger's reputation, they wanted a newer airplane to fly.

The crews who flew her and the 28 missions are as follows:

5 Nov 1944	Lt Alvin I. Caplovitz	Frankfurt M/Y
21 Nov 1944	Lt Donald C. Meyers	Mersemurg I/O
23 Nov 1944	1st Lt James C. Evans	Gelsenkirchen I/O
25 Nov 1944	Lt Alvin I. Caplovitz	Merseburg I/O
29 Nov 1944	Lt Max K. Rahn	Misburg I/O
30 Nov 1944	1st Lt George L. Mathews	Bohlen I/O
4 Dec 1944	Lt Ralph L. Hay	Kassel M/Y
11 Dec 1944	1st Lt James C. Evans	Frankfurt M/Y
12 Dec 1944	1st Lt. Clyde R. Weid	Merseburg I/O
15 Dec 1944	Lt Henry S. Blach	Kassel M/Y
19 Dec 1944	Lt Roy H. Kirk	Gemund T/T
1 Jan 1945	Lt Ero P. Salo	Kassel M/Y
13 Jan 1945	Lt Herbert A. Lawyer	Maxmilliansau RR/BR
21 Jan 1945	Lt Henry S. Blach	Aschaffenburg M/Y
29 Jan 1945	Lt Henry S. Blach	Siegen I/ORD
1 Feb 1945	Lt Willmore Fluman	Ludwigshafen M/Y
6 Feb 1945	Lt Carl P. Sundbaum	Schmalkaiden I/O
9 Feb 1945	Lt Carl P. Sundbaum	Lutzkendorf I/O
14 Feb 1945	Lt Carl P. Sundbaum	Dresden M/Y
20 Feb 1945	Lt Ralph W. Coons	Nurnburg M/Y
21 Feb 1945	Lt Joseph B. Maguire	Nurnburg M/Y
23 Feb 1945	Lt Carl P. Sundbaum	Ellingen RR
25 Feb 1945	Lt Joseph B. Maguire	Munich A/F
26 Feb 1945	Lt Carl P. Sundbaum	Berlin I/AREA

27 Feb 1945	Lt James H. Latimer	Leipzig M/Y
28 Feb 1945	Lt Frank R. Guca	Soest M/Y
1 Mar 1945	Lt Frank R. Guca	Gappingen M/Y
2 Mar 1945	Lt Frank R. Guca	Chemnitz I/O

Comes the time in every life when retirement becomes necessary and such was the case with 075—"Flak Dodger." She would be relegated to simpler duties, to gunnery training duties.

Sgt. Ralph E. Windell was assigned as crew chief and he and his crew stripped all of the armorplate and tools of war out of her. They then installed gun cameras and used her to train gunners, a mundane end to a once proud lady. But then the war was over in only about two months so the pain did not last long.

The troops were ordered home and in June 1945 Group Commander Col. Harris E. Rogner and Lt. Col. William F. Smith, Jr., chose her as the airplane in which to fly home because she was lighter and faster than the other B-17s.

Sgt. Windell flew home with Rogner and Smith and he said they flew the North Atlantic route along with the many other 8th AAF A/C.

One B-24 crew chief was nonplussed when at each air base on the return trip he found "Flak Dodger" there well ahead of his A/C. He was incensed that a B-17 could outfly a normally much faster B-24, and threatened Windell with bodily harm if he kept it up!

The trip to the United States terminated at Bradley Field, Connecticut, where "Skeleton Circus," a contract ferry company, picked up the A/C and flew her to Lubbock, Texas, and then Kingman, Arizona, for storage.

Sgt. Sumner Marshall, "Flak Dodger" crew chief, gave her a fitting epitaph:

"Her aerial number was 42-97075 and she was a real Boeing—there were differences and a Boeing was always the best. I could tell the difference as soon as I stepped into the cockpit—as I could about her Wright Cyclone engines.

"She was the first silver B-17 to be assigned to the 457th Bomb. Group and I got her."

Lt. Bejot's Crew: Standing left to right—P 1st Lt. Clayton Bejot, AE T/Sgt. Norman Depelteau, N F/O Andrew Solari, CoP 1st Lt. Augustus J. Harris, TG S/Sgt. Vinell L. Bush. Kneeling: WG unknown, BT S/Sgt. Oliver S. Orris, RO T/Sgt. Paul G. Parker, WG S/Sgt. Fernando G. Biancolana. The list of crew members given previously were his (Bejot's) original crew. The above list matches the picture—crew picture—taken after mission to Munich.

457th

Replacing the vertical stablizer and rudder assembly on "Flak Dodger" after it had been damaged by 50 calibre gunfire from the radio room gun. 31 October 1944

Sgt. Ralph E. Windell, Flak Dodger crew chief near end of WWII (Unidentified airman at left)

Mission

It is late afternoon, the date 19 June 1944, and the commanding general of the 8th AAF, Lieutenant General James Doolittle, and his staff are receiving a briefing by the weather officer concerning the weather forecast over the European Continent for the following day.

They learn that the cloud cover will be marginal for visual bombing although there is an even 50-50 chance that conditions will improve overnight. General Doolittle has been waiting for just such weather so that the 8th AAF heavy bombers can "hit" priority oil targets in Germany.

On 8 June 1944, two days after "D-Day" (Code name for the invasion was OVERLORD), General Carl Spaatz issued an historic order to USSTAF (United States Strategic Air Forces in Europe) – the 8th AAF and 15th AAF: "The primary mission of the 8th AAF and 15th AAF is to deny oil to the German armed forces." The 8th AAF would in the immediate future bomb synthetic oil plants at Merseburg-Luena, Politz, Zeitz, Magdeburg, and Ruhland, and crude oil refineries at Hamburg, Bremen, and Hannover. The 15th AAF based in Italy would attack crude oil refineries at Ploesti, Vienna, and Budapest, and synthetic oil plants in Selesia, Poland and the Sudetenland at Brux, Oswiecim, Blackhammer-north, Blecha-south, and Odertal.

While most of the missions flown by the 8th AAF immediately after D-Day were flown to satisfy the commitment to "OVERLORD" and "CROSSBOW" (V-weapon sites), missions flown against the German oil industry were flown as these commitments and weather permitted.

On 15 June oil targets at Misburg had been bombed by 8th AAF heavy bombers. Again on 18 June, oil targets at Hamburg, Oblebshausen, and again Misburg had been hit.

After some discussion with his staff, General Doolittle gave the word to "go" with the field order. The three 8th AAF divisions would attack oil targets in Germany on 20 June 1944.

The teletype began to clatter and the field order for the mission, which had been meticulously planned, the tape cut, and just waiting for favorable weather, went out over the teletype. The field order specified 14 industrial and oil targets to be attacked by 1360 (1257 actual) heavy bombers in Hamburg, Ostermoor, Misburg, Politz, and Magdeburg.

The field order also gave the aiming points at each target, the type and number of bombs, the routes both to the target and back to base, the bombing altitudes, the zero hour, the radio procedure, the fuel loads, and the number — 760 (728 actual) — of fighters flying support.

The time is 0110 hours and the field order has been sent to the three Divisions, who in turn transmitted it to the Wings, and they in turn to the individual bomber and fighter groups.

At 0112 at the 457th Bomb Group, the duty operations officer at Group operations awakens the S-2 officer (intelligence) and also informs each squadron that the field order is coming in on the teletype.

During the same period of time, the duty navigator and bombardier began to "work" the field order, the navigator calculating the time and distance between specific locations along the mission course. They each pass the information along to intelligence and ordnance personnel respectively, as well as providing the information to the lead teams.

The cooks are awakened, as well as are the personnel at the motor pool — The drivers of gasoline trucks, jeeps, personnel carriers, cleat tracks, and fire trucks all begin the day.

The hour is 0130, time to awaken the group commander, Colonel James R. Luper. All elements point to a rough mission for the 457th Bomb Group, for they are required to "put up" 36 aircraft — two 18 aircraft boxes of B-17s — more than the usual number.

The weather appears to be good over the Continent. While clear CAVU (ceiling and visibility unlimited) is good for bombing, it is also great for visual sighting of the "flak" guns — anti-aircraft defense — and also for launching enemy fighters.

Captain Frank Taylor, the 750th Squadron S-2, signed for and took the classified "secret" target folder from the file. He leafed through the folder to determine if all the necessary information was included in the file. Taylor noted particularly the large-scale map and the target photographs. He notices that the refinery should be relatively easy for the lead navigator and bombardier to locate because of its location on the Elbe River. Water is a geographical feature easily seen from altitude and the target was situated on the estuary at the mouth of the Elbe River.

Captain Taylor walked over to the planning table where he drew the course specified in the field order on a map of the area. He was taking particular note of the "flak" areas identified by intelligence and other sources of information from previous missions, along the route.

At 0205 Col. Luper entered the intelligence hut. Someone yelled "Attention" and everyone "pops to" (stands at attention). Luper savors the respect for a brief moment, takes the pipe from his mouth and quietly says, "At ease." Everyone goes back to the jobs they were performing.

Luper walks over to the table where Capt. Taylor is drawing on a map with a straight edge the course the 457th airplanes will follow on the mission. He rubbed his hand behind his neck as he characteristically did and said to Capt. Taylor, "What is today's target?" "The 457th is leading the 94th Wing to bomb a Hamburg oil refinery, sir," as Luper looked at a copy of the field order Taylor had handed him.

"Well, we've been waiting for good weather to visually strike their oil installations for some time now, and it appears we've got it," Luper said.

"This is the 749th Squadron lead today, isn't it?" Luper questioned (as he posed a positive question—he had been schooled in never asking a negative question. It shows weakness in your character, he always said.)

"It is, sir," Capt. Taylor answered. "Major Hoffman is air commander of the lead box but I have not been informed of the identity of the lead crew he is flying with. Shall I find out the identity of the lead team, sir?" "That's all right," Luper answered. "I'll find out from Ted." (Ted was Major Ted. C. Hoffman, Squadron Commander of the 749th Squadron.)

"I see we are 'putting up' two 18-ship boxes," Luper said as he read through the field order. "Yes," Capt. Taylor said. "Major Smith is the Air Commander of the low box. He is flying the right seat with Capt. Schuchmann as pilot, Lt. Byers as lead navigator, and Capt. Tonelli as lead bombardier."

"That should be a good team" Luper absent-mindedly offered as he puffed on his pipe.

* * * * *

457th

Main briefing map and target.

457th

Lead team briefing, right to left: Lt. Roland O. Byers (N), Capt. Irwin Rosen (B), Capt. Frank Taylor (S-2).

457th

Main briefing crews.

457th

Equipment room.

The two hinges on the outer door of the light lock of the 750th squadron "Q" hut, orderly room, squeaked harshly as Major J.M. Dickinson stepped out into the darkness. "Mac" hesitated a moment to allow his eyes to adjust to the darkness, and looked up at the sky and could see a few stars blinking through a 3/10 overcast sky. He thought to himself, "Looks like the weather is good enough to get a mission off."

The time was 0225 hours and Mac hurried over to Major William F. Smith's "Q" hut and, shining the flashlight away from his face, shook the squadron commander's shoulder and said, "Bill, the time is 0230 hours and y'awl wanted to get up early to go over today's mission with Capt. Frank Taylor before briefing." "Mac" Dickinson said this in his usual unhurried Tennessee drawl.

Bill Smith sat up on the edge of his bunk, blinked his eyes, yawned, looked at his watch as if he didn't believe it was time to get up. "Thanks, Mac. That sure was a short night," he said in his also unhurried Alabama drawl.

Smith dressed, putting on his long woolen underwear and O.D. woolen shirt and trouser (even though it was June, it would be cold at 25,000 feet), and ran his electric razor over his face, not spending much time trimming his thin mustache. It seems that mustaches were sprouting all over the Group since Colonel Luper showed up with one.

Smith pulled on his field jacket, climbed into his jeep, and drove through the darkness with what little light the blackout headlights made, toward Group headquarters and S-2 (intelligence) quarters.

At 0255 hours Major Dickinson again came out of the 750th orderly room hut and walked in the darkness over to the huts where 1st Lt. Roland Byers, lead navigator, and Capt. Dino Tonelli, lead bombardier, bunked and he awakened them. His next stop was the hut of Capt. Schuchmann, the lead pilot, and then to the eight other huts where the crew members lived, who would be flying today's mission from the 750th squadron.

Not every crew member had slept soundly that night, for as Major Dickinson said it, "As Squadron Operations Officer, I felt it was my duty to awaken my crews. It was then I learned what 'sweating it out' really meant—a great many of the men would be wet with cold sweat, dreaming about and reliving the missions they had flown, knowing they were alerted to fly the next day."

During the half hour between 0225 and 0255 "Mac" Dickinson had toured the flight line in his jeep and had stopped and talked briefly to the crew chief of each of the nine planes that he had put on alert for today's mission. He found that all were in flying condition and were ready for the mission. The ordnance men were loading each plane with twelve 500-pound G.P.s (General Purpose) bombs. The 100-octane gasoline load for the mission was specified as 2,500 gallons and gasoline trucks were filling the leakproof tanks up to that amount. (A full gas load was 2,680 gallons with Tokyo tanks.)

Mac stood and looked longingly at "Miss Ida," the lead ship and the ship in which Major Smith, Captain Schuchmann, Capt. Tonelli, and Lt. Byers, the lead team, would fly and lead the low box of the 94th wing. "Miss Ida" had been "his" ship. He had named it so to honor his mother and when he looked up at the name printed on the nose of the airplane it brought back to him fond memories of his home in Tennessee.

It would now be warm in Tennessee, he thought to himself for the briefest moment. In June, even at night, the warm breezes blew softly over the green bluegrass fields and whispered through the

457th

Major J. "Mac" Dickinson

maple trees. The frogs would be croaking in the marshes and the katydids would be "calling" from the hardwood trees. His thoughts were jolted back to the present by the ragged staccato backfiring of an airplane engine in the 749th squadron dispersal area. "Sounds like some crew-chief is having trouble getting a fortress ready for the mission," Mac mused to himself. Then as he glanced at the luminous dial on his "hack" wristwatch he noted the time to be 0250. He had five minutes to drive back the half mile or so to the 750th Squadron living area and to get "his" crews up for the mission.

The time was 0330 hours and 144 officers composing the combat crews who would fly the day's mission filed into the officers' mess two and three at a time. No one seemed to be in any rush even though briefing was set for 0400, a half hour ahead. Neither was there much conversation from the usually loquacious "fly boys." Part of the reason was due to the combat experience of this particular group of men. They were veterans of many rough missions over Germany and for some this would be their last mission. Some would complete their required tour of between 25 and 30 missions, depending on the date they started their tour, if they got back from this one. Almost all of the men had completed 20 or more missions. Most of the men in the chow line had been original crews coming to the ETO as members of the 457th Bomb Group and had been fortunate enough to survive when 27 of 72 crews (37%) of their friends, more than one out of every three crews, had been shot down. This was not counting the individual crew members who were wounded, or killed, on an airplane which had returned to base. This was a deadly business and with a mission into the very "crucible of affliction" facing them, there wasn't much levity or conversation in evidence. Each knew that some of the group would not return to eat dinner this day.

While combat crew members were usually given fried eggs for breakfast – sort of the last meal before the execution – the breakfast was tasteless, regardless of the fare. The hot coffee did give a little lift to the appetite. However, the men ate, because they knew it would be twelve hours before they would eat again when they returned from the mission.

It is one minute before 0400 hours. The combat crews are assembled in the briefing room awaiting the prompt arrival of Col. Luper. The faces of the men are without emotion – almost blank. There is no fear, apathy, or arrogance showing in the faces, only the desire to get a dirty job done. These were not the faces of overconfident killers out to conquer the world, only the faces of young men who would rather be plowing the soil back on the farm, going to college, riding with the cattle, selling suits, constructing buildings, selling insurance, teaching school—almost any civilian occupation you can think of was represented by the men assembled in the dimly lit room.

Then someone yells "Attention" and every man in the room stands at attention as Colonel James Luper, commanding officer of the 457th Bombardment Group, strides briskly into the briefing room. Luper, swinging his "swagger stick," savors the respect shown for the rank and uniform—possibly even confusing the military courtesy as respect for the man. Luper had only eight days previously, 12 June 1944, been promoted to the rank of full Colonel. He said "At ease" and the quiet men sat back down on the benches.

The S-2 sergeant pulled back the black curtain that was drawn in front of the wall map and the eyes of the crew members followed the long black ribbon extending from the coast of England across the North Sea to the coast of occupied Holland, across the Zeider Zee, and on into Germany, turning sharply north to Hamburg and the target.

There were a few murmurs in the back of the room, which subsided as Luper strode to the front of the rostrum and began to speak.

"Men, as you can see on the map before you, our target for today is once again the oil refinery at Hamburg. We attempted to hit this refinery two days ago. Some of you were probably on that mission. We were, however, unable to strike the target because of a 7/10 cloud cover and the effective smoke screen which obscured the target area. However, the weather report for the Continent is predicted to be CAVU and we should have good conditions for bombing. It is important that we demolish this refinery. We must deny the Wehrmacht and the Luftwaffe oil with which to fuel their war machines. We will have good fighter support today. Seven hundred and sixty fighters will patrol the bomber stream. However, be alert for the Luftwaffe—with good weather they will be up in numbers to protect their oil refineries.

"Col. Wilson informed me that our formation was ragged on yesterday's mission to Landes-de-Bassac Airfield in France. As you are aware, a ragged formation invites fighter attacks. After today's mission I want to hear from Major Smith and Major Hoffman that our formation flying has improved. Otherwise, we will spend our stand-down days learning the finer techniques of high altitude formation flying. That isn't a threat, men, that's a promise.

"We have two spares assigned to the mission today. However, I do not anticipate any need for them. If you check out your airplane adequately before take off, there is no excuse for an abort. You airplane commanders: If you do abort, stay with your airplane until your photograph has been taken and then report to my office immediately.

"Let's fly a good mission today, worthy of the 457th!" And he turned and strode crisply out of the room.

Combat had not mellowed the "Old Man" as it had many of the other commanders. He had been schooled at the "Point" and served his apprenticeship in the Training Command. He still adhered to the premise of "When I say squat, I want you to start straining."

S-2 Capt. Frank Taylor now steps forward as the projection screen is pulled down in front of the map and the S-2 sergeant turns on the opaque projector to show the photograph of today's target—the oil refinery at Hamburg.

Taylor says, indicating with a pointer the installation he is talking about, "This is your target, the oil refinery at Hamburg. This is one of 14 targets the 8th AAF will strike today with 1,360 B-17s and B-24s. Other locations targeted by the 8th AAF include: Harburg, Ostermoor, Misburg, Politz, and Magdeburg.

"The lower box under command of Major Smith will assemble over our base and the lead box commanded by Major Hoffman will assemble on the buncher of the 351st at Polebrook. The 351st will not participate in this mission."

Capt. Taylor nodded to the opaque projector operator who turned it off. Capt. Taylor raised the screen and with a pointer discussed the route to the target.

"You will depart the English coast at Cromer, cross the North Sea, and enter occupied territory at Bergen Ann Zee, just north of Amsterdam. There are two flak areas on the coast, but at your altitude of 19,000 feet you should not receive any flak if the group is on course. The bomber stream will cross the Zeider Zee and continue east toward Hannover. The 94th Wing will turn north to Hamburg just south of Bremen.

"Your route out of enemy territory after your bomb strike will be a course of 280° which will take you over the North Sea just south of Kuxhaven.

"You can expect fighter attacks at any time as you near the enemy coast. However, the VIII Fighter Command will put 760 fighters in the air along your route. Flak will be heavy and accurate over the target. The radio men will start dropping chaff (WINDOW) 3 minutes before the IP (initial point) and continue dropping for 15 minutes at 3-minute intervals."

Capt. Taylor then walked to the side of the rostrum and Major Smith, the air commander for the low box, now stepped to the platform.

Major Smith was a West Point graduate, one of the four West Point graduates assigned to the 457th. Col. James Luper, Major Leroy Watson, and Major William Snow were the other three. While Major Smith was a "good soldier" and expected his men to be likewise, he had empathy for his fellow man and was well liked by the men of his command. He listened to the needs of his charges and, when merited, stood his ground when the issue involved the individuals under his command.

In his low well-modulated southern drawl (Latham, Alabama), Major Smith said, "Stations are at 0630, we will start engines at 0730, we will taxi at 0810, and take off is at 0825. We will assemble on the Glatton buncher. Visibility is predicted to be excellent. However, I will be firing red and green flares for identification purposes. We will assemble at 8000 feet, and depart on a course magnetic heading of 40° at 0918. The 457th B.G. is leading the 94th Wing on this mission as well as flying the low box. The 401st B.G. at Deenethorpe will fly the high box. We will join the Division formation between Splashers 7 and 8. Zero hour is 1000, the time when we cross the English coast at Cromer.

"Our bombing altitude is 25,000 feet and if the weather holds as predicted we will bomb the primary target. If we for some reason cannot bomb the primary target we will seek a target of opportunity on our withdrawal.

Let's keep them tucked up tight and fly a good formation. Good luck and good bombing."

Major Ted Hoffman, commander of the lead group, now stepped to the rostrum and repeated for the lead box much of what Major Smith had said for his group.

Next came the weather officer, 1st Lt. Charles D. Weber, saying, "Weather for assembly will be 2/10 thin alto-stratus clouds above 12,000 feet, with a few cirro-stratus above 25,000. The weather over the Continent is CAVU, one of the few we have experienced in our time in this part of the world. The weather for your return to base will be excellent.

"The winds are 325 degrees at 10 knots at ground level and will be 340 degrees at 70 knots at 25,000 feet at the target. We expect this wind to hold for the next 12 hours.

"The temperature at bombing altitude of 25,000 feet will be -28 degrees."

Capt. Edwin R. Roberts, group intelligence officer, now stepped up on the rostrum and said, "We will not set our watches." He studied his watch for a moment and said. "The time will be 0447 hours at the cue." He waited for a minute or so, giving everyone time to pull the stem on their watch, set the watch, and stop the sweep second hand at 0447. Then he said, "In ten seconds the time will be 0447 hours—10-9-8-7-6-5-4-3-2-1-hack," at which time everyone in the room pushed the stem and started their watch.

"I will repeat the important time requirements for the lead and low box—Stations is 0630," etc., etc.

After he had repeated the time increments, he said, "The navigators may now go to the planning room and get their pilotage maps. The bombardiers are to go study the target pictures with the group bombardier. The lead teams will get together with your squadron intelligence officer—Capt. Frank Taylor for the 750th and Capt. Larry D. McDonald for the 749th.

"The co-pilots are to pick up the flimsies [a printed sheet made of rice paper, to be eaten if possible if bail-out is imminent] for themselves and the radio operator [lists all signals, frequencies, etc., for the day]. The co-pilots will also pick up escape kits [contained money and silk map of area flying over] for each crew member. When you return from the mission turn them in to the intelligence officer at de-briefing and you will get your left testicle back!" This brought a guffaw from some of the co-pilots and broke the tension that hung over the group. "Those of you who wish to talk with Chaplain, Capt. Victor F. Halboth, may do so in the back of the room after briefing."

The navigator and bombardier of the lead team of the low box, 1st Lt. Roland "Ron" Byers and Capt. Dino Tonelli respectively, sat at a table in the front of the planning room talking with Captain Frank Taylor about the bomb run from the IP (initial point) to the aiming point—the oil refinery at Hamburg. Capt. Taylor pointed out to Tonelli the location of the target in relation to the ship docking facilities in the estuary, just beyond the target. He also pointed out the location of the round oil storage tanks to the southeast of the target and the marshalling yard adjacent to the refinery.

Lt. Byers and Capt. Tonelli discussed the bomb run and

identified on the map the town of Soltau, Germany, 40 miles south of Hamburg at the IP. The bomb run would also take the group near the towns of Harburg and Wilhelmsburg only five miles from the target.

The target would be heavily defended and on a clear day the flak would be intense. Tonelli needed to have a mental picture of the target area well in mind so that the deadly distractions did not affect his setting the crosshairs of the Norden bomb sight on the target. The bombs from all 18 airplanes in the group would be dropped at the time the bombs dropped from the lead ship. On Tonelli's shoulders rested the success or failure of the mission. Three hundred and sixty men would put their very lives on the "line" to deny oil to the German war machine.

After briefing was over the crew members all walked to the equipment room to put on their flying equipment: the heated suit, gloves, and boots; the leather helmet, the goggles, the oxygen mask, the throat microphone, the Mae West, a parachute (back or chest pack), the heavy flak suit worn over all of it, and a flak helmet. You tie the laces of a pair of G.I. shoes to the harness of your parachute just in case you "hit the silk." Escape and evasion would be easier with a good pair of shoes. Under your left arm, in a shoulder holster, is your .45-calibre automatic pistol, to be used in case an incensed farmer is about to stick his pitchfork into you or sic his dog on you. If you are captured you hope it would be by the military. At least they knew about the Geneva Convention.

During the next hour or so from 0530 to stations at 0630, the gunners assembled their guns—the thirteen .50-calibre machine guns on a B-17 model G(the model G had a "chin" turret under the front end nose of the B-17 which was fired by the bombardier). All guns were taken out of the airplane after each mission and cleaned. A gun would freeze up in the below zero temperature if not cared for by experienced hands.

The co-pilot was meticulously checking over the airplane in the company of the crew chief, making sure that the airplane was as airworthy as was humanly possible to make it.

The pilot was with the Operations Officer discussing the formation and what to do in case an airplane aborted or was disabled by flak or fighters.

The lead team—air commander, pilot, navigator, and bombardier—flew in the lead airplane of the 18 "ship" box. Flying on the right wing of the lead airplane was the deputy lead in which also flew a lead team capable of assuming the duties of the lead airplane in case of malfunction of any of the equipment in the lead airplane or the lead airplane was shot down. In the event both the lead and deputy lead airplanes were unable to complete the mission, the lead ship in the high element (six airplanes) or the low element were equipped with a bomb sight and an experienced crew which could "take over" if necessary, and on occasion was called on to do so.

There is an aura of expectation hovering over the hardstands. The time for stations is only ten minutes away. The sun shines as a red ball through the mists of the "fens." In each crew member the hard knot that is his stomach does not seem to soften. On occasion one of the crew hurries to the back of the hardstand and "pukes" up his breakfast. Better now than in his oxygen mask. Stomachs will feel better when the airplane is airborne. This mission will go – the weather is good. This mission will not be "scrubbed."

The ground crew polishes the glass on the pilot's windshield and the plexiglas in the waist, nose and turrets. Visibility is important in seeing fighters, of flying formation, picking out targets, and doing navigation.

Time 0625 ... the crew has all been transported by trucks to the dispersed airplanes. One of the last acts by the crew before climbing into the ship is to answer "a call to nature" at the rear of the hardstand. Nine or ten hours in the air, in the below zero temperature, puts a strain on the body. There are no relief tubes, only a flak helmet. More than one flak helmet was used for relief and then the "flak" started coming up!

At 0630 hours all crewmen are in their positions in the airplane. Major William F. Smith Jr., the air commander, has not arrived but will wait at flight control until just before start engines at 0730 for any final instructions. In the lead airplane, "Miss Ida," number 152, Capt. Clare Schuchmann, a burly farm boy from Hawkeye, Iowa, and co-pilot 1st Lt. Franklin "Crash" Marra have taken their seats on the flight deck and with T/Sgt. Joe Hibbs kneeling between the seats are going through that part of the pilot's check list accomplished before engine start. Lt. Marra has completed the preflight check and will ride as tail gunner when Major Smith takes his position in the right seat.

The gunners, S/Sgt. Ed Lanzone and Harold Duseaux, waist gunners, and Robert Bridges, ball turret, have completed checking all of the guns and are nervously awaiting takeoff. Guns will be test fired when the formation is over the North Sea.

The radio operator, S/Sgt. H. R. Pike, waits for the power to come up so he can check his radio. He checks the packages of chaff (strips of aluminum foil) which will be pushed out the slot in the side of the airplane when the formation nears the target area. The aluminum strips jam the gun sighting radar used by the Germans, hopefully confusing the altitude at which fuses on anti-aircraft "flak" shells are set.

The navigation instruments would need to be checked when the engines were started and the power "came up."

The bombardier, Capt. Dino Tonelli, checked the twelve 500-pound G.P.s hanging from shackles in the bomb bay. The pins have been pulled and all appears to be in readiness for the mission. Tonelli also talked with the radio operator to check signals about turning on the strike camera just before bombs away.

The ambulance and the fire truck are in position for the takeoff. One asbestos-clad fireman is suited up in case of fire in any of the airplanes. He appears as if he were a monster club-footing around the fire truck, ready to walk into a fire to save the lives of any bomber crewmen who might survive a takeoff crash.

1st Lt. Roland Byers, lead navigator, and 2nd Lt. John W. McDonnell, dead reckoning (D.R.) navigator, climb through the hatch up into the nose. They take from briefcases navigation equipment which they lay out on the table located on the left side of the "nose" and just in front of the pilot's instrument panel: maps, flight log, an E6B computer, a Weems plotter, a pair of dividers, and pencils. The crew of a lead ship includes two navigators, a lead navigator and a D.R. navigator. A third navigator is used if the bombing is to be by instruments—H_2X through the clouds.

Start engine time 0730 is approaching and Major Smith in his plywood-topped jeep pulls to a stop in front of "Miss Ida" and Bill gets out and walks to the airplane and pulls himself up into the front hatch. The ground crew pull through the propellers in preparation for engine start. Propellers are pulled through to assure that a liquid-lock has not accumulated in the lines to the cylinders. No one wants a blown cylinder now.

The time is 0730 and a red flare is fired and arches above the control tower. The put-put (generator) is running beside the airplane providing power to start the engine. Capt. Schuchmann, the lead pilot, slides his window back and yells "All clear." The crew chief answers, "All clear" and stands ready with a fire extinguisher in case of engine fire. The pilot turns to the co-pilot (Major Smith acting as co-pilot) and calls out, "Master switches and ignition switches on." "On," comes back the answer. "Battery switches and inverters on." "On and checked." Etc., etc., until the entire check list has been accomplished and all four engines have been started.

When the power came up, the bombardier, the navigators, and the radio operator each checked their instruments and equipment. Lt. Byers, lead navigator, turned on the Gee set and the remote reading compass. He set the day's barometric pressure in the altimeter, and watched the instruments as each gave a reading. It soon became apparent that the reading from the remote compass (the remote compass is placed in the outer wing, well beyond the magnetic field set up by the engines—the display in the pilot's cockpit and at the navigator's position is a slave unit) was incorrect. Flying without a compass was impossible and would require the lead ship to abort the mission.

Lt. Byers called Capt. Schuchmann on the interphone, "Navigator to pilot." "Go ahead," Schuchmann answered. "It looks like our compass is giving a false reading. Seems to be 180° out of phase! What does the magnetic compass on your instrument panel read?" "About 340° Mag," Schuchmann answered back. "The remote compass reads 160°," Byers stated. "Ask the crew chief if the remote unit was worked on since the last mission."

After a time during which the pilot talked to the crew chief, it was determined that the remote compass had been installed backwards.

Major Smith called Lt. Byers and asked, "Ron, do you think we could fly the mission by using the reciprocal of each heading?" Byers thought a moment and answered, "We'll give it a try, sir!" And so the mission was flown "backwards," so to speak!

Capt. Schuchmann taxied "Miss Ida" out of the hardstand, brakes squealing as a turn is made on to the perimeter track. "Miss Ida," the lead ship, is first in line as all the other B-17s will play follow the leader and wheel into line behind the lead ship and each slowly taxi around the perimeter track to the end of the runway, awaiting the signal from the control tower for take-off. Lt. Byers sets the coordinates of the end of the runway on the Gee set just in case the weather does not hold as predicted and fog settles over the "fens."

Back at the "hardstand" from which "Miss Ida" had just departed, the crew chief leaned against the fire extinguisher cart and contemplated the oil leak in number 3 engine. The engine was not an original Curtis Wright Cyclone engine but rather was a replacement engine—Studebaker built—and tended to leak oil. He hoped it was all right as he "cocked his ear" and listened to the engines in the distance. He was also abashed that the compass had been installed incorrectly. Although the instrument section had installed the compass, it was his responsibility.

In "Miss Ida," the time for take-off was near. The engineer Joe Hibbs knelt down between the pilots and watched the instruments as Capt. Schuchmann ran through the check list prior to take off. All seemed to be in order as the brakes were set, awaiting the green flare from the control tower.

The time is 0825. The green flare arches high over the control tower. The Wright Cyclone radial engines of the B-17 increase in RPM as Capt. Schuchmann eases the throttle forward and the engines throb. The brakes are released, the lumbering B-17G heavy bomber rolls slowly down the runway. Schuchmann grits his teeth. The Hamilton-Standard propellers bite into the air and pull the airplane faster and faster. The tail of the airplane now lifts from the

457th

B-17s lined up for takeoff.

457th

Assembly for mission.

runway, but still the lumbering giant is earthbound. This is the time of decision. Will the airplane gain enough speed before it comes to the end of the runway? The twelve 500-pound bombs, 2500 gallons of gasoline, armor plate, contraband flak suits lining the nose of the airplane-by the navigator, eleven crewmen, all the extra ammunition toted by the gunners into the airplane—all increased the gross weight of the airplane. Now is the time of commitment. The speed of the airplane increase ... 110 ... 120 ... 130. Schuchmann pulls back on the control column. The controls still feel mushy. He pushes hard on the throttle. Seemingly they will not go far enough forward. The end of the runway is approaching fast and Schuchmann pulls back harder on the control column. The engines roar in a cacophony of sound. "Miss Ida" slowly but surely lifts off of the runway. We are airborne! The lumbering behemoth is now as light as a butterfly as it dances in the breeze and climbs slowly to the west. Schuchmann, Smith, and all the others of the crew breathe easier now. The mission was on—tensions were eased. The experienced crew would deliver the bombs to Hitler's 1000 year Reich.

The other airplanes of the group each in turn taxied onto the runway and at 30-second intervals repeated the take-off as had the airplanes before it. Turbulance, "prop wash," from the airplanes ahead made climbing difficult, but in spite of the rough air all climbed upward toward assembly.

The lead ship circled the Glatton radio buncher, the radio operator firing red and green flares at intervals so that the lead ship could be identified.

After circling the base for a while the lead navigator, Lt. Roland Byers, called the pilot, Capt. Schuchmann, on the interphone. "Navigator to pilot." "Go ahead," Schuchmann answered. "We have five minutes until departure and I would like for you to make a five-minute circle on the buncher. When you cross the buncher at 0910 hours come to a magnetic heading of 349° (169° on the remote compass). That will take us to the first checkpoint at Cottsmore." "Roger," Schuchmann answered back.

The formation was now formed. Radio silence was mandatory and the formation had been formed by each of the eighteen airplanes finding its place in the V-shaped formation. This was seemingly accomplished without apparent difficulty because of the long hours of practice and combat flying time of each crew. Luper's badgering had its good points: it saved lives.

From the ground Colonel Luper looked up at the sky as the roaring formation approached the base at 8000 feet elevation from the south. He noted that "Tail End Charlie," the end airplane in the low element, and also a "ship" in the high squadron were not "tucked" into the formation with their element leaders. He looked at his watch and noted the time to be ten seconds early—0909:50—ahead of departure time. Luper looked over at Lt. Col. Henry B. Wilson, deputy group commander, and said, "The group is on course and on time. Makes for a good mission."

Between Cottsmore and Lycester the three 18-ship boxes, two from the 457th Bomb Group and one box of 18 B-17s from the 401st Bomb Group—Deenethorpe—the high box of the 94th Wing, assembled in wing formation. The difference in elevation of each box was 1000 feet relative to the lead box. The lead box would at bombing altitude be at 26,000 feet, the high box at 27,000 feet, and the low box at 25,000 feet. The V-shaped formation would form into 1st Division formation between splasher 8 and Cromer.

Aircraft of the 1st Division would form the lead division in the bomber stream of 1360 B-17s of the First and Third Divisions and B-24s of the Second Division.

The heavily loaded bombers, pregnant with bombs, climbed steadily higher as they crossed the North Sea to the landfall along the Netherlands coast.

The co-pilot, now flying as tail gunner and observer, Lt. Marra, reports to the air commander Major Smith, "Tail gunner to air commander." Major Smith answers, "Go ahead." "Sir, the formation is intact except for the last aircraft in the high element. He seems to be having trouble keeping up with the formation. Also I have seen two aircraft from the 401st fall back and out of formation in the high box. One has been replaced by a spare aircraft." "Thanks, Marra," answers Major Smith.

Capt. Schuchmann calls on the interphone for an oxygen check and the crew answers quickly, "Tail, ok," "Left waist, ok," "Right

457th

8th AAF bomber stream.

waist, ok," etc. The check was completed quickly from lots of experience. On some crews the co-pilot performs the oxygen check while on others it is the pilot. Now comes the rattle of machine guns as the gunners fire short bursts to test their guns. The vibration is apparent when one of the turrets start squirting lead. Capt. Tonelli, the bombardier, tests the chin turret and finds it operative. Tonelli then moves out of the bombardier's chair and is replaced by Lt. Byers who occupies the position because of the good visibility of the plexiglas nose from which to do pilotage navigation. The visibility is good and only the difficulty of peering into the sun and frost that forms on the plexiglas limits the ability of the navigator to see the coastline ahead. Lt. Byers, lead navigator, now watches intently for the exact landfall along the Netherlands coast so as to avoid the "flak" areas on each side of the course. If Capt. Taylor had the correct intelligence information, the formation should "slide" right between the two flak areas. If not, some of the aircraft would probably be hit. The fault is that of the navigator or incorrect intelligence. A coastline with its harbors, estuaries, capes, and islands offers excellent landforms for pinpoint navigation and a precise course can be determined to steer the formation by anti-aircraft defenses.

The 94th Wing is now nearing the coast and Lt. Byers sees the low box of the wing ahead is receiving some flak. He decides that the box is two miles to the right of course. From 19,000 feet you can "spit" on two miles. However, he calls the pilot, "Navigator to pilot." "Go ahead," Schuchmann answers. "Turn five degrees to the left to a magnetic heading of 259° (79° actual) on your remote compass. This compass problem is confusing, isn't it. It looks like we're a little right of course and flak is hitting the low box in the wing ahead. When we make landfall we'll turn back right again to 264°," Lt. Byers states. "Roger," Capt. Schuchmann answers, and the other aircraft in the formation, which follows the movements of the lead ship, slowly swing five degrees to the left and then level out. A small change in either heading or speed is magnified by the time Tail End Charlie sees the change. The navigator of the 94th Wing lead box, the 749th Squadron, apparently also saw the "flak" exploding in the low box of the wing formation ahead, as Byers noticed that the lead box also eased to the left.

"Be alert for bandits," Schuchmann tells his gunners as the formation makes landfall exactly over Bergen Ann Zee. McDonnell, the D.R. navigator, notes the time of landfall in the log. Ahead across the narrow strip of land lays the Zeider Zee. It was a larger body of water now than pre-war as some land had been flooded during the German invasion.

There had been very few days during which the visibility was as good as it was on 20 June 1944. From the altitude to which the bombers had climbed, now 20,000 feet, the patchwork farmland below was a green panorama not often seen.

Escort fighters, P-51s and P-47s, could be seen carving hugh S's made visible by contrails high above the bombers as they followed the bomber stream eastward, alert to any Luftwaffe fighters that might try to attack their charges.

The gunners slowly rotated their turrets back and forth searching the skies for the German Air Force which of late had been noticeable by its absence except on selected instances. Air superiority in the skis over Germany had been wrenched from the Luftwaffe by the P-47, the P-38, and in particular the P-51, "The Mustang."

T/Sgt. Joe Hibbs, the engineer and operator of the top turret, let his mind wander for a moment because of the paucity of action and thought about his PX ration he had to pick up before the week was over. Although he didn't smoke, the ration of one pack a day could be used in trade to the English for fresh eggs and for other short rations. He also would get for the week two bars of candy, two razor blades, two boxes of matches, and one package of gum.

The steady drone of the four Wright Cyclone engines, still laboring to pull the heavily loaded bomber up to the 25,000 feet bombing altitude, could mesmerize one if he did not direct his attention at his job. The nascent sense of expectation, however, kept the experienced crew member alert. Those who let their minds stray too often were not flying anymore.

When the target of the massive wave of 8th Army Air Force bombers became apparent to the German warning system, the Luftwaffe would be directed to climb and intercept the bombers in an attempt to protect their depleted oil supply.

Aided by the 340 degree at 70 knot tailwind, the 94th Wing crossed the Zeider Zee and penetrated the patchwork land of occupied Holland in only twenty-two minutes. The narrow "flakless" corridor between the towns of Zwolle and Meppel was negotiated by pin-point navigation without the formation receiving any "flak." However, bursts of "flak" were seen at flight level on either side of the course.

At 1115 hours Lt. Byers, the lead navigator, turned in the bombardier's seat and handed Lt. McDonnell, the D.R. navigator, his pilotage map on which he had written "ETA for turn to IP at 1119 hours. Do you confirm?" McDonnell looked at his log on which he had previously calculated an ETA for the turn and held up his hand with his thumb and index finger forming a circle—the sign of confirmation. His D.R. wind calculation had been the same as that calculated from pilotage by Byers. D.R. wind direction and velocity is calculated by reading the drift on the drift meter on two or more "legs" of a flight and then plotting that drift on the E6B computer.

McDonnell looked at Byers with only the two eyes of his face visible, the remainder covered by his oxygen mask, nodded his head "yes," and handed Byers back his pilotage map, after which Byers called the pilot on the interphone. "Navigator to pilot." Go ahead," Schuchmann answered. "In two minutes, at 1119 hours, turn left to a heading 8° — 188° on the remote compass." "Roger," Schuchmann answered. "That is 8° — 188° on the confused compass at 1119 hours," Byers repeated.

The 94th Wing would leave the security of the bomber stream and fly north to bomb the refinery at Hamburg, while others in the 8th AAF would continue on deeper into Germany to bomb targets at Politz, Ostermoor, Misburg, and Magdeburg.

At 1119 hours the 94th Wing turned gradually to the left and into the teeth of the 340°/70 knot wind. The run to the IP would be slow. The bomb run from the IP to the target would be through intense anti-aircraft flak and would be at a speed of only 156 knots, practically standing still, sitting ducks.

The two boxes of 457th airplanes and one of the 401st—54 airplanes— labored northward into the wind. Other groups of B-17s were ahead and would also attack targets in the Hamburg area.

"Gunners, we're sitting ducks out here away from the bomber stream," Schuchmann cautioned his crew, although as he looked high above he could see the contrails of escort "little friends" following the formation north.

Then Sgt. Bridges, the ball turret gunner, calls on the interphone, "Bandits at seven o'clock low. They appear to be FW-190s out at about 3000 yards—about seven of them." All eyes in the airplane, and all guns that could bear, swung in that direction. "They don't seem to be heading our way," Bridges stated. "Watch them," Schuchmann said. "Hold your fire—unless they close."

Major Smith called Lt. Marra, "How is the formation, Lt.

Marra?" "Looks good, sir," Marra answered. "They're tucked in tight." "That's why the bandits aren't attacking," Smith mused to himself.

"Navigator to pilot." "Go ahead," Schuchmann answered. "We'll be at the IP at 11:36:30, in two minutes," Byers said. "At that time turn 5° to the left to 3° or 183° on the remote compass." "Roger, Capt. Schuchmann answered.

Lt. Byers and Capt. Tonelli now exchanged places in the nose, with Tonelli seated over the Norden bomb sight. The oxygen hoses were exchanged, each man making sure that the other had snapped in place the hose attached to their oxygen mask. Byers now checked the wind drift with McDonnell, the D.R. navigator, to be sure the wind drift was accurate that Tonelli would enter into the bomb sight.

Sgt. Joe Hibbs in the top turret excitedly came on the interphone. "We're not gonna have any trouble with the bandits," he said. "A flight of six P-51s just dove down from above and scattered the FW-190s."

At 11:36:30 Schuchmann swung slowly five degrees to the left, leveled out, and then set up the AFCE (automatic flight control). As soon as he was satisfied he called Tonelli and said, "She's all yours, Dino."

P-51 Mustang based at Kings Cliffe AAB, 55th Fighter Squadron, 20th Fighter Group.

457th (Bains)

P-47 Thunderbolt. One of the three "Little Friends" P-38, P-47, and P-51 which provided fighter cover for the 8th AAF bombers.

(Bains)

P-38 Lightning. 77th Fighter Squadron, 20th Fighter Group Kings Cliffe, Northamptonshire, United Kingdom.

Tonelli had been programming the bomb sight—setting in the bomb ballistics and wind drift. He also checked his bomb release switches and found all to be in readiness for the bomb run. The airplane was now being flown by the bombardier through the auto pilot connected to the bomb sight.

Ahead lay the city of Hamburg. Lt. Byers hunkered behind Tonelli, looking out over Tonelli's right shoulder through the plexiglas nose for the target. The visibility was excellent. There was some smoke coming up from bomb explosions in other parts of the city but now the target appears at the end of the estuary. Byers points toward the target and Tonelli agrees and leans over the bomb sight to pick the target up in the sight.

"Navigator to air commander." "Go ahead," Smith answers. "The bomb release time will be at 1147, sir—about three minutes," Byers says. "Thanks," Smith answers. "Navigator to pilot: When bombs are away turn left to a heading 280° (100° on the remote compass)," Byers said. "Roger," Schuchmann answered.

The flak ahead is heavy. The bomb run is straight and level. The anti-aircraft gunners can see clearly the formation as it approaches, knowing you will not deviate from the course. The ground speed is slow. The formation is flying almost directly into the 340° 70 knot wind.

Tonelli has completed his settings; he opens the bomb bay doors. The cold air surges through the airplane. He calls the radio operator, who is busy pushing "chaff" (window) out the slot. "Start the strike cameras." "Started," the radio operator answers.

Flak is now bursting in the formation—it is intense—a burst hits an airplane in the formation. Flames flash from number one engine. The airplane pulls away slowly at first and then peels off to the left, flames spreading to other parts of the airplane.

"Jump," Sgt. Harold Duseaux, the waist gunner, urges. "Jump before it blows!" Then the plane drops out of his line of vision. The airplane is number 615—Lt. Bomer's plane.

Tonelli checks his bomb sight again, making sure his original settings were on target. The indices in the sight move together and then the airplane lifts and the bombs drop. "Bombs away," Tonelli almost yelled over the interphone. He leaned forward watching the bombs fall in a ballistic curve toward the target. Now the bombs were out of sight. He waited ... waited ... and then came the explosion, the flash of fire and smoke as they hit the refinery dead center. Tonelli called the air commander, "That's one shack (target) we won't need to hit again." "Good show," Smith answers back, emulating the English exclamation.

Smith calls Lt. Franklin Marra, "Can you see anything of Bomer's airplane?" he queried. "No, sir," Marra answered back. "The plane dropped below the formation and I lost sight of it." "Thanks," Major Smith answered.

The crew of A/C No. 615 was lost to anti-aircraft fire over the target and are as follows: Lt. William G. Bomer, pilot; Lt. Jack A. Bade, co-pilot; Lt. Charles Curione, bombardier; Lt. Robin E. Hill, navigator; Sgt. William H. Kane, AEG, Sgt. Edward Kline, RO, Sgt. Edwin E. Teagler, RWG, Albert W. Leeing, BTG, and Richard A. Bohl, TG.

Capt. Schuchmann had swung left, away from the intense "flak" in a turn that was steeper than usual. The formation had "loosened up" somewhat after bombs away. Everyone was wanting to escape the intense "flak" following the formation.

Then it was over—the attention of the anti-aircraft gunners was directed at the other incoming bombers.

Again Major Smith called Lt. Marra, "Do you see any other aircraft in trouble?" Lt. Marra answered back, "I see two other aircraft each with a feathered propeller, but they seem to be keeping up with the formation."

The field order had specified that the group start descending just after leaving the target and Capt. Schuchmann now eased back on the throttle and dropped the nose. The maneuver also allowed the damaged aircraft to keep up with the formation.

"Navigator to pilot," Byers said. "Go ahead," Schuchmann answered. "We will cross the coast outbound at 1206 in about two minutes at which time take a heading of 296°—116°, the reciprocal, on your remote compass. Our ETA for the base will be 1317 hours." "Roger," Schuchmann answered back.

The "let down" across the North Sea was without incident. At 10,000 feet the oxygen masks came off. Those who had taken with them a candy bar hungrily chewed the delectable morsel. While the formation was loose, the integrity was maintained. More than one group had in the past been attacked by far-ranging Luftwaffe fighters over the North Sea.

The return trip home to base was without incident for the 35 airplanes which returned from the mission.

All was not well in all the airplanes, however. As the airplanes of the group came in over the field, two of the planes came in low firing red flares, an indication that wounded men were aboard. Those airplanes were allowed to land first so the men could be rushed to the hospital.

On aircraft 574, Lt. John B. Fowler, co-pilot, and Lt. Ralph C.

Jordan, bombardier, were wounded from a burst of "flak." On aircraft 689, S/Sgt. Joseph Schrapiro, engineer, had been wounded by "flak." These men were quickly loaded into the ambulances and driven to the base hospital for medical treatment.

Col. Luper looked up at the formations as they prepared to land and counted 33 airplanes. The group had been relatively fortunate today. Upon landing, however, several aircraft were found to be badly damaged from the fierce "flak," requiring major overhaul.

The war had not been so kind to the bombers which had bombed Politz, Magdeburg, Ostermoor, and Misburg that day. One hundred and twenty Luftwaffe fighters had attacked the bombers and all together the 8th AAF lost 48 bombers on the mission and 468 had been damaged. It turned out that this mission was one of the few occasions since 1943 that the German Air Force had temporary air superiority. The Luftwaffe lost only 28 airplanes.

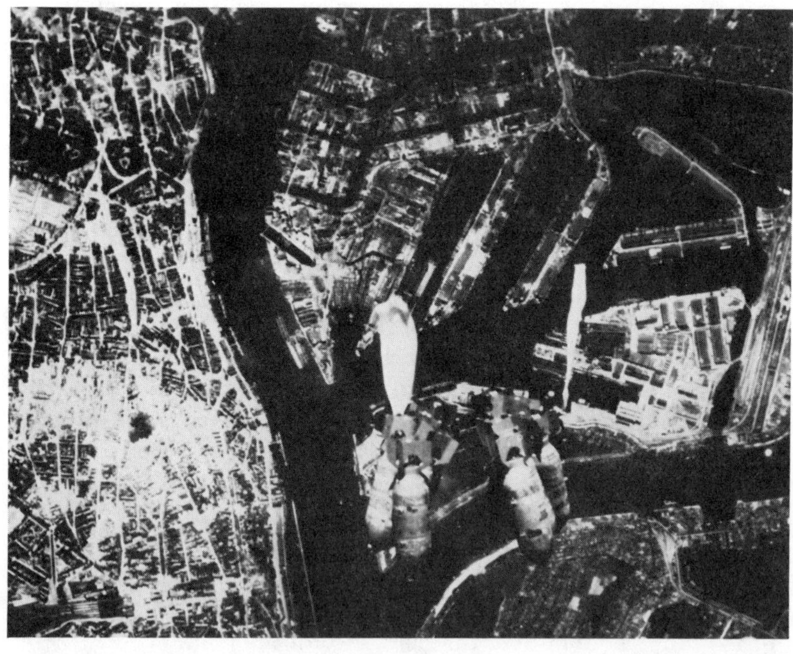

457th (Zemper)

"Bombs Away," Hamburg 20 June 1944.

The bombing results of the mission were excellent at all targets. The refineries at Politz, Hamburg, and Magdeburg were forced to shut down for repairs. The German armed forces were denied fuel for their sputtering war machine.

For Lt. William G. Bomer and his crew, the mission had been fatal. They were to join the 85 other crews which would make the ultimate sacrifice for their country from the 457th Bomb Group.

The crews climbed down out of and walked around their airplanes, looking at the holes punctured by bursts of "flak." The crews were then transported to base operations where they were given a shot of bourbon by the flight surgeon, if they wanted it, given doughnuts and coffee, and were interrogated by the S-2 intelligence officers. Many questions were asked: "Were there any unusual occurrences? Did you see any jet aircraft? Any ships in the North Sea? Was the 'flak' unusual?"

The formation had not been attacked by fighters and no "kills"

457th (Zemper)

Hamburg 20 June 1944.

were reported. Had anyone seen what had happened to Lt. Bomer's airplane? Were there any parachutes?

The mission had been the last mission of the tour for Lt. Roland O. Byers, lead navigator. He was given a cluster on the Distinguished Flying Cross (DFC) for navigating an airplane effectively with malfunctioning equipment. But he would return to the group to fly a second tour after R & R in the United States.

The mission was by men who were well trained and performed effectively, men who "placed their lives on the line" for their country.

457th

Ground crew waiting for the chickens to return from the mission.

457th

Watching A/C returning from tower: left to right, B.Gen. J. K. Lacey, C.O. 94th Wing; Col. James R. Luper, C.O. 457 B.G.; Lt. Col. Roderick L. Francis, Deputy C.O. 457th B.G.

457th (Zemper)

Bombs away at Merseburg.

Merseburg

2 November 1944 – Mission: Merseburg/Luena, Germany.

Although target selection priorities had shifted somewhat by the end of October 1944, German oil facilities still retained their position as first priority for the 8th AAF bombing attacks. Close behind oil though was the German transportation system. However, on 2 November 1944, the 8th AAF continued its attacks on the German oil industry and sent 1,100 heavy bombers to attack the synthetic oil plant at Merseburg/Luena, a target that the 457th Bomb Group had not visited since the 29th of July 1944.

Prior to the 2 November mission, the Luftwaffe had not made a significant appearance in the German skies for three weeks. The last mission on which the 8th AAF had lost many aircraft to fighters was the 7 October mission when the 8th AAF had lost 52 heavy bombers, 41 of which were attributed to fighter attacks.

The 457th B.G. had suffered severely on the 7 October mission to Politz when the Group had lost its commanding officer, Colonel James R. Luper, as well as other Group officers. However, losses incurred had been as a result of accurate and intense flak and not fighter attacks.

But today would be different – for the Luftwaffe filled the skies with Me 109s and FW 190s. They had conserved fuel for a period of time and launched fighters in significant numbers – 400 were estimated.

The Luftwaffe was also using improved weapons and tactics when attacking the heavy bombers. They were using explosive and incendiary projectiles as well as 20 mm cannon fire.

For the 457th Bomb Group the target selected for the day was Merseburg/Luena, Merseburg being the city in which the Luena synthetic oil refinery was located. The Group launched 35 B-17s, almost a complete 36-ship box. The 748th Squadron was designated to lead the Group as well as provide the lead team for the high 12-ship squadron. The 751st Squadron provided the lead team for the low box as well as the majority of the crews and aircraft in the low squadron.

The crew of the lead ship of the Group was as follows:

P	Capt	Donald L. Seesenguth
A/C	Major	Eugene A. Peresich
Lead Nav	1st Lt	Roland O. Byers
DR Nav	1st Lt	George A. Voris
PFF Nav	1st Lt	Joseph F. Ellis
TG	1st Lt	William D. Mock
Bomb	1st Lt	Kenneth B. Taylor
AEG	T/Sgt	Raymond D. Brodin
ROG	T/Sgt	George R. Mangowski
LWG	S/Sgt	William M. Thacker, Jr.

The crew of the lead ship of the high squadron was as follows:

P	1st Lt	Richard E. Fitzhugh
CP	1st Lt	Louis G. Mueller
Lead Nav	1st Lt	William J. P. Meng
DR Nav	1st Lt	Enoch T. Naverson
PFF Nav	2nd Lt	Felicisimo Basuil
Bomb	1st Lt	John Schwall
AEG	S/Sgt	Henley R. McDonald
ROG	T/Sgt	Howard Carson
LWG	S/Sgt	George L. Cole
TG	1st Lt	Kenneth E. Rohde

The lead ship of the low squadron was as follows:

P	1st Lt	William E. Dawson
CP	Capt	John B. Wallace
Lead Nav	1st Lt	Jerome Silverman
DR Nav	1st Lt	George P. Korb
Bomb	2nd Lt	Frank O. Pappenfuss
AEG	T/Sgt	John R. Roster
ROG	T/Sgt	Harold W. McDaniel
BT	S/Sgt	Joseph M. Giller
LWG	S/Sgt	George C. Hardin
TG	2nd Lt	Charles B. Ford

The group was well supplied with experienced lead crews and radar equipped A/C on this mission. The lead navigator of the lead ship as well as the navigator in the low squadron were original Group navigators and each had previously flown a combat tour as members of a lead team and each was flying a second tour.

The lead ship, the deputy lead, and the leader of the high box were all PFF equipped A/C.

The group assembled above briefed altitude because of clouds, however, they joined the wing and division formation as briefed. The navigation of the group as it entered Germany was under the control of PFF as the undercast was either 10/10 or partially broken during the complete mission.

Navigation by PFF on a lead ship flying over an undercast is performed by the "Mickey" (PFF) navigator providing the lead navigator with fixes which are determined by crossing two bearing

457th

Lead Crew on mission to Merseburg, 2 November 1944. Standing left to right: Lt. Roland O. Byers, Capt. Donald L. Seesenguth, Major. Eugene Peresich, Lt. Kenneth B. Taylor, Lt. Joseph F. Ellis. Kneeling left to right: T/Sgt Raymond D. Brodin, S/Sgt William M. Thacker, T/Sgt George R. Mangowski, Lt. George A. Voris, Lt. William D. Mock. A/C "Miss Ida" #152.

and distance (LOPs) lines of position from identifiable radar reflections of geographic locations, such as towns, etc., on the ground. The position of the aircraft can in this manner be determined in only a few seconds and a position can be maintained at all times.

Bombing by PFF is performed in much the same manner. The "Mickey" navigator uses the radar reflection of the target area rather than using a visual sighting at which the bombs are dropped. The method is effective for bombing a large target such as a town but is not effective for a small specific target such as a manufacturing plant.

The penetration of Germany and the course to the vicinity of the IP was flown as briefed.

Beyond this point there is a difference of opinion as to what happened thereafter. It is standard procedure for the lead navigator to give the lead pilot an estimated time of arrival (ETA) at the IP. The ETA is determined, in the case of PFF control, by using the PFF fixes to establish positions and from those positions determining a ground speed and with this ground speed forecasting an arrival time at a point ahead where the course will be altered. To add credibility to that position the dead reckoning navigator maintains a constant watch of the instruments—the magnetic compass, the altimeter (altitude), the indicated air speed, the drift of the aircraft in relation to the ground (if visible), and the outside temperature—and from these data calculates a D.R. position.

The one most credible source of information while flying over an undercast is of course PFF (radar) information.

The check of the ETA to the IP calculated by the PFF information did not in this case match that determined by the D.R. navigator. An additional check of the PFF information provided the same discrepancy. However, the ETA for the turn on the IP elapsed and as previous course and time had appeared to be correct the turn at the IP was made. The air commander was informed of this discrepancy as the turn was made. As soon as the turn on the IP was completed both Lt. William J. P. Meng in the high squadron, who also had PFF information on which to calculate an ETA for the IP, called his pilot and informed him that according to his calculations the lead ship had turned about five minutes early (about 20 miles) on the bomb run. Radio silence was broken and the information relayed to the air commander, Major Eugene A. Peresich, in the lead ship. About the same period of time the navigator in the low squadron, Lt. Jerome Silverman, although he did not have PFF information, had calculated an ETA based on briefed winds and what corroborating information—visual pilotage—he could obtain along the course. Silverman also informed his pilot to relay the information to the lead ship to "check your navigation," being aware that the Germans would be monitoring VHF radio transmission.

As a normal rule the lead navigator does not monitor VHF transmissions as does the air commander and was unaware of the radio messages by the other lead aircraft when they were made.

When the lead aircraft reaches the IP (if over an undercast), the coordination between the pilot, PFF navigator, and the bombardier now is instituted and continues until the bombs are dropped. The coordination occurred as is standard procedure.

It was obvious by watching the other aircraft in the bomber stream that the course taken by the 457th was to the left of the other aircraft of the 8th AAF, which were also bombing the Merseburg/Luena target. Only one factor added to the credibility of the route was the trail of two smoke bombs dropped by another group which lay directly ahead on the 457th course.

The 457th B.G. bombs were dropped by PFF and after bombs away the formation immediately turned to the right to get back into division formation which it was very obvious at this point had been violated.

There was no anti-aircraft flak visible at the selected target, neither were there any fighters visible at the time of bombs away.

The 457th had very obviously strayed away from the bomber stream and had the German Air Force not selected 2 November 1944 as a day on which to make an appearance for the first time in three weeks, the mistake in navigation would have been counted as another of the many mistakes which occurred during the 236 missions flown by the Group.

But such was not to be the case, for 40 or so of the German Luftwaffe—mostly FW 190 fighter aircraft—attacked the 457th Bomb Group and shot down nine of the bombers, seven from the low squadron and one each from the high and lead squadrons, before being driven off by escorting P-51s.

When the remnants of the 457th Group returned to base and nine aircraft were determined to have been lost, a hearing was called which included the lead crews, by the group commander Col. Rogner, in his office. There the story of the mission unfolded. The final decision of those at the hearing placed the blame for the error on malfunctioning PFF equipment in the Group lead ship.

But really was the equipment at fault or was there a breakdown in communication and should not the blame have been placed on lead crew error?

If the PFF equipment in the lead ship was malfunctioning should not this error have been detected earlier either by the lead navigator or the PFF navigator?

When the leader of the high box which also had PFF equipment informed the air commander that the turn on the IP was in error, should not the air commander have transferred the responsibility of the bomb run to the deputy lead A/C?

Was the PFF navigator lost and did he make an incorrect ETA for the IP?

If a wind shift had occurred why did not the lead crew correct for the shift as had apparently the other groups?

The answers to these questions were academic for the cause of the error, found at the hearing, was declared to be equipment malfunction and no blame was affixed to those flying the mission. The short time of only four or five minutes between the turn on the IP and the release of the bombs probably precluded any change in command and at that point the error had already been made and could not be reversed.

Whether the German Luftwaffe would have selected the 457th as the victim for 2 November 1944 is also academic, although time and location in this case was obviously detrimental to the 457th. However, the attack could even have been worse had not the escorting P-51s been in the immediate vicinity at the time of the attack.

1st Lt. Jerome Silverman, the lead navigator flying in the low box and one of those shot down on the Merseburg mission, gives his version of the mission as recalled nearly 40 years later.

"I was a member of the 751st Squadron and was flying as lead navigator on the 2 November 1944 Merseburg mission. 1st Lt. George Korb was D.R. navigator.

"As we taxied from the hardstand prior to take-off, Lt. Jerry Page, a 751st navigator, was standing there waving us off and I recall with a rather grim look on his face. Maybe he knew something we didn't.

"I have no specific recollection of the takeoff, the assembly or the route to the IP as they were generally as briefed. I recall very vividly what followed soon after, however.

"We were turning on the IP determined by the lead ship. I remember clearly calling the pilot, Lt. William E. Dawson, and asking him to call the lead ship on VHF and tell them 'Check your navigation.' I figured the lead ship would know what I meant, for we had turned on the IP much earlier than I calculated we should. Besides, the whole 8th Air Force was going one way and we were going another!

"The official report of the mission states that 'The formation was navigating by PFF when the Group began to deviate north of course, while the PFF operator believed he was on course.'

"Now I think I was on pilotage at times, however I do recall heavy cloud cover during most of the mission. However, we were obviously leaving the bomber stream regardless of our form of navigation.

"Time was obviously against us and soon the bomb bay doors were opened and the bombs were dropped but I knew we were no place near our target at Merseburg.

"Only God and some of the farmers know what we hit but I do recall seeing farm land through breaks in the undercast.

"Well, after bombs away we broke right and chased the rest of the 8th Air Force but we never quite made it! The tail gunner, Lt. Charles Ford, began calling out 'Fighters to the rear of the

(Bains)

A captured German Focke Wulf (FW) 190 with British markings. Merseburg, 1944.

formation — a whole "gaggle" of them, 30 or 40 or more." At first we hoped they were friendly but friendly fighters don't queue up like these were doing.

"Well, being in the nose I couldn't see much of the action but I knew they weren't friendly fighters when I saw white cottonballs exploding all around us.

"I did see enemy aircraft diving through the formation when they split S'd out. I also saw one FW 190 stall out ahead of us right at our level and our bombardier and I'm sure others drew a bead on him and cut loose all at the same time. One wing of the FW 190 was shot off and he fell away just before we would have run into the pieces of the airplane.

"At one point quite a shudder went through the airplane. I thought it was probably cannon fire, however, I found out a little later that a FW 190 had been shot up and had collided with our airplane.

"We were still flying straight and level when the pilot hit the bail-out bell. So I reached back into the navigator's hatch and jettisoned the entry door and prepared to bail-out. I remember hanging my legs out preparatory to jumping and I looked down. At this point Pappenfuss suggested that I untie the shoe string with which I had tied up my oxygen hose — taking the weight of the hose off the mask. He said, 'You might hang yourself,' and I said at the time, 'That's a good idea.'

"I recall at that point thinking, 'Hell, this is the only transportation I have back to England and I have a date I want to keep in a few days, up in Scotland.' So I climbed back in the airplane, hooked up my intercom, and called the pilot, and asked, 'Just what is wrong with this airplane anyway?' The pilot, Bill Dawson, answered back, 'We are on fire because an FW 190 fighter had flown into us and the wing and tail section of our airplane is on fire.' Now I'm not from Missouri, but I looked out of the window and saw the big hole in the wing and could see what looked like gasoline streaming out of the hole. Further back the gasoline was burning. I thought, 'Well, it appears there is enough of the wing remaining to fly with. If we can get the fire out maybe we can get back to the base.' I crawled through the hatchway back to the bomb bay and from there could see the whole rear of the airplane was on fire. I was convinced. I crawled back to the nose and prepared to bail out.

"I remember thinking, 'Plenty of guys have bailed out so it must be all right' and I dropped through the entry door. We had been flying at 26,500 feet and I knew I needed to delay my chute opening, for I had passed out in about a minute in an altitude chamber test back at Maxwell Field, Alabama, during preflight, so I counted to 10 and then pulled the ring. Nothing happened. So I pulled it harder the next time and the ring and wire both came out of the parachute pack in my hand. I recall checking to see if my GI shoes were still tied to my parachute harness and also thinking had the parachute straps denied me of a future as a father. Something I guess we always wondered might happen if we jumped.

"Then it struck me as to how quiet it was, except for the sound of the bomber engines getting fainter and fainter, going away without me.

"I could also hear the sound of fighter engines and I looked around but could not see any. About that time I dropped through a layer of clouds into a clear area with another undercast below. Then I saw the fighters—four or five of them in a big 'Luftberry' nose to tail—going around in a circle. At first I thought they were German fighters and were firing at parachutes, but not so. I could see that P-51s were following Me 109s and I could see the flashes along the front edge of the wings of the P-51s as they were firing at the Me 109s.

"Well, I soon fell into the undercast—and was I glad—then I broke out of the clouds again and could see the ground. Just below me, which I was sure I would hit, was the sharp steeple of a church in the middle of a small town. Well, fortunately, I missed the town and was not impaled by the steeple. I landed in an open field and was soon surrounded by people who took me prisoner. And I spent the remainder of the war as a POW.

"I was released from the prison camp on 29 April 1945 by units of the 14th Armored Division, Ninety-Ninth Division of the Third United States Army commanded by Lt. General George S. Patton.

"I was transported back to the United States and was home one month later on 29 May 1945."

Lt. William J. P. Meng, lead navigator of the high squadron, recalls the mission in this way:

"I was the high squadron lead navigator on the mission to Merseburg on 2 November 1944 (it was the group's 143rd mission). The bomb load was 12-500# GPs. The target was the oil refinery and was PFF (part visual). The Mickey operator (radar), Lt. Felicisimo Basuil, had control of the flight. I was doing visual plotting and the second navigator in the nose, Lt. Enoch T. Naverson, was following with D.R. All three navigators were in constant communication as to our location.

"We had had the ETA about five minutes and twenty miles early when the lead squadron turned at the IP. I advised the pilot, Lt. Richard E. Fitzhugh, of the error. He advised, on VHF, the air commander of the Group, Major Eugene A. Peresich, of the error. However, time was against me. We dropped our bombs on the lead ship smoke bomb. There was no record of what we hit as we had a 10/10 undercast.

"About ten minutes after bombs away and before we were back in the bomber stream about 40-50 Luftwaffe fighters hit us and we lost nine airplanes. I can still see men jumping out of their airplanes some with their chutes on fire. Yes, it was a bad day for the 457th."

Mission Ingolstadt

5 April 1945 — Mission Ingolstadt, Germany

Lt. William J. P. Meng, lead navigator of the 5 April 1945 mission to Ingolstadt A/F, was hard pressed to complete his preparation for the mission because the course and time intervals had been changed twice before the mission was finally set.

Bill Meng and 1st Lt. James P. Guyot, the D.R. navigator, worked rapidly in the lead team briefing room to change the briefed course lines they had drawn on their maps to conform to the latest change. By the time they were dressed in their flight clothing and were transported to the 748th Squadron dispersal area, start engines time had passed and the engines of the airplane were running on Miss Ida, A/C #44-8152, the lead ship.

Miss Ida was Major "Mac" Dickinson's ship. When he was relieved of his duties as operations officer of the 750th Squadron and made commander of the 748th Squadron on 17 September 1944, he brought the airplane with him.

Miss Ida was used as a lead ship on many missions thereafter. She was a lead ship because H_2X had been built into her "belly" where the ball turret would normally be located.

After laying out his maps and navigation equipment on the navigator's table, Lt. Bill Meng called lead pilot Lt. Donald L. Snow on interphone. "Navigator to pilot." "Go ahead, Bill," Lt. Snow answered. "Well we made it and we're finally all set to go," Meng said. "Glad you made it," Snow said. "I get lost too easy without a navigator. We've had a little trouble with number two engine—couldn't get it started—but it seems to be running OK now."

The time to taxi to the end of the runway was nearing and Major Edward B. Dozier, commanding officer of the 748th Squadron, who was flying as air commander on today's mission, drove up in his jeep and climbed into the airplane through the front hatch.

Major Dozier had joined the 457th Bomb Group at Ephrata, Washington, on or about 28 October 1943 along with the thirty-five combat crews from Moses Lake AAB.

From Nanafalia, Alabama and married to Elsa Dozier of Bessemer, Alabama, he had joined the Army Air Force and had graduated from Cadets as a pilot in June 1943. A gregarious man, he soon became the center of attention at the officers' club or wherever a group of "flyers" would gather.

He and his crew flew the first mission flown by the group on 21

February 1944 to Lippstadt / Gutersloh. The airplane was shot up so badly it was salvaged when he returned from the mission.

20mm cannon fire and flak had knocked out the number 3 engine, almost all of the controls, the oxygen system, and the interphone. The control surfaces on the tail were shot off. Unbelievably, Dozier brought the airplane back and made an almost perfect landing. One man, Sgt. Seymour C. Pliss, radio operator on the crew, was seriously wounded and died of his wounds. Others on the crew suffered from frostbite. For his display of airmanship, Lt. Dozier was awarded the D.F.C.

Major Dozier became a key member of the 457th Group and was promoted to captain and appointed assistant Group operations officer on 26 August 1944. On 30 October 1944 he was appointed as operations officer of the 748th Squadron. The author was appointed squadron navigator of the 748th Squadron on the same orders as was Dozier. The author and Dozier moved into one half of the Quonset hut, the other half of which was occupied by squadron commander Major Wilbur D. Snow and flight surgeon Capt. Shelby G. Bale.

All four of the men were addicts of the card game of bridge and spent many cold damp winter evenings enjoying the game. Capt. Bale always provided a bit of medicinal bourbon from his footlocker to warm up the occasion, however.

Dozier had subsequently, without an R and R in the United States as had the author and many other men, elected to fly a second tour of missions. He was soon promoted to major (16 March 1945) and on 19 March 1945 made squadron commander of the 748th Squadron.

* * * *

At 0530 the signal flares arched over the control tower, indicating it was time to taxi. Lt. Donald L. Snow increased the speed of the outboard engines, waved to the ground crew, taxied out of the hardstand, and, with brakes squealing, turned on to the perimeter track. Other airplanes in turn followed Miss Ida, the lead plane, around the perimeter track to the end of the 2,000 foot 340°/160° runway.

Lt. Snow braked Miss Ida to a stop and he and Major Dozier went through the check list, the routine performed just before take-off: set the trim tabs, check the generators, check RPM, exercise the turbos and propellers, etc., etc.

The time is 0600—take-off time—the tower flashes a green light. Lt. Snow glances over to Major Dozier, who nods his head, and Snow eases forward his throttles while holding his toes on the brakes. the engines roar in a cacophony of sound. Snow releases his brakes and Miss Ida surges forward, slowly at first and then picking up speed, reaching for the speed that would lift the heavily loaded bomber into the air.

Seated on a .50-calibre ammunition box on the right side of the nose,—the D.R. navigator sat in the navigator's chair at the navigator's table—as Miss Ida labored to gain enough speed to clear the tarmac runway, Bill Meng had no feeling of impending doom. His thoughts were on the assembly that was immediately ahead and was wondering if, in his haste to complete the preparations for the mission, he had neglected to include any vital information in the flight plan.

The speed of the airplane increased and Meng could feel the undulating motion of the airplane caused by the uneven surface of the tarmac briefly launch the struggling Miss Ida into the air — only to drop again onto the surface of the runway.

457th

Lt. Edward Dozier's original crew:

2LT	*(1024)*	*Edward B. Dozier*	*0803089*	*P*
2LT	*(1024)*	*Charles E. Newmeyer*	*0751186*	*CP*
2LT	*(1034)*	*Alexis P. Umoff*	*0755204*	*N*
2LT	*(1035)*	*Charles L. Hilton*	*0679515*	*B*
S Sgt	*(748)*	*Dwight M. Anderson*	*35561847*	*AEG*
Sgt	*(748)*	*Hyman Kalb*	*13127586*	*AAEG*
Sgt	*(757)*	*Seymour C. Pliss*	*12216617*	*ROG*
Pfc	*(748)*	*Frederick L. Exley*	*13109916*	*AROG*
Sgt	*(612)*	*Gerald E. Poston*	*15340923*	*AG*
Sgt	*(612)*	*Frank L. Ridenhour*	*34598066*	*AAG*

457th

Lt. Edward B. Dozier

How many times before had he "sweat out" this same take-off in an airplane loaded with 12-500 GP bombs and enough volatile 100 octane gasoline to fuel the four 1200 horsepower Wright Cyclone engines with power to carry the bombs to their target—today's mission, the Air Field at Ingolstadt, Germany. Meng had already completed twenty-five missions. He had flown on both the 100th mission on 3 August 1944 and the 200th mission on 7 March 1945, flown by the airplanes and crews of the 457th Bomb Group.

Meng had flown 3 group leads, 7 squadron leads, and 9 deputy leads and was squadron navigator of the 748th Squadron, having replaced Capt. Roland O. Byers on 28 February 1945.

Meng could feel Miss Ida lift from the runway as she gained flying speed. One could sense the feeling of lightness when the airplane became airborne.

Blond haired and pleasant Lt. Harry G. Vaal, seated forward in the bombardier's chair, turned his head and looked at Bill Meng, smiled, and held up his hand showing a connected index finger and thumb forming a circle, the sign of "We made it again—all is OK."

Harry Vaal was an original member of the 457th Bomb Group. He was the bombardier on Lt. Kenneth R. Johnston's crew which had been one of the 36 Hutchison Provisional Group crews which had joined the 457th B.G. at Wendover, Utah.

Lt. Harry Vaal had, as had Major Dozier, the air commander of the mission, elected to fly a second tour of missions, as a bombardier with the 8th AAF.

Miss Ida slowly climbed above the trees of Holme Woods on the north side of the airfield but seemed to hang in the air, not rising as rapidly as she should have. Even though Lt. Donald L. Snow had the throttles pushed forward toward the "fire wall" as far as possible, Miss Ida was not responding as she should. He was not getting full power out of engine number two.

Out of the corner of his left eye, Lt. Meng saw a flash outside the left window just above the navigator's table. Bill turned his head and looked more directly at the flash which had attracted his attention and saw fire coming out of the front of and curling around the cowling of number two engine.

Lt. Jim Guyot, D.R. navigator seated at the navigator's table, also saw the fire and with wide eyes looked over at Bill Meng, aware of the situation but saying nothing.

The airplane continued to climb for only a few moments. She seemed to hover for a time and then at the top of the rise about one mile beyond the end of the runway lost flying speed and started to fall. "It felt like an elevator descending," Meng said.

Lt. Snow saw the fire out of his window and turned and pointed outside his window and said to Major Dozier, "Number two engine is on fire!" Dozier immediately called on the radio and informed the tower that #2 engine of the airplane was on fire and they would try to return to base. Those were the last words heard on the radio by personnel in the tower. Any uncertainty by those people in the tower as to what was happening was soon dispelled, however, by a flash on the horizon and soon after the sound of an explosion.

Bill Meng felt the airplane dropping and knew that they would crash. He prayed to God, hard! He prayed that he could be again with his mother and spare her all the heartache that his possible death would cause her.

Out in front of the plexiglas nose of the airplane, Meng could see ahead a hay stack which Miss Ida struck almost squarely. The nose of the airplane broke off, dumping the three occupants of the nose – the bombardier, D.R. navigator, and Bill Meng – out on the ground at a speed of over 100 miles an hour. The bombardier, Lt.

457th (Zemper)

"Miss Ida" A/C #44-8152 crash at the end of runway 5 April 1944

Harry G. Vaal, struck his head on the yoke of the bomb sight and died immediately. "Lt. Jim Guyot and I were dumped onto the freshly plowed dirt of a potato field which probably saved my life," Meng said.

At the moment of impact the bombs and 100 octane gasoline exploded, blowing a large hole—over eight feet deep and thirty feet across—in the soft ground.

After the explosion, parts of the airplane fell around Lt. Meng and Lt. Guyot, a gasoline tank falling on Lt. Guyot. Lt. Meng was not hit by any of the falling debris but when he "came to" and he was aware of .50-calibre ammunition exploding, he struggled to get behind one of the nearby smoking engines.

"I heard Jim Guyot calling and I crawled and walked over to him and tried to pull him out from under the tank, but I passed out. The next thing I can remember is waking up on the X-ray table. I immediately passed out again and woke up again two days later in the hospital ward with a nurse trying to feed me pancakes.

"I learned that my injuries included a 30% compression fracture to each of the #3 and #4 lumbar vertibrae, a cracked rib, a fracture of my left ankle, some abrasions and burns, and a cut on the top of my head, the result of the blow which probably knocked me out."

The ambulance driver who was the first person to arrive at the scene of the crash saw Meng walking around in circles, apparently in shock, and he waited for Meng to stop, which he did at the edge of the crater. The ambulance driver noted that Meng was moving with his arms hanging almost to the ground and at that time thought Meng probably had suffered an injury to his back.

Fifteen days later, Meng returned to his "Q" Hut at Station 130, encased in a body cast, to get his personal belongings.

One of the crews in the hut had, on their next mission, experienced the same engine failure that had occurred to Miss Ida. However, they were more fortunate than had been the crew of Miss Ida. They had gained enough altitude to be able to dump the excess fuel and salvo their bombs in "The Wash" and return to base without mishap.

Another strange occurrence concerned the same crew on the day of the crash of Miss Ida. They heard the explosion and because of the time of take-off thought it to be the lead ship. When they learned of the one survivor, they knew without being informed that it was Meng who had survived.

All of the members of the crew except Vaal, Adams, and Todd were interred in Madingly, a U.S. military cemetery at Cambridge. Only Lt. William J.P. Meng survived the crash.

The following are the members of the crew which crashed on 5 April 1945:

P	1st Lt	Donald L. Snow
A/C	Major	Edward B. Dozier
N	1st Lt	William J. P. Meng, Jr.
N	1st Lt	James P. Guyot
PFF N	1st Lt	Herbert L. Stempler
B	1st Lt	Harry G. Vaal
AE	S/Sgt	Joseph R. Adams
RO	T/Sgt	Robert W. Pinkney
LW	S/Sgt	Robert L. Todd
TG	2nd Lt	Jack E. Taifer

(W. J. P. Meng)

Lt. William J. P. Meng and original crew (Meng kneeling 3rd from left).

P	1st Lt	William H. Flannery
CP	2nd Lt	Jewell L. Lowery
LEAD N	2nd Lt	William J.P. Meng
D.R.N	2nd Lt	Morris Armovitz
PFFN	2nd Lt	Raymond C. Moon
B	2nd Lt	John H. Schloondorn
AE	T/Sgt	Floyd K. Lagrassa
RO	T/Sgt	Duane E. Stowits
BT	S/Sgt	George L. Petty
TT	2nd Lt	Walter C. Strossner

457th

100th Mission Lead Crew, August 3, 1944. Left to right: Capt. Clarence Schuchmann P, Lt. Marsh Galloway N, Unknown, Lt. Col. William F. Smith A/C, Col. James R. Luper, 457th Commanding Officer.

Personalities

Lt. Col. William Franklin Smith, Jr.

Instruction in refresher navigation classes held during the summer months—July—in southeast Texas—Ellington Field—in the almost 100% humidity falls on almost deaf ears. Lunch time was only a few minutes away and the profusely perspiring instructor, his shirt wet from sweat, was doing his best to keep interested the dozing class of veteran combat navigators in the subject, Over Water Navigation.

The war in the ETO (European Theatre of Operations) had been over for almost three months (8 May 1945) and navigators from the 8th Army Air Force in England, the 9th AAF in France, and the 15th AAF in Italy were being trained for transfer to the 20th AAF with operations in the Western Pacific Ocean. Others, as was I (author), were being trained as instructors and flight commanders at navigation schools.

The Saturday morning class was dismissed and the student officers filed out of the hot classroom into the equally hot hazy sunshine to either wend their way to the cafeteria or, for those living off base, to climb into their hot automobiles and drive home for the remainder of the weekend.

I walked over to the parking lot, climbed into my two-tone black and gray, 1941 Pontiac two-door sedan and drove out to the main gate and turned west toward Houston where my wife of only eleven months—seven months of which I was in England—Elaine Hohenberger Byers and I had rented an apartment located on Clay Street.

I squirmed a bit on the hot plastic seatcovers and reached over and turned on the radio. I heard the news reporter tell of attacks by B-29s of the 20th AAF on targets in Japan including an oil refinery in Shimotsu and of B-24s of the FEAF claiming direct bomb hits on a Japanese battleship and an aircraft carrier at Kure. The announcer then told of an AAF B-25 Mitchell bomber which had been flown into the Empire State Building in New York City. The airplane had been piloted by a Lt. Col. William F. Smith, a highly decorated veteran of many heavy bombing missions with the 8th AAF.

I was immediately alert to the news item for Bill Smith had been my squadron commander, with whom I had flown several lead missions as a member of the 457th Bombardment Group (H) while based in England. But then, Bill Smith was a common name — there must be hundreds of "Bill Smiths" in the AAF. Besides, he would have been flying a B-17, not a B-25. It would be coincidental if he was the same Bill Smith I knew and I almost dismissed the news item from my mind as I drove up Telephone Road and turned off to Clay Street and our apartment, thinking about my lovely wife who awaited me there.

Lt. Col. William F. Smith, Jr., had departed Bedford Army Air Field near Boston, Massachusetts, where he had visited his wife Martha and son Billy, at 0855 AM on 28 July 1945 with destination

457th

Lt Col William F. Smith Jr. C.O. 750th Squadron.

to be Newark Field, New Jersey. He had arranged to meet there Col. Harris E. Rogner, the 457th Bombardment Group Commander, with whom Smith had flown to New York where Rogner visited his family. Together they would fly back to Sioux Falls AAB, South Dakota, where the 457th B.G. was currently based.

On the journey of less than an hour by air, Col. Smith became lost in the low clouds which also obscured the high buildings in New York City. He drifted off of his intended course to Newark Field and had flown into the 79th floor of the Empire State Building. He had been killed instantly along with his two passengers.

But then, as I found out later, when the news story appeared in the newspaper, the pilot of the B-25 twin engine bomber was Lt. Col. William Franklin Smith, Jr., the same Bill Smith with whom I had flown so many missions bombing Hitler's 1000 Year Reich!

457th

Majors W.F. Smith and Fred A. Spencer, C.O.s 750th and 751st Sqdns respectively. 18 May 1944.

Lt. Col. Smith, a 1942 West Point graduate, was one of four West Point graduates assigned to the 457th B.G. before the group was transferred overseas to England in January 1944. The other three "Point" graduates were Col. James R. Luper, Lt. Col. Wilbur D. Snow, and Lt. Col. Leroy Watson, Jr. Col. Luper was later replaced by Col. Harris E. Rogner on 11 October 1944, four days after Col. Luper was shot down on 7 October 1944 on the mission to Politz. Col. Rogner was also a West Point graduate, having graduated in 1938. Each of these men would assume command of either the Group, a Squadron, or be selected as Asst. Group Commanders. Lt. Col. Wilbur D. Snow was an original 457th B.G. Squadron operations officer of the 748th Squadron and was later selected squadron commander of that Squadron (27 October 1944).

Lt. Col. Leroy Watson, Jr., was appointed squadron commander of the 748th Squadron while the Group was stationed at Wendover Field. He was later appointed as group operations officer. Lt. Col. Smith replaced Lt. Col. Watson as group opera-

457th

Lead crew May 30, 1944, Mission to Oschersleben. Left to right: Lt. Roland O. Byers (N), Major William F. Smith Jr. (A/C), Lt. John B. Blachley (B), Capt. Clarence Schuchmann (P).

tions officer on 16 February 1945 and later was appointed deputy group commander on 10 April 1945.

Col. Smith was one of the original members of the 457th Bombardment Group. He was the operations officer and eventually would be appointed deputy commander of the 457th B.G. on 10 April 1945 near the end of the war in the ETO (8 May 1945).

For the majority of the period while the Group was based at Glatton, England, Col. Smith served as squadron commander of

457th Lead Crew Dresden Mission, 15 February 1945:

1.	*P*	*Capt*	*Donald L. Seesenguth*	*0-815976*
2.	*AC*	*Major*	*William F. Smith*	*0-24859*
3.	*N*	*Capt*	*Roland O. Byers*	*0-675976*
4.	*N*	*1st Lt*	*John A. Frank*	*0-718274*
5.	*BN*	*1st Lt*	*Felicisimo Basuil*	*0-552175*
6.	*B*	*Capt*	*Kenneth B. Taylor*	*0-755250*
7.	*TT*	*T/Sgt*	*Raymond D. Brodin*	*16146931*
8.	*RO*	*T/Sgt*	*Jack J. Ham*	*16081947*
9.	*FG*	*S/Sgt*	*William M. Thacker*	*18032378*
10.	*TG*	*1st Lt*	*James Manspeaker*	*0-385796*

the 750th Bombardment Squadron (25 April 1944 to 16 February 1945). It was during this period of time that I served as lead and squadron navigator of the 750th and later the 748th Squadrons.

The first mission on which I flew with Col. Smith was to Epinal, France, on 23 May 1944. The target was a M/Y at Blainville. This mission was my first lead mission and I flew as navigator with Lt. Tom Goff. Tom was lead navigator on Capt. Schuchmann's crew at the time, but would complete his prescribed number of missions (25) with one more mission (27 May 1944 to Ludwigshafen) after which I assumed the 750th Squadron lead team duties until I too completed my first tour of combat missions on 20 June 1944 (described in chapter "Mission").

Lt. Col. William F. Smith, Jr., epitomized the mental picture that the average "man on the street" visualized an Air Force officer to be.

He was confident, loquacious, intelligent, of even temper—I never knew him to be indecisive even under fire—pleasant, swaggered a bit, stern if necessary, yet had empathy for his fellow man.

Dressed in his thousand mission crush hat, his green "Eisenhower" jacket, chest emblazoned with silver wings set on a blue field, colorful combat ribbons, shoulder epaulets surmounted with silver leaves, and "pink" trousers, he cut quite a figure.

Capt. Clarence Schuchmann, the lead pilot with whom Col. Smith flew as many of his missions as he did with anyone, describes Smith's crash in this way:

"I never could understand why Col. Smith flew into the Empire State Building. I flew a lot of the missions with Smith in the right seat. He was an excellent pilot. He knew the peculiarities of an airplane as well as anyone I ever knew. When we returned from a mission he would say, 'Schuchmann, let me grease this one in for the troops!'

"Col. Smith would fly training missions with me as often as he could so he could keep his hand in. He enjoyed flying and was in the air as often as he could get away from his squadron duties.

"I told Col. Smith that he would be a general one day and I wanted to be his pilot. We wouldn't fool around though with a big bomber as our airplane. We would fly a B-25. I had flown a B-25 during bomber transition before being assigned to B-17s.

"I really think that what happened to Col. Smith in the crash into the Empire State Building was a peculiarity about the B-25 that was different than was the case in a B-17. The airspeed of a B-25 would not change when the pilot 'let up' on the throttles. This was different than was the case in a big heavy bomber. I really think that Smith was more familiar with the peculiarities of the B-17 and when he became disoriented in the soup he was in trouble before he knew it in the B-25 because the airspeed did not change appreciably when he let up on the throttles."

Lt. Col. Smith and Col. Rogner flew back to the United States in "Flak Dodger," A/C #42-97075. They selected the A/C because it had been stripped of all the armour, making it lighter than the combat planes and consequently much faster. Sgt. Ralph Wendell, crew chief of 075, tells of a landing made by Col. Smith at Goose Bay. The landing was at night and when Col. Smith "set the airplane down," Wendell said he was still waiting for the "bump" of the landing when Col. Smith looked over at Col. Rogner, grinned, and said, "That's a pretty good night landing for not having made one for 18 months!"

He had really greased "Flak Dodger" in, which again gave credence to the comments of Lt. Clayton Bejot that she was like a Farmall F-20 tractor, "dependable."

457th

Col. Harris E. Rogner and Lt Col. William F. Smith Jr. on the occasion of being awarded the Croix de Guerre.

457th

First crew from 457th B.G. to complete 25 missions.

P	*2nd Lt*	*Robert D. Lane*	*0-803227*
CP	*2nd Lt*	*Howard E. James*	*0-754350*
N	*2nd Lt*	*Robert C. Dvorak*	*0-690639*
B	*2nd Lt*	*Thomas C. Guest*	*0-752667*
AEG	*S/Sgt*	*Winfred C. Kincaid*	*35564985*
ROG	*Cpl*	*John E. Misener*	*32672948*
AAEG	*Sgt*	*Joe D. McCall*	*38473037*
AROG	*Sgt*	*George J. Shukaitis*	*35515670*
AG	*S/Sgt*	*Garvin E. McBride*	*18193608*
AAG	*Sgt*	*James O. Vaughan*	*14045604*

Bits and Pieces

19 May 1944, less than three months after crews of the 457th had flown their first mission, the crew of Lt. Robert D. Lane completed its tour of 25 missions. They were the first crew of the 457th B.G. to do so.

Lt. Lane's crew had been a member of the Hutchison Provisional Group which had, along with 35 other crews, joined the 457th B.G. at Wendover Field, Utah. The crew had been assigned B-17G #42-97468 which they named "Tujunga."

"Tujunga" not only brought the crew to England, but it was in "Tujunga" that the crew completed their tour.

Their last mission, the 25th, was to Berlin on 19 May 1944. While the target potentially could have been a tough one, that day the mission was a "milk run."

Lt. Robert C. Dvorak, navigator of the crew, from Schuyler, Nebraska, was as elated as the quiet reserved farm boy from middle Nebraska ever became and celebrated with his usual glass of milk!

* * * * *

Lt. Clayton E. Bejot tells a story of what happened to the bulletin board located in the 750th Squadron area, just outside of the orderly room.

Seems there was a gathering of assorted crew members one evening in the "Q" hut occupied by the officers of Bejot's crew. Such a gathering was not unusual particularly on a rainy day after a scrubbed mission.

The conversation drifted from one subject to another including English women, poor food, dirty quarters, miserable weather, warm beer, Luftwaffe jets, V-1 buzz bombs. The mood of the discussion took on a mischievous tone as the contents of the bottle of White Cloud Scotch disappeared. The cause of most of their problems, they decided, was the information posted on the bulletin board.

What to do about it? The only solution to the problem was to get rid of the bulletin board!

A committee was selected from the most inebriated of the men and during the wee hours of the morning the bulletin board was "heaved" from the ground, taken to the "Q" hut, cut up with machetes and burned! The hut was warmed to a temperature quite unlike it had been since their arrival in England! Since the evidence had been disposed of, there has never been any culprit identified until this date! The troubles suffered by the troops did not cease, however, as the "Limey" maintenance men soon produced a new board.

* * * * *

Capt. Clarence Schuchmann, a lead pilot of the 750th Bombardment Squadron, tells the following story about his recovery from a "spin" in a B-17 loaded with bombs:

"Flying formation in a heavily loaded bomber in the rarefied air at the extreme upper limits of the service ceiling of a B-17 was very difficult. The aircraft did not respond quickly to changes in direction and altitude with the same efficiency above, as it did below 20,000 feet altitude.

"Comparatively, however, the lead airplanes were much easier to fly than that of tail end Charlie back there in purple heart corner. Any change in course or altitude found 'Charlie' alternating between 'hanging on his props' to catch up with, or of 'chopping his throttles' to keep from overrunning, his element leader.

"The weather condition that I despised more than any other in which to fly formation was fog. There were many bomber collisions which occurred from trying to fly a combat mission in fog and bad weather.

"On one of the early missions the Group flew to Berlin, March 4, 1944, the weather was miserable—we took off in the soup (fog), climbed through it, and assembled above the 10/10 undercast. I was leading the high squadron following the lead squadron of the Group of which Capt. Rod Francis was the Air Commander. Capt. Norman A. Kriehn I recall was the lead navigator of the Group.

"We penetrated occupied territory and were well on our way into Germany. The 10/10 undercast was coming closer and closer to our flying altitude of 25,000 feet the deeper we went into enemy territory. Soon we were flying in the soup. The visibility deteriorated and we lost sight of the wing of B-24s ahead of us in

457th

Capt. Clarence Schuchmann

the clouds. Then I lost sight of the lead squadron and soon the wing men could barely see the element leaders.

"About this time we received over VHF (very high frequency radio) a mission recall order — abort the mission and return to base. This was only the Group's seventh mission and we had not developed a decent procedure for flying formation in thick fog.

"The visibility was terrible and the wing men flew as close to our plane as was prudently possible so as to keep in contact. When I made a left turn so as to obey the recall order to return to base my right wing man, Lt. Robert Lane, didn't roll out quite as quickly as he should have when I rolled out. Lt. 'Crash' Marra, the co-pilot, saw Lane's airplane coming at our airplane and he 'figured' they were about to crash into us. He yelled something over the interphone and hauled back hard on the control column. I felt what was happening and reached down and switched off the automatic pilot and pushed the throttles forward as far as possible — too late of course. Well, we went straight up as quickly as you can in a B-17 loaded with three ton of bombs. We stalled out — fell off-I don't remember whether it was to the right or left—but I do recall the safety belt tightening on my lap.

"One of the wingmen, Lt. Bill Rogers, told me later he had told his co-pilot Lt. Stanley Wolczanski, 'Well, I guess Schuchmann's had it.' So he was real surprised when he made it home and found us there before he arrived.

"Anyway, we spun down and I tried to get control of the airplane but was having extreme difficulty. I glanced over at 'Crash' Marra and saw that he was holding the 'stick' back into his lap. I hit him in the shoulder with my fist and got his attention. 'Crash' released his 'frozen grip' and I pulled the airplane out of the spin! We had lost about 12,000 feet of altitude by the time I leveled out, glanced at the altimeter and saw we were down to about 13,000 feet."

Lt. Tom Goff, the navigator, said "I was in the 'nose' and when the plane started spinning the 'G' force was so strong I couldn't move."

Goff says, "As soon as I got my bearings and the compass quit swinging, I saw that we were going southeast. I called Schuchmann and told him, 'Schuchmann, we're going the wrong direction!'

457th (Dickinson)

Capt. Clarence Schuchmann right, Lt. Thomas Goff left.

Schuchmann then asked for a heading and I gave him a 270° heading until I could get my equipment together and find out where we were. I took some GEE fixes which fortunately was not being jammed as badly as it was usually and from that position calculated a course back to the base.

"We then had a crew discussion as to whether we would return to base 'on the deck' or start climbing again. We decided to go home as high as possible. The bad weather precluded any fighter attacks, so our only problem was flak areas," Tom says. "I continued to get GEE fixes. As we approached Dunkerque I again calculated a D.R. position and found that only 12 miles existed between my D.R. and the GEE location even after all of that manuervering around.

"We came out of the 'soup' at one point and there below us were three Luftwaffe fighter planes. They were close enough we could see the swastika insignia on the wings! For some reason they didn't attack us and continued on the course they were flying. There was a cloud bank just ahead and Schuchmann headed for it at full throttle.

"I had been lost once while in training in the United States and I thought this was a good time to build up the confidence of the crew in my navigation ability and didn't say anything about the GEE fix. We climbed up out of the clouds and when we crossed the coast between Dunkerque and Calais we slid right between the flak which came up on either side of us.

"We dumped the bombs in the Channel and dropped back into the clouds and when we broke out again below the clouds there we were right over Glatton AAB.

"Marra wanted to be sure that the base was in England and not a German base. I told him 'Glatton is the only base in Europe that has a farm inside the triangle of runways.'

"We landed and created quite a stir. It was almost an hour before any more airplanes showed up."

"I would guess that very few B-17s carrying a full bomb load ever recovered from a spin," Schuchmann said. "But now we know it is possible."

* * * * *

M/Sgt Ralph Windell tells a story about a young corporal—name withheld for security purposes—a welder by trade.

"The VD rate was a perpetual problem among the troops and an attempt was made to reduce the swelling incidence by Squadron officials with a concerted VD campaign. Rubber prophylactics became a required part of the 'uniform' before the troops were permitted off-base liberty.

"Seems the corporal, a shy, Catholic boy, found no use for the rubber prophylactics distributed free by the squadron docs. However, on a particularly rainy day after a couple of scrubbed missions and with scheduled work at a minimum, the corporal was passing the time in the welding shack. He happened to pull one of the unused prophylactics out of his pocket and the germ of an idea sparked his thoughts. He inflated the 'balloon' with acetylene gas and some oxygen from the handy nearby tanks.

"Things had been too quiet around the flight line and he decided to explode his invention. To do so, however, he needed a fuse, so he walked over to the nearby latrine and with a length of toilet paper manufactured a fuse and inserted it in the 'balloon.'

"Well, not wishing to be in the vicinity when the explosion occurred, he set the paper afire. The balloon ascended to the ceiling and the corporal vacated the premises.

"Well, the expected occurred! There was a loud explosion. Also, the top of the latrine went flying through the air.

"There was the usual inquiry but the lack of any evidence as to what had blown the roof off the latrine brought no indictments and the case was dropped.

"To this day the mystery had not been solved." Until now!

* * * * *

Lt. Col. Tom Goff tells about one of the "Q" huts in the 750th Squadron area.

"As you may remember, one of the officers' 'Q' huts was located close to the road. It was next to the parking area where all the trucks and cars parked. Liberty runs from Peterborough came in late at night loaded with 'loaded' troops making all kinds of racket!

"Well, the people in the 'Q' hut soon found out that that particular hut was poorly located and when a crew was shot down or a vacancy occurred in another hut, they soon moved to a more auspicious location.

"When a new replacement crew arrived, they were assigned to a vacant bunk and that was usually in the undesirable 'Q' hut.

"The hut came to be known as the replacement 'depot' hut in the 750th Squadron. Some 'joker' went into the hut and painted a sign over the door saying, 'NO ONE RESIDING IN THIS HUT HAS EVER COMPLETED A TOUR!' They also listed the names of the crews that had been lost!

"So, except for the original crews in the group, most of the officers had at one time lived in that hut.

"Anyone shot down was eligible to have his name included in the list. Believe me, there were lots of names listed. Can you imagine how a new crew member must have felt when he first arrived at the base, and found himself assigned to the 'depot'!

"You can bet each crew moved to another 'Q' hut as soon as another was available!"

* * * * *

100TH MISSION
AUGUST 3, 1944

Two milestones, given special attention by members of the 457th Bombardment Group (H), were the 100th and 200th missions.

The 100th mission was led by Major William F. Smith, Jr., as air commander and riding with the lead crew commanded by Capt. Clarence Schuchmann. The 457th B.G. launched 36 aircraft, and the target was a M/Y at Strasbourg, bombed to support "OVERLORD"—the Allied troops which had for two months been battling the German Wehrmacht!

The bombing results were excellent and there were no serious casualties or damage to 457th personnel or aircraft. All in all the mission was performed with expertise befitting the experience gained by personnel of the 457th B.G., both ground and air crews, of a veteran 8th AAF combat unit.

To celebrate the event, two dances were held—one for officers on 12 August at the Officers' Club and one for enlisted men on 11 August 1944. Free beer was served at the "Aero Club" for all enlisted men. The "Fireballs" station band played at both parties.

200TH MISSION

On 2 March 1945, the target was a M/Y at Chemnitz. Captain Edward B. Dozier flew as air commander. The bombing results of the mission were unobserved as the bombing was by PFF. There were no casualties and relatively minor damage to any of the aircraft.

The 200 missions flown by the 457th Bomb. Group had been accomplished in just one year and ten days—376 days—a mission flown every other day. Considering the scrubbed missions due to miserable flying weather, the achievement is commendable.

While the 457th Bombardment Group commanded by Col. Harris E. Rogner entered the European theatre later than had many Bomb. Groups, the 457th led the 8th Army Air Force in bombing results during the last five months of 1944.

Upon return to the base the crews were greeted by representatives of the 8th AAF 1st Division including the Commanding Officer, Brigadier General Bartlett Beaman.

* * * * *

A trip by train, 2nd class compartment, to London was the favorite off-duty recreation of the American flight crew members. London provided, even during the worst of the "Blitz," places to satisfy almost any desire, be it a stage play, a cinema, historical buildings, bridges, parks, castles, palaces, pomp and circumstance, Scotland Yard, blocks of bombed-out buildings, barrage balloons, double-decker buses, the Underground (subway), air raids by the

457th

100th Mission Party

457th (Bains)

Col. Harris E. Rogner, Commanding Officer 457th Bomb. Group

457th

Squadron Commanders at time of 200th mission. Left to right: Major Eugene Peresich 751st; Major Harry E. Lawrence, Group Engineering Officer; Lt. Col. William F. Smith Jr. 750th; Major Edward B. Dozier 748th.

German Luftwaffe, anti-aircraft barrages, flood lights stabbing into the sky, the putt-putt of V-1 flying bombs, V-2 rockets that slammed down and exploded without warning. Thick yellow fog—smoke spawned—through which taxi cab drivers walked carrying a lantern and guided the taxi. The Regent Palace Hotel—with breakfast in bed and white sheets. If your desires were slanted toward the baser things in life you could stumble through the blackout in Picadilly Circus and approach one of the myriads of Picadilly Commandoes, fallen doves who there plied their trade, women who, for the asked price of twenty pounds—$80.00—but who could be had for less—would provide bed and breakfast. Total conscription in England during World War II included all adults. Men and women alike were conscripted into the armed services or into industry. The Picadilly Commandoes were draft evaders and became lost in the masses of London and lived off of the carnal desires of the foreign soldiers as well as native "Limeys." Most of the women would probably have gravitated into the world's oldest profession, war or no war.

* * * * *

457th (Bains)

200th mission bomb drop. Major Edward Dozier A/C #44-8706 and Lt Smithson, Lead Pilot.

If one desired strong drink to dim the thoughts of lost friends or dreams of flak and fighters, such was readily available in London. The "Pubs" catered to all with warm beer—albeit often short of Irish or Scotch whiskey. Terrible tasting orange gin was dispensed until the daily ration was sold at specified hours—say 4 PM—Bourbon whiskey was scarce but could be found at the private clubs or at the Rainbow Club. Bourbon was expensive and was available to the "Yank" only through the Black Market. One could wonder who were the people who smuggled bourbon in the ships—the convoys—across the Atlantic Ocean when that space would have been better used for transportation of food and war materials.

Food was rationed to the English civilian economy. The bill of fare at the restaurants and hotels was sparce and not particularly palatable—even less palatable than the usual bland English diet. Allied military officers on leave in London prudently ate at the Grosvenor House, a "mess" operated by the United States military for Americans stationed in London but which was also available to officers on leave.

The English system of education shunted at the eleventh year most women into the vocational field rather than toward higher education. It was difficult for a relatively well educated American military man to meet the class of English woman who was educated beyond the secondary school level. The average English woman who voluntarily climbed into the back of an American 6 x 6 truck and was transported to a dance at the nearby Army air base was usually not educated beyond secondary school. Rather, the base commander was forced to publish in the Daily Bulletin that women attending dances on the base must be off the base by 0200 the night of the dance. I must admit that the willingness of the English women to attend the dances was appreciated by all. Certainly there was need for female companionship even if only for dancing and talking. To be able to talk to anyone other than a fellow airman was needed to keep the mind off of the next mission.

Not all American men were looking for a philosophical conversation and some of the women were on occasion amenable to a visit to the quarters of the base personnel, whether they be enlisted men or officers. Flying combat does strange things to men and the desire to survive often made God-fearing chaste Christians out of some. The carnal desire for solace of the body was for some precluded by the desire to survive. Only by imbibing in an excess of alcoholic beverage were inhibitions dimmed—inhibitions built up by living a life style developed to survive a tour of missions.

* * * * *

A bar of soap was often included in the duffle when the airman went on a pass. Body cleanliness was not the same in England as it was in the United States, and a visit to the water closet (WC) was on occasion a precursor of intimacies.

* * * * *

Reluctant female companions were often tempted by the promise of a pair of impossible-to-get nylon stockings, nylons which had been sent from the United States to the designing airman for just such a purpose.

* * * * *

Lucky talismen and superstition had their place in the mystique of survival. Even the author carried through the war a silver dollar won on the crap (dice) table in Ephrata, Washington. That silver dollar is still in my possession.

Many airmen carried lucky charms. One I recall was a cloth dog carried by Capt. Kenneth Taylor, a lead bombardier with whom the author flew many missions. We both came through the war unscathed—be it because of my silver dollar or his dog, we will never know.

* * * * *

The "short snorter"—a dollar bill (or several pieces of paper money pasted end to end and rolled up) on which many other airmen signed their names often served as a lucky charm. The "short snorter" carried by the author was signed by many of the 457th Bomb. Group members including Col. Harris Rogner. Many men who did not survive the war signed the four-foot-long "short snorter"—Edward Dozier, Bill Doherty, Alfred W. Fischer, Lt. Delmar Spatz—and others who were shot down or interned in Sweden—Lt. Robert M. Krumm, Lt. Leo R. Green, Lt. Clarence R. Jennings.

* * * * *

Lt. Clayton E. Bejot tells about the movies shown in the Officers' Club. The movies were provided in several reels and at the end of each reel, while the next reel was being threaded into the projector, the men made a dash for the bar. As the movie progressed and some of the audience became inebriated, the comments from the audience usually became loud and off color.

* * * * *

Sgt. Ralph Windell recalled the "Red Cross" Club-mobile, the "South Dakota," that cruised the flight line when the ground crews were working until the wee hours of the morning to repair the damaged bombers and have them available for the next mission. The hot cup of coffee and doughnuts provided did wonders for the tired and lagging constitution of many a crew member.

The "Red Cross" was also on hand when the bombers returned from a mission. Coffee and doughnuts were handed out to those who had flown the mission, a welcome tidbit after many hours in the air.

The "Red Cross" also provided hostesses at the "flak houses," establishments available to flight crewmen who had completed about half their tour and were given a week of leave to rest and recuperate before continuing their tour.

The establishments were often hotels which during peacetime were seashore resorts such as were those at Southport, England.

Other "flak houses" were English manor houses provided by well-to-do British. Such a place was "Furzdown" near Winchester, England, at which the author spent the Christmas of 1944, along with Ralph Stutzman, Charlie Lower, and Paul Umoff. The Red Cross hostesses were Mariane Pederson, Jeanne Helber, and Kathleen Regan. These names are recalled because they signed the "Short Snorter" of the author.

* * * * *

Mail call was probably the most looked forward to time of day. Mail from home—the wife, the girl-friend, the family—did wonders for a homesick airman. There could be a package—often badly crushed—but containing the recollections of home: chocolate chip cookies, candy, good American cigarettes—Lucky Strikes for a time and not "Sunshines" we had been smoking. I often wondered who the Army purchasing officer was who was responsible for contracting for "Sunshine" cigarettes. I guess either the price was right or they knew we would smoke anything—again they were right. Certainly someone probably became rich by selling the soldiers inferior tobacco.

Letters often came in bunches, five or six at a time, then there would be a long dry spell. Answering letters was an almost daily activity. Getting mail was such an important event that letter writing was for many men a daily routine. Even if it was only a V-mail letter, at least the message was sent: I am still OK and have only a given number of missions to complete my tour. Letters were censored and specific information about the war was cut from a letter by censors. The censors were officers assigned the duty by the squadron executive officer. Each officer took his turn at censoring mail.

* * * * *

The following are aircraft assigned to the 457th which were given names by their crews. (Compiled by Bernard Bains)

43-38540	Mysterious Witch
42-97558	'Tis Me Sugar
42-97562	Evening Folks How Y'All
43-37567	Willie III
43-37574	Butch
42-97579	Local Mission
42-97590	Virgin Mary
43-38594	Lady Be Good
44-6603	Jaynee
43-37603	BTO
42-97630	Geraldine, Pakawalup
42-97649	Paper Warrior
43-37694	Patty Ann
42-31706	Slow But Sure
42-31726	Duration Plus
43-37733	Ace of Hearts
43-37765	The Duchess
43-37782	Lady Margaret
44-8785	Crack Up
43-37785	Tarfu
43-37796	Stinky
42-97827	My Mary Myrtle
43-37828	Georgia Peach-Remember Me
43-38831	Screaming Eagle

44-8832	Battle Baby
43-38885	Ruthanne
43-38887	Perpetual Help
43-38889	Fish n' Chips
43-38909	Kraut Krusher
42-31923	Prop Wash
42-97934	Rene V
42-38021	Mission Maid
42-98024	Que Up
42-107026	Hamtramack Mama
42-32051	Lady Luck
42-38063	The G.I. Virgin
42-38064	Arf n' Arf
42-97067	Black Puff Polly, Georgia Peach
42-28073	Luck of Judy Ann
42-97075	Flak Dodger
42-32079	Delayed Lady II
42-32084	Li'l Satin
42-32086	You Never Know
42-97087	Tujunga I
42-32098	G.I. Virgin II
42-32101	El Lobo
42-38113	Rene III
42-97131	Home James
44-8152	Miss Ida
43-39200	Rattlesnake Daddy
43-39211	Maguires Chop House
44-8414	G.I. Virgin III
42-97451	Nancy B
42-97456	Mighty Little John
42-97460	Delayed Lady
42-97468	Tujunga III
44-8479	Susie Sag Sump
42-31505	Miss Cue
43-28534	Wolf Pack

* * * * *

20TH FIGHTER GROUP MEMORIAL

Memorial constructed at King's Cliffe, home of the 8th AAF 20th Fighter Group located just northwest of Glayton AAFB. The base was at various times home of the RAF and the USAAF.

The memorial reads:

Kings Cliffe Airfield
Station 567

To commemorate the eternal memory of
those American, British, Belgian, and
Commonwealth airmen who gave their
lives in the cause of freedom
1939-1945
LEST WE FORGET

The memorial is constructed of two stone pylons to which are attached a replica of a wing of an American P-51 and an English Spitfire.

* * * * *

351ST BOMBARDMENT GROUP MEMORIAL, POLEBROOK

A sister B-17 Group, the 351st Bombardment Group, located at Polebrook was one of the groups which composed the 94th Bombardment Wing. The 457th B.G. and the 401st B.G. at Deenethorpe were the other two.

Illustrated below is the memorial constructed by the members of the 351st Bombardment Group.

The memorial reads as follows:

In memory of
the
351st Bombardment
Group (heavy)
of the United States Army
Air Force
The group combat bombing missions
were flown from this airfield over
occupied Europe between 1943-1945
175 B-17 Flying Fortresses and their
crews were lost. 303 enemy aircraft
were destroyed in aerial combat

Byers (1984)

Kings Cliffe Airfield Memorial

Byers (1984)

351st Bombardment Group, Polebrook Memorial

OFFICERS CLUB – 457TH BOMB. GROUP

The brick end wall of the "Q" hut, Officers Club, was festooned with the carved fireball motif denoting the combat missions on which the crews of the 457th Bomb. Group had flown.

Centered on the end wall—above the fireplace—was the popular "fireball" insignia of the 457th Bomb. Group, the "fireball" symbolically traveling counterclockwise through the Black Hills (Rapid City AAB), the mountains of the western United States (Ephrata AAB and Wendover Field), and the White Cliffs of Dover, England. Below the insignia was the Latin phrase *Fait Accompli*, translated as "An Accomplished Fact."

A "fireball" replica was painted with name and date of the mission and posted on the end wall of the "Q" hut officers club.

* * * * *

COL. JAMES R. LUPER

Among other assignments after World War II, Col. James R. Luper was assigned as Deputy Inspector General with station at the

Byers

351st Group Identification Letter

Strategic Air Command (SAC) Headquarters at Offutt Field, Omaha, Nebraska.

While flying to Offutt Field from Colorado Springs 19 February 1953 in a B-26, he was attempting to land at Offutt Field on G.C.A. (Ground Control Approach). He had made his final turn and was approaching the field. About nine miles from the field the aircraft suddenly lost altitude and crashed, killing Col. Luper.

As commanding officer of the 457th Bomb. Group, Col. Luper had flown 20 combat missions during World War II. He had been decorated with the Silver Star, the DFC with cluster, and the Air Medal and two clusters.

He was survived by his widow Rene and three children and two children from a former marriage.

* * * * *

457th (Bains)

"Wall of Missions" at end of "Q" Hut Officers Club

(Bains)

Col. James R. Luper assists at the piano at a dance held in the 457th B.G. Officers' Club.

COL. HARRIS E. ROGNER

After World War II, Col. Harris E. Rogner, who succeeded Col. Luper as commander officer of the 457th Bombardment Group, was given command of a B-29 Bombardment Unit and stationed in Korea in 1951.

Col. Rogner was killed when he was returning to Barksdale Field at Shreveport, Louisiana, from Travis AF Base, Sacramento, California. He was one of four men who were killed when the B-29 crashed and burned.

Col. Rogner had been decorated with the DFC and five clusters, the Air Medal and three clusters, and the French Croix de Guerre w/palm.

Col. Rogner was survived by his widow Kathryn and three children.

* * * * *

BLACK OUT!
DAILY BULLETIN 26 May 1944

New light bulbs will be issued only when the old burnt out bulb is turned in to the supply room

* * * * *

457th (Zemper)

457th B.G. 1945. Original memorial monument.

Memorial Monument

457th Bombardment Group Memorial Monument

Located in the churchyard of All Saints Evangelical Church and facing the 457th Bomb. Group Base in England is a newly constructed memorial, dedicated to those men of the 457th B.G. who made the supreme sacrifice for their country.

The monument was reconstructed in 1982 to replace the original memorial designed and built by Sgt. Lester Fried, of S-2 (intelligence), a 457th B.G. member.

The original monument was dedicated at a ceremony attended by Col. Harris E. Rogner, 457th B.G. commander, Chaplain Capt. Robert D. Newcombe, Canon Wayne of Conington Church, and Sgt. Lester Fried, on 30 May 1945.

Thirty-seven years of English weather had wrought havoc with the original memorial, even though local English residents had maintained the monument.

In 1979 at the 457th reunion held in Colorado Springs, it was decided to rebuild the monument. A committee of five people was selected to raise funds, and rebuild the monument. Bernard Bains, an Englishman who had over the years sought to preserve the history of the 457th B.G. and who had attended the Colorado Springs reunion, was selected by the committee to be the English representative.

The committee was composed of:

Thomas A Goff, Chairman
Joseph Falcon
Lester Fried
Leslie R. Peterson
Neil C. Schroeder

The new memorial was constructed of Portland stone which is very hard and often used for facing on British government buildings. "The Wall of the Missing," and the chapel of the American Cemetery in Cambridge, are also constructed of the stone.

Connington Church

457th (Bains)

Dedication of Original memorial on 30 May 1945. Canon St. John Wayne, Col. Harris E. Rogner, and Sgt. Lester Fried

Goff

Memorial at Glatton located in Connington All Saints Church yard

The memorial is six feet tall and the original memorial designed by Lester Fried was used as a model. A picture of the memorial is shown hereafter. The All Saints Evangelical Church is a large church which was built in the 15th century and provides an appropriate setting for the placement of the memorial.

MADINGLY CEMETERY

Established on 7 December 1943, the second anniversary of the Japanese attack on Pearl Harbor, Madingly Cemetery is the resting place of 3,811 American War Dead. Most of the air bases of the 8th Army Air Force were located in the vicinity of the cemetery and a large proportion of those interred were members of the Army Air Force.

Adjacent to the fan-shaped quarter circle of grave sites is located a mall, through which a reflecting pool runs from the flagpole platform to a memorial chapel at the east end.

On the south side of the mall is located the 472 foot long "Wall of the Missing." Recorded, in Portland stone, are 5,125 names of men who gave their lives for their country and whose remains have never been recovered.

Interred at the Madingly United States Military Cemetery at Cambridge are the following listed 457th Bombardment Group (H) airmen:

Richard T. Bennett
Everett Broadie
Owen B. Coffman
William K. Doherty
Edward B. Dozier
Walter B. Graves
James P. Guyot
Charles Held
Raymond V. Hunter
Roy E. Kerr
Joseph L. Kilmer
Richard L. Mack
Vinton H. Mays
Donald L. Moore
Joseph J. Paddock
Donald R. Peacock
Robert W. Pinckney

Byers

"Wall of the Missing." Memorial Chapel and Reflecting Pool, Madingly Cemetery.

Byers

Major Edward B. Dozier's grave at Madingly Cemetery, England.

Joseph T. Schembri
Bernard E. Sidebottom
Donald L. Snow
Herbert L. Stempler
Jack E. Taifer
Edwin D. Waggoner
Earl E. Whitnack

Listed on the "Wall of the Missing" are those men from the 457th Bombardment Group (H) who are missing in action:

Oscar A. Gascon, Jr.
Edward A. Grover, Jr.
Oscar C. Hightower
Chester V. Hudec
James J. Kilroy
Roy H. Kirk, Jr.
Willard Krueger
Earl A. Markwalder
Edward A. McNeal, Jr.
Francis A. Minturn
Paul R. Moore
Keith W. Morgan
Leroy E. Wetzel
Glenn M. Wisdom

Lt. Clayton E. Bejot reflected on the memorials erected in memory of the men who gave their lives for their country: the recently erected memorial in our nation's capital—Washington, D.C.—erected in memory of the men who died in the Viet Nam War and the memorial at Madingly Cemetery, Cambridge, England, erected in memory of the American men who gave their lives in Word War II. Standing before the Wall and reading the inscribed names forty years after brings back with dramatic suddenness the recollections of friends with whom you shared confidences. Might not it have been just as easy for one's own name to have been inscribed in the stone rather than theirs? It was only the "luck of the draw" that protected you. Only God knows why you were spared and these unfortunate men were not.

Lost and Missing

457TH BOMBARDMENT GROUP (H)
LOST AND MISSING CREWS AND AIRCRAFT

The tour of operations of the 457th B.G. in the European Theatre of Operations (ETO) is officially listed to be from 21 February 1944, the date crews of the 457th B.G. flew their first mission to Lippstadt and Gutersloh, to the last mission the 236th, to Seddin, on 20 April 1945.

During this tour of operations the record lists 86 aircraft lost, 729 men killed, taken prisoner, or interned in neutral countries.

There is a discrepancy between the number of 86 recorded as lost and the listing taken from several sources by the author. Why this discrepancy exists is probably a matter of what types of accidents were counted. The author will list those aircraft as taken from the sources researched which were available to him. The following is the list of officers and enlisted men who did not return to base while flying combat missions over Germany and occupied territory.

Some of the men were forced down in the neutral countries of Switzerland and Sweden and were interned for much of the European War.

Some of the men evaded capture and, with the help of the underground forces and allied sympathizers, were eventually returned to allied territory.

Other men were captured and confined in prison camps for the duration of the European War.

There were also those men, to whom this book is dedicated, who made the supreme sacrifice for their country. The bodies of some of these men were buried in foreign lands, some were lost at sea, still others were returned to the United States after the cessation of hostilities in the ETO.

21 February 1944 – Lippstadt-Gutersloh. The 8th AAF sent 764 heavy bombers on this mission of which 3 heavy bombers were lost.

This was the first combat mission flown by crews of the 457th Bombardment Group. The crew of Lt. Llewellyn G. Bredeson flying A/C #42-31596 was the first crew to be shot down by enemy action.

The record states only that one crew from the 750th Squadron was missing and did not return to base.

The crew is as listed below and was a member of the "Hutchison Provisional Group" which joined the 457th B.G. at Wendover AAB.

P	2nd Lt	Llewellyn G. Bredeson
CP	2nd Lt	Wayne G. McLeod
N	2nd Lt	Robert A. Whitby
B	2nd Lt	Samuel Kalman
AE	T/Sgt	Howard R. Collins
RO	T/Sgt	Leonard V. Luchonok
LW	S/Sgt	Louis P. Rigaud
RW	S/Sgt	John F. Lewis
BT	S/Sgt	Walter J. Jutze
TG	S/Sgt	William H. Schenkel

(Dickinson)

Lt. "Lew" Brederson's Crew first shot down in group, 21 February 1944, A/C #42-31596

24 February 1944 – Schweinfurt. The 8th AAF sent 231 B-17s to attack a Schweinfurt ball bearing plant, 11 of which did not return to base.

The 457th B.G. furnished 18 aircraft and flew the high box in the 94th wing formation. One aircraft was lost to flak damage, that piloted by Lt. Max Morrow. The crew bailed out and was taken prisoner by the Germans.

Lt. Robert G. Horn, the bombardier from Lt. Robert M. Krumm's crew, flew the mission as a replacement on Morrow's crew. It was Horn's first mission and he spent the war as a P.O.W.

The record also states that one man was killed, identity unknown, and two men were wounded on aircraft which returned to base.

Battle damage of A/C #42-31588 piloted by Lt. Edward Dozier which occurred on the 1st mission flown by crews of the 457th Bomb. Group. 21 February 1944.

Lt. Morrow's crew is listed hereafter:

P	2nd Lt	Max R. Morrow
CP	2nd Lt	Thomas G. Davis
N	2nd Lt	Daren A. McIntyre
B	2nd Lt	Robert G. Horn
AE	S/Sgt	George B. Lee
RO	S/Sgt	David E. Wallace
LW	Sgt	Everett M. Tyler
RW	Sgt	Bernard E. Harris
BT	Sgt	Italo Stella
TG	Sgt	Merton R. Cattanach

25 February 1944—Augsburg. The 8th AAF launched 680 heavy bombers to attack aircraft factories at Augsburg, Regansburg, and Furth, and a ball bearing factory at Stuttgart. Thirty-one A/C were lost to fighter attacks and flak.

457th

Lt. Max R. Morrow, Escape and Evasion picture. Shot down 24 February 1944.

The 457th launched 27 A/C, some of which flew in both the high and low boxes of the wing. One A/C aborted and two A/C were lost when they collided in mid-air.

A/C #42-31517, piloted by 2nd Lt. James R. Chinn, did not return from the mission and no report was made as to what happened to the aircraft and crew.

The crew of A/C #42-31517 is as follows:

P	2nd Lt	James R. Chinn
CP	2nd Lt	R. F. Cooper
N	2nd Lt	Frank J. McNichol
B	2nd Lt	John C. Vollmuth
AEG	S/Sgt	Vite (NMI) Peragine
ROG	Cpl	Robert J. Mullins
AAEG	Sgt	Marion D. Ross
AROG	Cpl	William J. Sullivan, Jr.
AG	Sgt	Dillard V. Engdahl
AAG	Sgt	Jeremiah B. Rolison

(Dickinson)

Lt. Morrow's crew was shot down on Schweinfurt Mission 24 February 1944. The Bombardier, Lt. Robert G. Horn flew as a replacement for Lt. John B. Blachely, kneeling at left. The mission was Horn's first. He was a member of Krumm's crew.

The crew was a member of the Hutchison Provisional Group.

A/C #42-97457, piloted by 2nd Lt. Archie F. Bower, did not return from the mission and no report was made as to what happened to the aircraft and crew.

The crew of A/C #42-97457 is as follows:

P	2nd Lt	Archie F. Bower, Jr.
CP	2nd Lt	William R. Baxendale
N	2nd Lt	Lee E. Hoskins
B	2nd Lt	Richard W. Cooke
AEG	S/Sgt	Frank S. Giordano
ROG	Sgt	Joseph M. Snyder
AAEG	S/Sgt	John W. Popowitz
AROG	Sgt	Jesse J. Hirschberg
AG	Sgt	John J. Waskovich
AAG	Sgt	Wesley W. Schneider, Jr.

The crew was a member of the Hutchison Provisional Group.

457th

Lt. Clarence Schuchmann's airplane damaged on the 25 February 1944 mission to Augsburg.

Lt. Col. Tom Goff recalls the mission in this way:

"It was our second mission and we flew to Augsburg, Germany, to bomb the Messerschmitt factory. We were leading an element and the 401st at Denethrope was leading the wing. We carried 12-500# GP bombs in some of the planes and incendiaries in others.

"On the run into the IP we were hit by flak which reduced power in one of our engines. On the bomb run we were hit again by flak which knocked out my oxygen system at the navigator's table. I plugged into the oxygen system on the right side of the nose but was too far away from the navigator's table to do effective navigation. I tried to follow the instruments and maintain our position as best I could, however.

"On the way home we were hit by flak as we flew in the vicinity of Laon, France. The flak knocked out one of the good engines and reduced power in another and we dropped out of the formation. Flak came through the plexiglas nose and two pieces went through the plexiglas dome on the top turret, one behind and one in front of Sgt. Hibb's head.

"The flak that came through the nose sprayed plexiglas about and injured Lt. Charles Gelbert the bombardier. Two gunners were also slightly wounded by flak. Gelber was screaming he couldn't see. The pilot, Lt. Schuchmann, was calling on the interphone for magnetic heading information, how far was the English channel, what would our ETA be to the base.

"Cold air blowing in the holes in the nose didn't help the matter at all, either.

"I opened the medical kit and used some of the salve to spread over the part of his face that was exposed above Gelber's oxygen mask and taped gauze over it. I thought we might have to bail out, so I snapped his chest pack to the harness which, he not being able to see, (only temporarily) scared the hell out of him. He grabbed hold of me and wouldn't let go.

"Well, we got back to the base and found the group in trail landing from the west on the east-west runway. Schuchmann said he had to set the airplane down, as we were losing power and couldn't circle the base. With wounded aboard the gunners were firing flares 'like mad.'

"We landed on the runway to the west as another airplane came toward the east. Luckily the pilot of the other airplane saw us in time, took a touch-and-go, and skimmed over the top of us."

6 March 1944 — Berlin. Six hundred and fifty-eight bombers from the 8th AAF bombed targets in Berlin. The German fighter resistance was fierce and 69 heavy bombers were shot down. This loss represented up to this date the highest loss incurred by the 8th AAF in a single day.

The 457th launched 18 A/C for the mission to Berlin. They returned to the same target, Erkner, Germany (Berlin vicinity), they had failed to reach, because of weather problems, on two previous occasions.

The intense fighter opposition, including Me 109s, FW 190s, twin-engined Me 210s, and JU 88s, resulted in the loss of two crews: those of Lt. Eugene Whelan flying A/C #42-31627 and Lt. E. Graves flying A/C #42-31595.

Reports by observers stated that a German fighter, a Me-109, held its pursuit curve too long and collided with Lt. Graves. Parts of the A/C also struck Lt. Whelan's A/C. All three A/C fell to the earth. No parachutes were observed.

457th

Lt. Eugene H. Whelan. He and crew were lost on 6 March 1944 on the mission to Berlin.

The crew of A/C #42-31627 is as follows:

P	2nd Lt	Eugene H. Whelan
CP	2nd Lt	James R. Cawley
N	2nd Lt	George S. McPeake, Jr.
B	2nd Lt	Robert J. Kuncl
AE	T/Sgt	Robert H. Vaughn
RO	T/Sgt	Jerome J. Hartings
LW	S/Sgt	J. D. Bartoe
BT	S/Sgt	John C. McVey
TG	S/Sgt	Virgil L. French

The crew of A/C #42-31595 is as follows:

P	2nd Lt	Roy E. Graves
CP	2nd Lt	Wayne G. McLeod
N	2nd Lt	James Salay
B	2nd Lt	Herbert W. Witte
AE	T/Sgt	Horace J. Gillespie
RO	T/Sgt	Weldon F. Brown
LW	S/Sgt	Donald L. Lillehaug
RW	S/Sgt	Robert R. Kent
BT	S/Sgt	Harold M. Moberg
TG	S/Sgt	Eldon A. C. Williams

The crews were members of the "Hutchison Provisional Group."

29 March 1944 — Waggum-Brunswick. One hundred and eighty-seven B-17s of the 8th AAF bombed industrial targets in Brunswick. Seventy-seven B-24s bombed V-Weapon sites.

Aircraft #42-31594 piloted by Lt. Lewis W. Lennartson was shot down by an ME 109 at Flittman. Observers reported #4 engine was feathered and #2 engine was on fire. Eight to ten parachutes were seen to have opened as the aircraft descended apparently under control. Other members of the group reported that the aircraft exploded at about 8000 feet altitude.

P	2nd Lt	Lewis W. Lennartson
CP	2nd Lt	Everett L. Keesee, Jr.
N	2nd Lt	Mariford Barkowitz
B	2nd Lt	Ralph C. Jordan
AE	T/Sgt	Thomas B. Haag

RO	T/Sgt	William T. Graham
LW	S/Sgt	Clyde E. Garnbart
RW	S/Sgt	Anthony J. Nunes
BT	S/Sgt	Cosmo J. Fazzio
TG	S/Sgt	James E. Blackwell

The crew was a member of the "Hutchison Provisional Group."

9 April 1944 – Gdynia. Three hundred and ninety-nine 8th AAF heavy bombers attacked targets in Germany and Poland. Thirty-two heavy bombers were lost by the 8th AAF on this mission.

The 457th bombed a FW 190 factory at Rahmel near Gdynia, Poland. This mission was the longest mission which had been flown by bombers of the 8th AAF up to this date. The bombing results of the mission were satisfactory for which the lead crew received a commendation.

Three aircraft were lost by the 457th B.G. on this mission, two to Luftwaffe fighters and one to unknown causes. Lt. Amos Shepard's aircraft #42-97537 was hit by both flak and fighters at 1320 hours while in the target area. At least one engine was on fire as the aircraft pulled away from the formation. Five crewmen were seen to parachute from the burning aircraft.

Lt. Shepard's plane was flying in the number 4 position and Lt. Robert Krumm and crew in "Flak Dodger" were flying on Shepard's right wing.

457th (Bains)

Lt. Amos W. Shepards A/C #42-97537 shot down by flak on mission to Gdynia, Poland 9 April 1944.

Number three engine on Lt. Shepard's aircraft was set on fire by flak just after "bombs away" at 1320 hours.

THE AUTHOR AS NAVIGATOR ON LT. KRUMM'S CREW:

I can recall Shepard's aircraft holding in tight but slightly ahead of our aircraft, seeking protection from the enemy fighters. I was thinking at the time, "Why don't they bail out?" Also I was thinking "If the aircraft blows up it will take us with him." Although one has empathy for someone in trouble, I was also thinking of my own self preservation.

The aircraft soon veered away from the formation and I saw the waist door fly off and then counted three men as they jumped out of the aircraft before it was lost to sight behind the formation. Other observers reported that three FW 190s attacked the plane soon after it fell from the protective formation of bombers.

P	2nd Lt	Amos W. Shepard
CP	2nd Lt	Ralph O. Hammerstrom
N	2nd Lt	Kenneth Galyean
B	2nd Lt	Herbert W. Spaulding
AE	T/Sgt	Joseph E. Fasone
RO	T/Sgt	Jon (NMI) Roberts
LW	S/Sgt	Amos T. Bunch
RW	S/Sgt	Arnold E. Kaufman
BT	S/Sgt	William H. Good
TG	S/Sgt	Harold E. Smith

This crew was a member of the "Hutchison Provisional Group."

Lt. Walker's aircraft #42-97465 was reported to have been shot down by German fighters after dropping its bombs. It was observed to go down in a spin. Two parachutes were observed to have opened in the area of the damaged aircraft.

The crew of A/C #42-97465:

P	2nd Lt	Robert K. Walker
CP	2nd Lt.	Unknown
B	2nd Lt	Lloyd T. Belanger
AE	Sgt	Albert L. Rothbauer
RO	T/Sgt	Jack F. Berry
LW	S/Sgt	Jack D. Bush
BT	S/Sgt	Cecil D. Burroughs
TG	S/Sgt	James V. Ambrose

Lt. Park's aircraft #42-31629 did not return from the mission and was reported to have crash-landed into a small lake in the vicinity of Gdynia. However, the reports of crew members were conflicting and the official report indicated no observation was reported as to what caused the loss.

The crew of A/C #42-31629, piloted by Lt. Parks, is as follows:

P	2nd Lt	David P. Parks
CP	2nd Lt	Floyd O. Grove
N	2nd Lt	William C. Ellerbusch
B	2nd Lt	Harold W. Dershimer
AE	T/Sgt	Donald J. Kesselmeyer
RO	T/Sgt	Ruben H. Halverson
LW	S/Sgt	Cosmo J. Fazzio
RW	S/Sgt	Charles M. Kerr
BT	S/Sgt	Anthony M. Pasce
TG	S/Sgt	George H. Grebe

(Byers)

The target referred to as "Crossbow" or "No Ball" — a V-1 "Buzz Bomb" —the flying bomb with which the Germans proposed to terrorize England.

20 April 1944 – Gorenflos. The 8th AAF bombed targets in the Pas de Calais and Cherbourg area with 566 heavy bombers.

The 457th bombed a NO BALL-CROSSBOW target at Gorenflos, located 13 miles southwest of Daullens. The target was a ski shaped launching ramp for V-1 flying bombs. Bombing results of the Group was excellent with a good pattern falling within 200 feet of the assigned MPI. The flak encountered was moderate but accurate. The fighter support was good.

The aircraft piloted by Lt. Milne flying as deputy lead of the "B" group exploded in mid-air. There were no parachutes observed.

The crew included the following men:

P	Lt	Walter S. Milne
CP	Capt	Robert E. Ensmenger
N	Lt	John D. English
B	Lt	Edward C. Cannon
AE	T/Sgt	Jerome A. Fogleman
RO	T/Sgt	Lyle W. Johnson
LW	S/Sgt	Alton A. Schaffner
RW	S/Sgt	Ralph L. Haldiman
BT	S/Sgt	(Unknown) Beck
TG	Lt	Carl E. Gamblin

25 April 1944 – Nancy/Essey Airfield. The 8th AAF "put up" nearly 300 B-17s and B-24s to bomb M/Ys at Mannheim and Landau, and A/Fs at Nancy/Essey, Metz/Frescat, and Lyon/Longvic.

The target for the 457th was the Nancy/Essey airfield. The airdrome was used for military transport flying between France and Germany.

The mission was a failure as the target was obscured by 9/10 to 10/10 cloud cover and no bombs were dropped.

On the trip back to base the lead aircraft, A/C #42-97070, caught on fire just as the group reached the English Channel. The bombs were dropped in the channel and the aircraft turned back into France where 11 parachutes were counted as the crew bailed out of the burning aircraft.

The 750th Squadron commander, Major Roderick L. Francis, was flying as air commander on this mission. He parachuted to safety, evaded capture, and returned to the 457th B.G.

The crew included the following:

P	Capt	Edward M. Bender
CP	Major	Roderick L. Francis (air commander)
N	Lt	Earl E. Woodward
N	Capt	Arthur T. Cavanaugh
N	Lt	Edwin K. Fuller
AE	T/Sgt	James L. Free
RO	T/Sgt	Lynon M. Mahan
LW	S/Sgt	John P. Sarico
RW	Lt	Jack Hotaling
BT	S/Sgt	Michael Woyurka
TG	Lt	(Unknown) Soules

457th

Lt. Col. Roderick Francis evaded and returned to 457th on 25 April 1944.

12 May 1944—Lutzkendorf. Eight hundred B-17s and B-24s bombed oil plants in Merseburg, Lutzkendorf, Zeitz, Zwickau, Bohlen, Gera, Brux, and Chemnitz. An estimated 430 German fighters attacked the bombers and 46 bombers were lost.

The 457th put 36 aircraft, two boxes of 18 aircraft, into the air to bomb the synthetic oil plant at Lutzkendorf. Lt. Col. Henry B. Wilson was air commander of one box and Major Fred A. Spencer was air commander of the second.

Although the weather over the target was CAVU, the bombing results were only fair.

Fighters were reported in the area but they did not attack the 457th B.G. formation.

One aircraft did not return from the mission, that piloted by Lt. John Akers. There were no reports from the other crews on the mission as to what happened to the aircraft.

(Dickinson)

Capt. Edward M. Bender, Lead Pilot (kneeling at right) and crew shot down 25 April 1944. Capt. Bender had previously assumed command as pilot of Major J. M. Dickinson's model crew when Dickinson was made operations officer of 750th Squadron.

The crew of this aircraft included the following:

P	Lt	John Akers
CP	Lt	Charles T. Scott
N	Lt	Lloyd C. Dell
B	Lt	Leo F. Kruszynski
AE	T/Sgt	Edward White
RO	T/Sgt	Robert J. Marsteller
LW	S/Sgt	Harold T. Peterman
RW	S/Sgt	Christopher W. Hilgo
BT	S/Sgt	Austin F. Moore
TG	S/Sgt	Wallace V. Taft

19 May 1944—Berlin. Four hundred and ninety-three B-17s bombed the Friedrichstrasse section of Berlin, while 49 B-17s bombed port facilities at Kiel. Two hundred and seventy-three B-24s bombed industrial targets at Brunswick. Twenty-eight 8th AAF bombers and 20 escort fighters were lost. One hundred and sixty-four German fighters were claimed destroyed.

The 457th B.G. put up two boxes of 18 aircraft, which bombed Berlin. The MPI was the government buildings in the center of Berlin. Thirty-two of the aircraft dropped their bombs, however, the results were unobserved because of an undercast.

The group was attacked by 50-60 German fighters, mostly ME 109s and a few FW 190s. The GAF shot down one of our bombers, that of Lt. Phillip Birong. The complete list of the crew is as follows. There was no report of what happened to the aircraft.

P	Lt	Phillip H. Birong
CP	Lt	Robert A. Patty
N	Lt	Frank Partinjak
B	Lt	Paul V. Owens
AE	T/Sgt	Max L. Hull
RO	T/Sgt	Norman Musial
AG	S/Sgt	Albert L. Missinger
AG	S/Sgt	Sacco M. Pasquale
AG	S/Sgt	William N. Farrar
AG	S/Sgt	Franco H. Luis

24 May 1944—Berlin. Four hundred and forty-seven B-17s bombed Berlin, 400 B-24s bombed airfields at Orly, Melun, Criel, and Poix. Seventy-two B-17s bombed T/O in the Berlin area.

Fighter opposition was heavy and 33 heavy bombers were lost.

The 457th B.G. put only one box of 16 aircraft in the air, which led the 94th wing. This was the 457th's 50th mission.

The results of the bombing were unobserved due to the 7/10 cloud cover.

The flak was intense and accurate. Although German fighters were reported in the area of the target, they did not attack the 457th B.G.

One aircraft was lost and was reported to have ditched in the North Sea and the crew was rescued. The aircraft was piloted by Lt. Harry Stafford. The complete crew is listed below.

P	Lt	Harry Stafford
CP	Lt	Bernard Maverosky
N	Lt	Arthur Flach
B	Lt	Anthony G. Wodek
AE	T/Sgt	Virgil D. Naylor
RO	T/Sgt	Virgil R. Meek
LW	S/Sgt	Reginald Buxton
RW	S/Sgt	Francis Craven
BT	S/Sgt	Robert Rodge
TG	S/Sgt	Walter H. Osika

27 May 1944—Ludwigshafen. Nine hundred and twenty-three B-17s and B-24s struck M/Ys, A/Fs, and industries at Ludwigshafen, Mannheim, Karlsrühe, Strasbourg, and other targets in Germany and France. Opposition from fighters was intense and the 8th AAF lost 24 heavy bombers.

The 457th B.G. "put up" 36 aircraft, the crews flying both the lead and low box. The group bombed the primary target, however, the results were poor. Col. Luper was air commander of the lead box and Capt. "Mac" Dickinson was a/c of the low box.

The group encountered accurate flak at the target and was also attacked by 30-50 German fighters resulting in the loss of three crews.

The three crews were as follows: Lt. Artie J. Whitlow, Lt. William E. Dee, A/C #42-97460, and Lt. Roger W. Birkman, A/C #42-38055.

The Me 109s made a pass through the 457th B.G. formation and shot off the end of the right wing of Lt. Whitlow's A/C. The aircraft fell in a spin, until it was lost from sight. Three parachutes were observed in the area of the disabled aircraft.

The crew of the A/C of which Lt. Whitlow was pilot is listed hereafter:

P	Lt	Artie J. Whitlow
CP	Lt	Robert H. Cunningham
NB	Lt	Daniel L. McLaughlin
AE	T/Sgt	Paul R. Isker
RO	T/Sgt	Paul R. Clerk
LW	S/Sgt	Lovell O'Masters
RW	S/Sgt	Robert V. Towle
BT	S/Sgt	Roe S. Woodis
TG	S/Sgt	James V. Ambrose

A/C #42-97460 piloted by Lt. William E. Dee was observed to be having difficulty keeping up with the formation as the group was returning to base. It was also observed that the bomb bay doors of the aircraft were not closed. The aircraft descended rapidly at one point and was caught in a heavy barrage of flak. The aircraft was last seen descending at about 12,000 feet, under control.

457th (Bains)

Lt. Clyde Knipfers A/C #42-31520. Shot down 28 May 1944 on mission to Dessau.

The crew of A/C #42-97460 is listed hereafter:

P	Lt	William E. Dee
CP	Lt	Robert M. Cotterell
N	Lt	Lawrence Oberstein
B	Lt	Donald S. Jay
AE	T/Sgt	William H. Jones, Jr.
RO	T/Sgt	George L. Hatcher
LW	S/Sgt	Orval Sterner
RW	S/Sgt	Stephen L. Floyd
BT	S/Sgt	Steve J. Sak
TG	S/Sgt	Thomas L. Treadwell

A/C #42-38055 piloted by Lt. Roger W. Birkman was observed flying homeward in the 457th formation until about 1225 hours at which time the aircraft made a 180-degree turn. The number 3 engine was on fire and when last observed the aircraft was losing altitude and heading south under control, possibly going to Switzerland?

P	Lt	Roger W. Birkman
CP	Lt	Alexander Kuckerenko
N	Lt	Michael N. Stanko
B	Lt	James M. Cochran
AE	T/Sgt	Raymond Koch
RO	T/Sgt	Andrew Kafka
LW	S/Sgt	John L. Toney
FW	S/Sgt	James C. Jones
BT	S/Sgt	John Buechel
TG	S/Sgt	Errol Bailey

Lt. Birkman's crew was a "Hutchison Provision Group" crew.

28 May 1944—Dessau. Nine hundred heavy bombers attacked industrial targets at Dessau, Ruhland, Merseburg, Zeitz, Konigsberg, Lutzkendorf, and Magdeburg. An estimated 450 German fighters opposed the penetration, most of the fighters intercepting bombers in the Magdeburg area. Thirty-two 8th AAF heavy bombers were lost.

The 457th B.G. "put up" one 16-aircraft box which led the 94th Wing. Major Hozier was the air commander with Lt. Brannon as lead pilot flying a PFF aircraft.

The results of the bombing were unobserved at the primary, and fair at the secondary, which was Leipzig.

The formation was attacked by 60-80 German fighters. The flak at the target was moderate but accurate.

The group lost three aircraft, two as a result of fighter attacks and a third to unknown causes.

The three aircraft which were lost are as follows:

A/C #42-97067

P	Lt	Rudolph M. Stohl
CP	Lt	David W. Schellenger
N	Lt	John D. Millham
B	Lt	James E. Thomas
AE	T/Sgt	Robert C. Kriete
RO	T/Sgt	Walter W. Wagoner
LW	S/Sgt	Irvin A. Welling
RW	S/Sgt	William F. Bemis
BT	S/Sgt	Sheldon E. Moore
TG	S/Sgt	Charles L. Stewart

A/C #42-97452

P	Lt	Emanuel Hauf
CP	Lt	Donald V. Swain
N	Lt	William R. Hawley
B	Lt	William E. Jaqua
AE	T/Sgt	Willis H. Johnson
RO	T/Sgt	James J. Kilroy
LW	S/Sgt	Paul R. Moore
RW	S/Sgt	Walter Furtta
BT	S/Sgt	Unknown
TG	S/Sgt	Oscar A. Gascon

A/C #42-31520

P	Lt	Clyde B. Knipfer
CP	Lt	Richard H. Bruha
N	Lt	George R. Dardinski
B	Lt	Stanley V. Gray
AE	T/Sgt	Stephen T. Voit
RO	T/Sgt	Nicholas F. Bendino
LW	S/Sgt	Percy Waltho
RW	S/Sgt	Unknown
BT	S/Sgt	Nicholas D. Furrie
TG	S/Sgt	Joshua Goldstein

Lt. Clyde B. Knipfer gives the following account of the 28 May 1944 mission, as he recalls the memorable incident 40 years later:

"Our mission was to Dessau and we were flying "Purple Heart Corner"—in the low squadron. We had just reached the IP and had opened the bomb bay doors. A large number—60-70—of German fighters hit our group, coming at us from seven o'clock high. #520, our airplane, was hit by 20 millimeter shells and our numbers one and two engines caught on fire. I peeled away from the formation, leveled out, dropped our bombs as the fire was really burning at the time. I saw no way to put out the fire so I hit the bail-out bell for everyone to bail out, which everyone did.

"The entire crew safely parachuted to earth, were all captured, and spent the remainder of the war in various prison camps."

Clyde Knipfer also relates that a Mr. Ivo M. de Jong of The Netherlands has been researching shot-down 8th Army Air Force aircraft and says there is in existence a picture of the shot-down #42-31520 "A" A/C.

Both Hauf and Knipfer were "Hutchison Provisional Group" crews.

14 June 1944—La Bourget/Melum. One thousand three hundred and fourteen heavy bombers of the 8th AAF bombed selected targets in France including 16 air fields and other tactical targets. The 8th AAF lost 14 heavy bombers, most of which were lost as a result of having been hit by flak.

The 457th furnished five 12-ship boxes on this mission, a maximum effort. Bombing results of the mission were fair.

The flak was intense and accurate and was responsible for the loss of five aircraft.

Major Raymond A. Syptak, flying as air commander of a lead aircraft, was awarded the Silver Star for his part in bringing the heavily damaged lead airplane back to base.

The lead airplane was damaged by German fighter 20mm fire which knocked out one engine and damaged a second as the Squadron approached the IP. However, Lt. William L. Gibbons, the lead pilot, maintained the lead position through the bomb run. Over the target flak further damaged the aircraft, causing damage to the control system and oxygen system. A fire also started burning in the A/C.

Lt. Gibbons set the automatic pilot, hit the bail-out button, and bailed out. Major Syptak also attempted to bail out but was unable to do so. He was unable to open the escape hatch in the nose.

Syptak returned to the flight deck to find the engineer had put out the fire and he flew the A/C back to base.

457th (Bains)

D-Day, 6 June 1944.

The five aircraft which did not return to base included the following:

P	Lt	Roy W. Allen
CP	Lt	Verne H. Lewis
N	Lt	Lawrence Anderson
B	Lt	Joseph C. Brusse
AE	S/Sgt	Ray E. Plum
RO	Sgt	William C. Goldsborough
AG	Sgt	Leonard S. Renson
AG	S/Sgt	Earnest L. Smith
AG	Sgt	Gorden Long

P	2nd Lt	Malcolm E. Johnson
(AC)	Lt Col	(Unknown) Cobb
N	2nd Lt	Donald E. Huston
N	2nd Lt	Roy A. Hough, Jr.
B	2nd Lt	William G. Patry
AE	S/Sgt	Randall M. White
RO	Sgt	Molton R. Davison
AG	Sgt	Clarence A. Ray
AG	Sgt	Steve Vargo
AG	Sgt	Raymond L. Osborn
TG	2nd Lt	David Wilks

457th

Major Raymond A. Syptak was awarded the Silver Star for his part in flying the damaged aircraft back to base 14 June 1944: Mission to La Bourget A/F France.

P	2nd Lt	William F. Rogers
CP	2nd Lt	Stanley J. Wolczanski
N	2nd Lt	Wilbert J. Collard
B	Sgt	Milton E. Bunch
AE	T/Sgt	Joshua D. Lane, Jr.
RO	T/Sgt	John Chumas
AG	S/Sgt	David H. Quick
AG	S/Sgt	Ray (NMI) Jones
AG	Sgt	Orion H. Shumway

P	2nd Lt	Charles R. Blackwell
CP	2nd Lt	Theodore R. Baskette
N	2nd Lt	Irving H. Byers
B	2nd Lt	Verne M. Boone
AE	T/Sgt	Thomas W. Howard
RO	T/Sgt	Edward Nabozny
AG	S/Sgt	Francis W. McCall
AG	S/Sgt	Thomas G. Leahy
AG	Sgt	Sylvester C. Kuraszkiewicz

The aircraft piloted by 2nd Lt. LaPaze was severely damaged and ditched in the English Channel. Five members of the crew were rescued.

F/O	Louis W. McGranahan
F/O	Keith W. Morgan
Sgt	Chester V. Hudic
S/Sgt	Henry L. Baker
S/Sgt	Oscar C. Hightower

Lt. Charles R. Blackwell, pilot of an A/C shot down at La Bourget A/F, relates the following story 40 years later:

"It was my 29th mission and 28th for the others on the crew. I had flown my first mission as co-pilot with Lt. Al Fischer on the 457th B.G. first mission to Berlin on 3 March 1944.

"Our target was La Bourget A/F in Paris. I'm not sure why, but we circled and went in up-wind at the target. We had a strong headwind and our ground speed was only about 80 knots and we were really 'clobbered' by the intense and accurate flak.

"We were hit by a burst of flak and we lost three engines, only one of which could we get feathered. There was gasoline running

457th

Lt. William F. Rogers, 1st Pilot, A/C shot down 14 June 1944 at La Bourget A/F.

457th

"Loading Up" crew checking equipment before climbing into airplane. Lt. William F. Rogers' crew shot down 14 June 1944 at La Bourget A/F.

457th (Dickinson)

Lt. Charles R. Blackwell shot down on 14 June 1944. Lt. Blackwell was Col. Dickinson's co-pilot before taking over his own crew.

all over the flight deck and I was really worried about fire. Two engines were 'running away' and the whole thing gave me a weird feeling. We rode the airplane down to about 3,000 feet where we flew into some clouds and I decided this would be a good time to 'hit the silk.'

"I set the autopilot, hit the bail-out button, and we all jumped. The airplane evidently made a big circle for Lt. Baskette, the co-pilot, said it came back and he thought the airplane was going to fly right into his 'chute.

"I landed in a tree and it took me some time to 'shinny' down and to also pull the 'chute down. Some French people found me before the Germans did and I stayed with a group of Free French for some period of time. Those 'French underground' people really would get 'frisky' at night—blowing up bridges, and shooting Krauts. One day they learned that some Kraut soldiers were coming around looking for shot-down American flyers. We had been living in an old barn and we hid in a nearby ditch. The French gave me two hand grenades and an old double barrel shotgun.

Thank goodness the Krauts did not find us. Nothing happened, but I decided to travel west with another downed flyer, a Polish pilot who had been flying with the R.A.F.

"We had been given civilian clothing and we walked west toward the American lines for two days. One night we slept in the hay-mow of an old barn. In the morning a 'Frenchie' with a bunch of cherries in his hand came to the barn and motioned for us to follow him. He took us to the small town of Blonville. There he introduced us to a French woman by the name of Mme. Jane Vaillant, who took us into her house and hid us for about five weeks, until we were liberated by the American soldiers."

20 June 1944—Hamburg. The 8th AAF launched 1257 heavy bombers to attack 14 strategic targets in Germany. The weather was CAVU and the 8th AAF used this break in the weather to hit the priority oil targets—the synthetic oil plants and the oil refineries.

The attacks on the oil targets were not without high cost, however, for the 8th AAF lost over 500 men, 50 heavy bombers, and 7 fighters. Gunners of the bombers and the fighters evened the score somewhat as they claimed 76 German aircraft destroyed.

The 457th Bomb Group supplied two boxes of 18 aircraft to the effort. Major William F. Smith led the low box and Major Ted Hoffman was air commander of the lead box of the 94th Wing.

The bombing results were excellent and members of the lead team Lt. Roland Byers and Capt. Dino Tonelli received DFCs for completing the mission with excellent results in spite of malfunctioning equipment.

Flak was heavy at the target to which was attributed the loss of one aircraft, that of Lt. Bomer. Sixteen of the 457th aircraft received minor damage and two major damage.

The crew of Lt. Bomer's A/C is listed hereafter:

P	Lt	William G. Bomer
CP	Lt	Jack A. Bade
N	Lt	Charles Curione
B	Lt	Robert E. Hill
AE	T/Sgt	William H. Kane
RO	T/Sgt	Elwood Kline
LW	S/Sgt	Albert W. Leeing
RW	S/Sgt	Unknown
BT	S/Sgt	Edwin E. Tengler
TG	S/Sgt	Richard A. Bohl

21 June 1944—Berlin. Nine hundred and thirty-five 8th AAF heavy bombers bombed motor industry targets in Berlin, Genshagen, Basdorf, Belzig, Potsdam, Stendal, Trebbin and Rangsdorf. Nineteen heavy bombers were lost on this mission. One hundred and forty-four 8th AAF bombers flew to Russia on operation "FRANTIC"—a shuttle mission from England to Russia to Italy and back to England again. During the night of June 21/22 the German Air Force attacked the base at Poltava, Russia, and destroyed 47 of the 73 B-17s which had landed there.

The 457th B.G. furnished 37 aircraft, two boxes of 18 (and a spare) for the mission. Major Leroy Watson was air commander of the lead box and Captain Belcher the pilot. Major Ted Hoffman was air commander of the low box with Capt. Mays the pilot.

The bombing results were considered good at T/O (target of opportunity).

Flak was described as moderate at the target and of 10 minutes duration. Two of the 457th aircraft were missing: one was reported to have blown up at the target and a second left the formation over the Baltic Sea and flew north in the direction of Sweden, a neutral country.

The crew that flew to Sweden was that of Lt. Robert M. Krumm which was interned in Sweden. His aircraft lost two engines from equipment malfunction and could not maintain flying speed to keep up with the formation.

The crew of A/C #42-107015 included the following:

P	Lt	Robert Krumm
CP	Lt	Leo Green
LW	S/Sgt	Tony Tozzi
AEG	T/Sgt	Joe Hibbs

A second A/C, #42-31656, was lost and reported to have blown up at the target, however, the crew was not identified.

29 June 1944—Leipzig. Two hundred and fifty-five 8th AAF B-17 bombers struck targets at Bohlen, Wittenberg, Leipzig/Taucha aero engine works, Leipzig/Heiterblick fighter assembly plant, and T/O. Three hundred and ninety B-24s bombed aircraft assembly plants at Bernburg and other locations. Fifteen heavy bombers were lost.

The 457th B.G. bombed a T/O and the results were unobserved. Trouble was encountered at assembly and only 22 aircraft completed the mission.

A/C #42-37562 flown by Lt. Albert Gumuslauskas was struck by flak and later attacked by enemy fighters and did not return from the mission.

P	Lt	Albert Gumuslauskas
CP	Lt	William Delhardt
N	Lt	Harry Hill
B	Lt	Paul Beatty
AE	T/Sgt	Ralph Delemart
RO	T/Sgt	Louis McPeake
LW	S/Sgt	Charles Campbell
RW	S/Sgt	Eros Sampler
TG	S/Sgt	Jay P. Stacy

7 July 1944—Leipzig. The 8th AAF bombed oil targets, aircraft assembly plants, A/Fs (air fields), and M/Ys (marshalling yards). Thirty-seven heavy bombers were lost. Six hundred and forty-nine fighters escorted the bombers. Fighters claimed 77 German fighters destroyed. Six fighters were lost.

The 457th bombed industrial targets at Leipzig. The bombing results were considered good in spite of the fact that smoke obscured the MPI when bombardier Lt. Harry B. Vaal dropped the bombs on the target.

One A/C, #42-30731, was lost, that of Lt. Owens, an F model B-17. Lt. Owens could not transfer adequate fuel to keep up with the formation and turned toward home. He did not have enough fuel to make landfall and ditched. Four of the crew were killed when the A/C broke up as it ditched. The others on the crew were picked up by air/sea rescue. The following crewmen died in the crash.

2nd Lt	Franci A. Minturn
T/Sgt	Phillip M. Murillo
T/Sgt	Theodore C. Roland
S/Sgt	Earl A. Markwelder

11 July 1944—Munich. Lt. Gazzale's A/C caught fire during assembly over England on the mission to Munich and the crew bailed out. The A/C blew up and the pilot, Lt. Gazzale, was blown out of the A/C and parachuted to the ground as had five of his crew.

Those who died in the explosion and resultant crash were

2nd/Lt James R. Phillips, T/Sgt Ralph R. Hipman, and S/Sgt Everett Broadis.

12 July 1944—Munich. One hundred and seventeen heavy bombers from the 8th AAF bombed M/Ys, A/F and an aero engine plant at Munich. Twenty-four heavy bombers were lost, 13 to flak and the remainder to accidents and unknown causes.

The 457th B.G. launched 33 bombers, providing the lead and low box of "B" wing. The 401st B.G. at Deenethorpe provided the high box of both "A" and "B" wings. The 351st B.G. at Polebrook provided the lead and low box of "A" wing. Two aircraft were lost to flak over the target, which was intense and accurate.

Lt. Edward Kozel's aircraft was hit by flak while on the bomb run. The propeller on number one engine was blown off. The aircraft #44-6111 was reported to be losing altitude and lagging behind the formation but under control. The aircraft was landed in Switzerland and the crew interned. The crew of A/C #44-611 is as follows:

P	Lt	Edward Kozel
CP	Lt	Alvie J. Phares
N	Lt	Selig Patchick
B	Lt	Carl F. Altimus
AE	S/Sgt	Robert E. Nichols
RO	Sgt	Jacob L. Alpert
LW	S/Sgt	Dwight F. Sranson
RW	S/Sgt	William H. Koester
TG	Sgt	Thomas D. Dalrymple

Lt. Gerald L. Kerr was the pilot of the second crew lost on the mission, A/C #42-31552. The aircraft bombed the primary target, had the number one engine knocked out by flak, and then was reported flying south under control, probably heading for Switzerland. It was later learned that the aircraft crashed into a mountain in Switzerland. Two crewmen survived the crash and were interned. The crew of A/C #42-31552 is as follows:

P	Lt	Gerald L. Kerr
CP	Lt	Arthur H. Lindsborg
N	Lt	Edward A. Schilling
B	Lt	Melvin L. Levine
AE	T/Sgt	Leon Finneran
RO	T/Sgt	Ernest J. Hegedus

LW	S/Sgt	Harold E. Alhfors
RW	S/Sgt	Samuel P. Younger, Jr.
TG	S/Sgt	Donald B. Boyle

19 July 1944—Augsburg. Eleven hundred heavy bombers of the 8th AAF operating in five forces attacked strategic targets in Germany. Targets included aircraft factories, chemical plants, ball bearing plants, M/Ys and A/Fs. Fifteen heavy bombers were lost.

The 457th B.G. launched 34 aircraft and lost one A/C, #42-97601, that piloted by Lt. Noel A. Cunefare. The aircraft was attacked by some of the 25 Me 109s which attacked the group just before turning on the IP. Engines #2 and #3 were reported to be on fire. The aircraft dropped out of the formation with no report of parachutes or of what happened to it.

The crew is listed as follows:

P	1st Lt	Noel A. Cunefare
CP	Capt	Jerome E. Godfrey
N	1st Lt	Wesley C. Akins
B	1st Lt	Donald W. Barton
AE	T/Sgt	Howard S. Drake
RO	T/Sgt	Frank L. Nunn
LW	S/Sgt	Ralph T. Hodson
RW	S/Sgt	Joseph W. Duvall
TG	2nd Lt	John C. Sampson

21 July 1944—Schweinfurt. Nine hundred and sixty 8th AAF bombers attacked targets in Germany including four aircraft plants, 2 ball bearing plants, and targets in 11 other towns and cities. Thirty heavy bombers were lost.

The 457th provided a high box of twelve aircraft for two 36 aircraft formations. The bombing results were unobserved.

A/C #42-38103, piloted by Lt. Norris H. Gerber, received a direct hit by flak in the #3 engine. Fire was observed coming out of the engine nacelle.

The aircraft dived, leveled off and then was lost to sight. No parachutes were reported.

The crew of A/C #42-38103 is as follows:

P	1st Lt	Norris H. Gerber
CP	1st Lt	Richard J. Colter
N	1st Lt	George K. Sipp

B	1st Lt	William A. O'Conner
AE	T/Sgt	Norman Hirsch
RO	T/Sgt	Floyd T. Stitely
LW	S/Sgt	Harold R. Moore
RW	S/Sgt	Herve J. Paquin
TG	S/Sgt	Charles Minter, Jr.

31 July 1944 – Munich. Six hundred and fifty-one B-17s bombed M/Ys at Munich and aero engine factories at Munich-Allach. Ten B-17s were lost at Munich.

The 457th put up a complete wing of 34 aircraft. The group bombed Munich-Allach, however, the results of the bombing were unobserved because of cloud cover.

One aircraft was lost, that being A/C #42-97087, piloted by Lt. Byron S. Schiffman. The aircraft was lost to flak while over the target. Number 1 engine was set on fire and the end of the wing blown off. The A/C went into a spin and exploded. Three parachutes were reported.

The crew of A/C #42-97087 is as follows:

P	2nd Lt	Byron S. Schiffman
CP	F/O	William L. Barton
N	F/O	Irving J. Cohen
B	F/O	Finn Firing
AE	T/Sgt	Joseph H. Westwood
RO	T/Sgt	Nathaniel Hostow
LW	S/Sgt	John R. Wilkerson
RW	S/Sgt	Alfred Kunz
BT	S/Sgt	Welbur L. Epley
TG	Sgt	Vernon A. Nelson

6 August 1944 – Genshagen. Nine hundred and fifty-three 8th AAF heavy bombers attacked targets including five aircraft factories, a torpedo plant, seven oil refineries, and other targets. The results of the bombing were one of the best in the war.

The 8th AAF launched its second shuttle mission to Russia on this date. Seventy-eight heavy bombers participated in the mission, accompanied by P-51s. The bombers landed at Poltava and Mirgorod, the P-51s at Piryatin.

The 457th B.G. launched 34 aircraft, each carrying ten 500-pound GP bombs. The group supplied enough aircraft for a wing. The bombing results were excellent for two of the 12-ship boxes and fair for the third.

457th (Dickinson)
Lt. Windred Pugh, shot down 24 August 1944.

457th
Lt. Windred L. Pugh's crew. Shot down on mission to Weimar on 24 August 1944.

One aircraft was lost, that of Lt. Vincent L. Frost, A/C #42-97131, which was hit by flak while over the target. Number two engine caught fire when the A/C was 10 miles SE of Brandenburg. Six to eight parachutes were reported by observers. The parachute of one man fouled on the ball turret and the man fell away without it. Soon after the A/C blew up.

The crew of A/C #42-97131 is as follows:

P	2nd Lt	Vincent L. Frost
CP	2nd Lt	John S. Folson, Jr.
N	2nd Lt	Cabert W. Danaher
B	2nd Lt	Earl N. Perouto
AE	S/Sgt	Soloman N. Bernstein
RO	S/Sgt	Chester F. Bartozewicz
LW	Sgt	Daniel D. Rice
RW	Sgt	Daniel C. Taylor
BT	Sgt	Hubert D. Rempp

24 August 1944—Weimar. Four hundred heavy bombers from the 8th AAF bombed strategic targets in Germany. The targets included 17 oil installations, aircraft assembly plants, and aero engine plants.

The 457th B.G. launched 34 aircraft, flying all three boxes of a wing. The bombing results were fair for two boxes and poor for the third.

The group lost two A/C on the mission. A/C #42-97571, piloted by Lt. Windred L. Pugh, peeled off and spiralled down for a distance, leveled out and then stalled and spun down. The A/C exploded between 5,000 and 10,000 feet. Observers counted five or six parachutes.

The crew of A/C #42-97571 is as follows:

P	1st Lt	Windred L. Pugh
CP	F/O	Arthur Richards
N	2nd Lt	Julius Drummond
TO	S/Sgt	Clifford Page
AE	T/Sgt	Edward Szumierz
RO	T/Sgt	James Woodgate
LW	S/Sgt	Joseph Wheatley
RW	S/Sgt	John T. Poshefko
TT	S/Sgt	Howard W. Martin

Dickinson

Lt. Teddy D. Shaw and crew. Shot down on 24 August 1944 mission to Weimar.

A/C #42-09755, piloted by Lt. Teddy G. Shaw, dropped out of formation and was not seen again. No enemy aircraft were seen in the area and no flak had been encountered. The A/C did not appear to be damaged.

The crew of A/C #42-09755 is as follows:

P	2nd Lt	Teddy G. Shaw
CP	2nd Lt	Richard H. Parsons
N	2nd Lt	Jack M. Thames
B	2nd Lt	Paul J. Terjak
AE	Sgt	Robert P. Stewart
RO	Sgt	Lawrence Erlings
LW	Sgt	J. I. Perry
RW	Sgt	Elbert Q. Allen
TT	Sgt	Clarence W. Cox

25 August 1944—Pennemunde. Eleven hundred heavy bombers—B-17s and B-24s—were launched by the 8th AAF. They attacked four A/C plants, three A/Fs, two experimental research stations, and fifteen T/Os in Germany. Nineteen heavy bombers were lost. Fifteen fighter groups escorted the bombers and shot down 11 enemy aircraft.

The 457th Bomb Group launched 34 A/C and bombed Pennemunde. The results of the bombing, using five 1000-pound bombs, bombing in trail were excellent for two boxes and fair for the third.

The group lost one A/C on the mission, that piloted by Lt. Donald K. Goss. The A/C, #42-9818, was hit by flak while in the target area just after the bombs were dropped. The flak blew a large hole in the left wing and #2 engine was feathered. No parachutes were observed.

The crew of A/C #42-9818 is as follows:

P	2nd Lt	Donald K. Goss
CP	2nd Lt	Phil B. Adreau
N	2nd Lt	Gerhardt Hoelzel
TO	S/Sgt	William H. Sokolowski
AE	S/Sgt	Peter G. Stern
RO	S/Sgt	Henry M. Githens
LW	S/Sgt	John A. Roe, Jr.
RW	S/Sgt	Ruben L. Hernandez
TT	Sgt	Charles E. Gentile

10 September 1944—Gaggenau. The 8th AAF launched over 1,000 A/C which attacked motor transport, tank, aircraft, aero engine, and jet propulsion plants and A/Fs in south central Germany. Two A/C were lost. A/C #42-97451 collided with A/C #42-97456. The latter A/C broke in two parts at a point near the rear door. Two parachutes were observed by American soldiers. The two men who parachuted to safety were Lt. Jerome W. Page, navigator, and Sgt. Jacob Z. Chimerinsky, tail gunner.

The crew of A/C #42-97456 is as follows:

P	2nd Lt	Homer M. Passmore
CP	2nd Lt	Gerald W. Esser
N	2nd Lt	Jerome W. Page
B	2nd Lt	Milton R. Long
AE	S/Sgt	Herman E. Taylor
RO	S/Sgt	Wade C. Hensen
LW	Sgt	James M. Fauls
BT	Sgt	Elmer M. Abel
TT	Sgt	Jacob Z. Chimerinsky

On the mission, a second A/C, number unknown, caught fire

and the crew bailed out over Allied Territory. All but one man, Lt. Anthony J. Wodek, returned to base.

12 September 1944—Ruhland. Eight hundred heavy bombers of the 8th AAF escorted by 15 fighter groups bombed two oil refineries, four synthetic oil plants, an oil depot, an aero engine plant, and several T/Os. The German air force attacked the bombers in defense of their oil facilities and shot down 45 of the heavy bombers. The Germans lost 63 fighters as well as 26 claimed destroyed on the ground to United States fighters. Bomber gunners claimed 27 German fighters.

The 457th lost one A/C, #42-31383, to German fighters, that piloted by Lt. Harry H. Selling. Reports were contradictory; however, apparently the A/C was attacked by one German fighter, the 20mm shells of which hit the B-17 in the cockpit and #3 engine. The aircraft was reported to be on fire. Another report stated the A/C blew up. One report stated one parachute was seen.

The crew of A/C #42-31383 is as follows:

P	1st Lt	Harry H. Selling
CP	2nd Lt	Floyd D. French
N	2nd Lt	Robert F. Marcum
B	2nd Lt	Howard L. Peterson
AE	T/Sgt	James P. Shadman
RO	T/Sgt	Edwin C. Drueger
LW	S/Sgt	Donald W. Conley
BT	S/Sgt	Stephen V. Gallucci
TG	S/Sgt	Leo A. Ryder

A second A/C, identity unknown, is listed on the 457th Bomb Group Mission Board. However, 8th AAF Missing in Action Crew Report does not list another A/C as lost.

17 September 1944—Nijmegen. The 8th AAF bombers flew a tactical mission in support of the First Airborne Army which was making parachute and glider drop of 20,000 troops in The Netherlands. The heavy bombers attacked flak batteries and installations in the vicinity of the drop.

The 457th encountered moderate but accurate flak at the target. One lead A/C, that piloted by Lt. Douglas Grananhan with whom Major George C. Hozier (air commander) was riding, was hit by flak in one and possibly two engines soon after turning at the I.P.

After being hit, Major Hozier flashed a green light, the bombardier salvoed the bombs as the A/C veered away from the formation. The bombardier then closed the bomb bay doors and the pilot dropped the wheels.

Four and possible five crewmen were seen to parachute from the aircraft. When last seen the A/C was flying apparently under control.

The crew of the A/C is listed as follows:

P	1st Lt	Douglas Granahan, Jr.
AC	Major	George C. Hozier
CP	F/O	Arthur Gennari
N	Capt	Patrick W. Henry
N	2nd Lt	Howard P. Quinn
N	2nd Lt	Robert C. Douglas
B	1st Lt	Robert E. Costello
AE	T/Sgt	William N. Suggs
RO	T/Sgt	Buford R. Milner
LW	S/Sgt	August E. Kugala
BT	S/Sgt	Sophus C. Rucker

26 September 1944—Osnabrook. The 8th AAF launched 400 B-17s which bombed targets in the cities of Bremen, Hesipe, Osnabrook and Hamm, Germany. The targets included two M/Ys, two A/Fs, two aircraft plants, a steelworks, and T/O.

The 457th was assigned a M/Y target at Osnabrook. One aircraft, #42-32079 flown by Lt. Carl H. Gooch, was hit with flak as the formation crossed the Dutch coast. The tracking flak blew off the top turret and also apparently damaged the cockpit and radio room. One witness reported two engines knocked out and the nose of the A/C blown out. However, the aircraft seemed to be in control when last seen.

The crew of A/C #42-32079 is as follows:

P	2nd Lt	Carl H. Gooch
CP	2nd Lt	John P. Quillin
N-B	2nd Lt	Rupert L. Phipps
AE	T/Sgt	Alexander P. McDermott
RO	S/Sgt	Wilbur M. Parker
LW	S/Sgt	Clement W. Kelsey
BT	S/Sgt	Leo J. Chermark
TG	S/Sgt	Thomas V. Angott
CHIN	S/Sgt	Donald J. Reilly

28 September 1944—Magdeburg. One thousand heavy bombers from the 8th AAF continued the attack on the German oil industry. Targets at Merseburg, Kassel and Magdeburg were bombed. Thirty heavy bombers failed to return to base.

This mission to Magdeburg by the crews of the 457th B.G. proved to be the most disastrous since the group began operations in February 1944.

Nearly 50 German fighters, ME 109s and FW 190s, attacked the formation just before the turn at the I.P. The fighters came in low from four to nine o'clock, attacking the rear of the bombers.

In a period of about twelve to thirteen minutes, 1146 to 1159, six aircraft were damaged enough by the fighter attack that they dropped out of formation.

A/C #43-37518, flown by Lt. Harold D. Gay was struck by 20mm shells in the area of the #3 engine and right side of the fuselage. Black smoke and fire was reported by observers just before the A/C slid off to the left away from the formation. The bombs were salvoed and then the A/C went into a steep dive. No parachutes were reported.

The crew of A/C #43-37518 included the following:

P	1st Lt	Harold D. Gay
CP	2nd Lt	Earl M. Johnson
N	2nd Lt	Fabian F. Hordan
B	2nd Lt	Carl C. Flander
AE	T/Sgt	Arthur G. Beck
RO	T/Sgt	Donald W. Anderson
LW	S/Sgt	Arthur G. Rounseville
BT	S/Sgt	Fred M. Cogswell
TT	S/Sgt	Thomas McDee

Six more A/C, two from the high flight and four from the low flight, were also shot down from the eighteen-ship box during the thirteen-minute attack. The white puffs of 20mm shells were seen bursting in the formation and almost immediately six A/C scattered and left the formation. Reports were few because the gunners were busy firing at the German fighters when so many A/C were leaving the formation.

The following A/C did not return to base.

The crew of A/C #43-38181, piloted by 1st Lt. Albert L. Sikkenga, is as follows:

P	1st Lt	Albert L. Sikkenga
CP	2nd Lt	Paul P. Reichert
N	2nd Lt	Angelo A. Archiopoli
B	2nd Lt	Vivian C. McWhorter
AE	T/Sgt	Charles T. Darnell
RO	T/Sgt	Anthony Villane
LW	S/Sgt	Robert S. Christofferson
BT	S/Sgt	Alton T. Eason
TT	S/Sgt	Stanley B. Hojnowski

A/C #43-38026, piloted by Lt. Charles J. Schultz, was not specifically identified by observers when it fell out of formation. A general observation was made of the five A/C lost from the low squadron that two of the five A/C blew up. Only two parachutes were observed in the area.

The crew of A/C #43-38026 is as follows:

P	2nd Lt	Charles J. Schultz
CP	F/O	Alfred P. Wilson
N	2nd Lt	Alfred A. Houghten
B	2nd Lt	George E. MacDermott
AE	T/Sgt	Richard D. Dickinson
RO	T/Sgt	John R. Palladina
LW	S/Sgt	Augustus R. Herrmann
BT	S/Sgt	W. J. Peppers
TT	S/Sgt	Calvin K. Carter

A/C #42-102948 is as follows:

P	2nd Lt	Keylon C. Clarke
CP	2nd Lt	Robert M. Newland
N	2nd Lt	Walter Sundling
B	2nd Lt	Robert F. Smith
AE	Sgt	Albert Griffith
RO	Sgt	William C. Sethloff
LW	Sgt	David R. Cooley
BT	Sgt	Lee S. Simpson
TT	Sgt	Richard H. Anderson

A/C #42-97470, piloted by Lt. Robert I. Ellsworth, was knocked out of formation by the 20mm shells fired by the first wave of German fighters which attacked the 457th B.G. There were no reports of what happened to the A/C.

The crew of A/C #42-97470 is as follows:

P	2nd Lt	Robert I. Ellsworth
CP	2nd Lt	John V. Van Ingen
N-B	2nd Lt	Thomas O. Metcalfe, Jr.
AE	S/Sgt	James D. Kreichbaum
RO	S/Sgt	James A. Mellin
LW	Sgt	Walter W. Maher
RW	Sgt	Joseph J. Smolinski
BT	Sgt	Melvin Milbauer
TT	Sgt	Robert J. Stubbs

The A/C #43-37834, piloted by 1st Lt. Fred J. Lockwald, was knocked out of the formation by 20mm shells fired from the first wave of German fighters which struck the 457th B.G. formation.

There were three or four A/C which fell from the formation at about the same time and no specific information was reported of what happened to Lockwald's A/C.

The crew of A/C #43-37834 is as follows:

P	1st Lt	Fred J. Lockwald
CP	2nd Lt	Joseph Jirik
N	2nd Lt	James R. Rawls
B	2nd Lt	Seymour Salganick
AE	T/Sgt	Charlton Killgo
RO	T/Sgt	Harry S. Jacobson
LW	S/Sgt	John Wranesh
BT	S/Sgt	Drew L. Sheffield
TG	S/Sgt	Everett A. Mohannah

30 September 1944—Munster. The 8th AAF launched more than 750 heavy bombers to attack M/Ys, A/Fs at Munster, Bielefeld, Hamm and Handorf.

The 457th bombed targets at Munster, Germany. One A/C was lost to flak at the target.

A/C #43-38538 received a direct hit by a burst of flak. The nose section appeared to crumple, parts of both wings broke off; also parts of the tail section broke off. An explosion was observed near the bomb bay. The A/C dropped immediately after the explosion, leveled out, and then dropped straight to the ground.

Two men apparently without parachutes were seen to leave the A/C.

The crew of A/C #43-38538 is as follows:

P	1st Lt	William A. Millea
CP	2nd Lt	Lymon C. Plyer
N	2nd Lt	Terrence E. Rice
N	1st Lt	John W. Tadje
B	1st Lt	Lee E. Kohn
AE	T/Sgt	Albert S. Levy
RO	T/Sgt	Albert E. Young
LW	S/Sgt	Edward J. Roos
BT	S/Sgt	John W. Philsley

7 October 1944—Politz. The 8th AAF launched four forces of bombers totaling 1300 aircraft to bomb high priority strategic targets in Germany. The targets included five synthetic oil plants, an aero engine plant, a tank factory, and 16 other targets in central and northeast Germany. Fifty-two heavy bombers were lost.

The mission for the members of the 457th Bomb Group would be one of the most memorable in the short history of the Group. The Group Commander, Col. James Rhea Luper, did not return to base. The aircraft in which he was flying was shot down by flak over the target, a synthetic oil plant at Politz, Germany.

This mission was a maximum effort for the 457th B.G. and 48 A/C were launched. The A/C formed one complete 36 A/C box and the low group of a composite box by the 94th Wing (457th, 401st, and 351st).

A/C #44-38046, piloted by Capt. Alfred W. Fischer, was hit by flak as it approached the target. #2 and possibly #3 engines were hit and caught fire. Fire also burned inside the A/C. The A/C was observed in a spin and then blew up. From two to nine parachutes were reported. One parachute was reported to be on fire.

The crew of A/C #44-38046 is as follows:

P	Capt	Alfred W. Fischer
AC	Col	James R. Luper
N	Major	Norman A. Kriehn
N	1st Lt	William J. Morrow
B	Capt	Henry P. Loades
N	1st Lt	Frederick A. Asbell
	Major	Gordon H. Haggard (Group Surgeon)
AE	T/Sgt	John W. Koahler
RO	T/Sgt	Ancil V. Shepherd
TG	1st Lt	Edward A. McNeal
LW	S/Sgt	John J. Derling

457th

Capt. Alfred W. Fischer. Lead Pilot of 7 October 1944 crew that was shot down on the mission to Politz.

A/C #42-97638, piloted by Lt. William H. Flannery, was hit by flak while in the vicinity of the target. Number three engine caught fire and flames were observed streaming out as far back as the tail of the aircraft. One crew member was observed to leave the aircraft, however no parachutes were seen to open. The airplane dove downward in an apparent attempt to extinguish the flames.

The crew of A/C #42-97638 is as follows:

P	1st Lt	William H. Flannery
CP	2nd Lt	Jewell L. Lowery
N	2nd Lt	Paul Moll III

N	2nd Lt	Morris Arnovitz
N	2nd Lt	Raymond C. Moon
B	2nd Lt	John H. Schloondorn
AE	T/Sgt	Floyd K. Lagrassa
RO	T/Sgt	Duane E. Stowits
BT	S/Sgt	George L. Petty
TT	2nd Lt	Walter C. Strossner

A/C #44-6469, piloted by Lt. Vernon M. Moland, was hit by flak in the nose section of the A/C. The burst of flak blew the crew members out of the nose section. The A/C dropped below the formation and was not observed after dropping away. No parachutes were seen.

The crew of A/C #44-6469 is as follows:

P	2nd Lt	Vernon M. Moland
CP	2nd Lt	Scott S. Millis, Jr.
N	2nd Lt	Leo J. Higgins
B	2nd Lt	Arthur H. Jensen
AE	T/Sgt	William D. Ackerson
RO	T/Sgt	Cecil D. Woodruff
LW	S/Sgt	Earl S. Howell
BT	S/Sgt	John R. Koziel
TT	S/Sgt	James A. Gunnels

A/C #43-38529, piloted by Lt. Salzer, was shot out of the formation but ditched in the English channel and the crew was saved.

A/C #42-102905, piloted by Lt. Clarence R. Jennings, was not observed to have been in difficulty when it dropped out of formation. The A/C dropped its bombs before it reached the BRL (bomb release line) and when last observed was on a northerly course.

Lt. Jennings landed the A/C in Sweden with two crew members dead and one injured. The other crew members were interned for the remainder of the European conflict.

The crew of A/C #42-102905 is as follows:

P	2nd Lt	Clarence R. Jennings
CP	2nd Lt	Richard R. Garland
N	2nd Lt	Martin Schwartz
B	2nd Lt	Stewart W. Jakku

AE	T/Sgt	Hardy S. Bell
RO	T/Sgt	Walter W. Karr
LW	Sgt	William N. Barth, Jr.
RW	S/Sgt	Charles Sparnick
BT	S/Sgt	John D. Wood
TC	Capt	Floyd A. Cox

15 October 1944 – Cologne. The 8th AAF attacked 9 M/Ys and a gas unit plant in the Cologne vicinity with over 1,000 heavy bombers.

The 457th B.G. supplied 36 A/C for the mission. The target was the M/Y in Cologne, Germany. The target was partly obscured by cloud cover; however, by coordination between the PFF navigator and the bombardier the target was hit. For this fine teamwork the crew received a commendation from B. General J. K. Lacey, Commanding General of the 94th Wing.

The lead crew was:

P	Capt	Donald L. Seesenguth
AC	Lt Col	Leroy H. Watson
N	Lt	Roland O. Byers
B	Capt	Irwin Rosen
PFF Nav	Lt	Oscar B. Stauff
DR Nav	Lt	Norman K. Nail
AEG	T/Sgt	Raymond D. Brodin
RO	S/Sgt	Willaim M. Thacker
AG	T/Sgt	George R. Mangowski

Two A/C are listed as being shot down by A/A flak on this mission; however, the A/C and crews were not identified in the available records. The 457th B.G. Mission Board lists zero crews lost. Apparently the report is incorrect.

17 October 1944 – Cologne. The 8th AAF attacked M/Ys and 2 T/Os in Cologne with 1,200 heavy bombers.

The 457th launched 36 A/C and attacked a M/Y in Cologne. The results of the bombing were unobserved due to cloud cover.

A/C #43-7606, piloted by Lt. Norman M. Chapman, was hit by flak just before bombs away. Two burst of flak were observed, one under each wing of the A/C. The A/C swung away from the formation and turned to the left. The wingmen turned with the A/C until they realized the A/C was in trouble and was leaving the

457th

Lead crew on 15 October 1944 mission to Cologne. Standing left to right: Lt. Roland O. Byers, Lt. Oscar Stauff, Capt. Irwin Rosen, Lt. Col. Leroy Watson Jr., Unknown, Lt. Norman K. Nail. Kneeling left to right: T/Sgt. Raymond D. Brodin, S/Sgt. William M. Thacker, T/Sgt. George R. Mangowski, Capt. Donald Seesenguth.

formation. For as long as the A/C was visible no parachutes were seen. There had been no visible damage or fire seen by observers.

P	1st Lt	Norman M. Chapman
CP	2nd Lt.	Raymond K. Mills, Jr.
N-B	F/O	Kenneth H. Johnson
AE	T/Sgt	Robert T. Brady
RO	T/Sgt	Marshall T. Windham
LW	S/Sgt	James R. Dixon
RW	S/Sgt	Carl M. Weibel
BT	S/Sgt	Joseph M. Budich
TT	2nd Lt	Oliver W. Wicks

25 October 1944—Hamburg. The 8th AAF launched 1,200

457th (Dickinson)

Lt. Norman M. Chapman, 1st Pilot A/C #43-7606 shot down over target, Cologne, 17 October 1944.

heavy bombers in five forces to bomb three oil refineries, an A/F, and a synthetic oil plant, all at several locations including Gelsenkirchen, Scholven, Buer, and Hamburg. M/Ys at Munster and Hamm were also bombed.

The 457th launched 36 A/C. They found the primary target obscured by the cloud cover and bombed a secondary target.

One A/C #42-97899, was lost, that piloted by Lt. John F. Angier. The A/C was struck by flak in the right wing. The A/C peeled off to the right, leaving the formation. A gasoline leak was observed and then it caught fire. Number 4 engine was feathered. The A/C was under control for two or three minutes during which time two crewmen bailed out. The A/C then exploded.

The crew of A/C #42-97899 is as follows:

P	1st Lt	John F. Angier
CP	2nd Lt	Samual E. Cashman
N	2nd Lt	Samuel A. Plestine
B	F/O	Robert J. Maitland

AE	T/Sgt	Howard H. Lang
RP	T/Sgt	William M. Thomas
LW	S/Sgt	Charles D. Osborn
BT	S/Sgt	Edwin C. Vantine
TT	S/Sgt	Maynard E. Judson

2 November 1944—Merseburg. The 8th AAF launched over 1,000 heavy bombers in five separate forces which attacked synthetic oil plants, M/Ys, and T/Os. The targets were located at Merseburg/Luena, Castrop-Rauxel, Sterkrade, and Bielefeld/Schielesche along with other T/Os. Opposition by the German Air Force was the most fierce in some time with over 500 fighters defending the Merseburg/Luena area. Forty heavy bombers were lost.

For the 457th B.G., November 2nd proved to be another disastrous day, as nine A/C were lost to enemy fighters.

The results of the bombing were unobserved due to cloud cover. However, the primary target was not attacked due to what the record states was a malfunction of PFF equipment.

The story of the mission "Merseburg" is given elsewhere in this book.

Between 1248 and 1258 hours, for ten minutes, 40-50 German fighters attacked the 457th Bomb Group about 17 to 27 minutes after bombs away.

The attack came from the rear of the formation at 5 to 8 o'clock. The attack was made in waves; however, it appeared each fighter was firing at a specific A/C. Nine bombers were shot down.

A/C #43-37766 was shot down. However, there were no reports of what happened to the A/C.

The crew of A/C #43-37766 is as follows:

P	1st Lt	Earl M. Morrow
CP	2nd Lt	William M. Stemach
N	2nd Lt	George J. Schaffer
B	F/O	Samuel J. Lisica
AE	T/Sgt	Clifford J. Upton
RO	T/Sgt	Charles E. Lindquist
LW	S/Sgt	Robert H. Koerner
BT	S/Sgt	Harry W. Pannell
TG	S/Sgt	Joseph P. Salerno

A/C #43-38561 was flying #6 low section, low squadron and

one eye witness observed the A/C going down in a spiral. The A/C was one of seven from this squadron. One A/C was lost from each of the high and lead squadrons.

The crew of A/C #43-38561 is as follows:

P	2nd Lt	Bruce F. Harrison
CP	2nd Lt	Robert C. McGuire
N	2nd Lt	Edward W. Mullen
B	2nd Lt	Peter G. Elsbeck
AE	S/Sgt	Robert F. Rhyner
RO	S/Sgt	Martin Silverman
LW	S/Sgt	Anthony T. Coerone
BT	Sgt	Joseph A. Youngross
TG	Sgt	Charles I. Gordon

E/A 20mm shells struck A/C #43-39123 just outboard of #4 engine and blew a four-foot hole in the wing. The A/C immediately caught fire and the pilot pulled the aircraft up over the #2 wingman and peeled off to the right. The pilot then dived the A/C, possibly attempting to evade fighters in the clouds or to put the fire out. Observers counted four parachutes and they did not see the A/C blow up.

The crew of A/C #42-39123, piloted by 1st Lt. Gordon E. Gallagher, is as follows:

P	1st Lt	Gordon E. Gallagher
CP	1st Lt	Donald W. Johnson
N	1st Lt	Joseph C. Isaacson
B	1st Lt	Roy E. Gleason
AE	T/Sgt	Paul W. Johnson
RO	T/Sgt	William J. Moore
LW	S/Sgt	Harold E. Sturman
BT	S/Sgt	Delos N. Riegle
TT	S/Sgt	Melvin D. Thompson

A/C #43-37782 was hit by 20mm shells from enemy aircraft (E/A), in the tail section and the #3 engine. Flames could be seen coming from the engine, from the radio room, and under the ball turret.

The A/C stayed in the formation for several minutes, then peeled off away from the formation. One parachute was seen by observers. The A/C was observed as having exploded and from two to eight parachutes were reported after the explosion.

The crew of the A/C #43-37782 is as follows:

P	1st Lt	William J. Murdock
CP	F/O	Albert F. Porta
N	2nd Lt	Robert J. Huels
B	2nd Lt	Paul D. Richardson
AE	T/Sgt	William F. Hunter
RO	T/Sgt	Ray L. Zirbel
LW	S/Sgt	Ben W. Berg
BT	S/Sgt	Charles C. Martiny
TG	S/Sgt	Edmund C. Caruso

A/C #43-37556 was hit by E/A 20mm shells in the tail section and the #2 and #3 engines. The aircraft peeled out of the formation to the left, zoomed up and then dove to an elevation of about 25,000 feet. The pilot then held the A/C straight and level during which time five crewmen were seen to jump out of the A/C. A description of the mission by one member of the crew, Lt. Jerome Silverman, is given in another section of this book.

The crew of A/C #43-37556, a lead crew, is as follows:

P	1st Lt	William A. Dawson
CP	Capt (A/C)	John B. Wallace
N	1st Lt	Jerome Silverman
N	1st Lt	George B. Korb
B	2nd Lt	Frank O. Pappenfuss
AE	T/Sgt	John R. Roster
RO	T/Sgt	Charles E. Lindquist
LW	S/Sgt	Joseph M. Geller
BT	S/Sgt	George C. Hardin
TG	2nd Lt	Charles W. Ford

A/C #43-37532, piloted by 2nd Lt. James B. Corriher, was not observed at the time it departed from the formation.

The crew of A/C #43-37532 is as follows:

P	2nd Lt	James B. Corriher
CP	2nd Lt	Jeremiah J. Healy
N	2nd Lt	Earl L. Hill
B	2nd Lt	Harold A. Doerr
AE	S/Sgt	George P. Levassauer
RO	S/Sgt	Harry F. Gormley

LW	Sgt	Gail E. Schatz
BT	Sgt	Daniel M. Willis
TG	Sgt	Robert J. Gunther

A/C #44-6155 was hit by E/A 20mm and was observed to have peeled out of formation; however, no other reports were made as to what happened to the A/C.

The crew of A/C #44-6155 is as follows:

P	1st Lt	Samuel H. Schimel
CP	2nd Lt	Edward F. Crudzien
N	2nd Lt	Donald E. Scheuch
B	2nd Lt	Dick E. Coffman
AE	T/Sgt	Henry W. Short
RO	T/Sgt	Bob B. McFarlane
LW	S/Sgt	Albert P. Schmitz
BT	S/Sgt	Dominic Staszwski
TG	S/Sgt	Robert L. Kaer

A/C #42-106998 was not observed at the time it broke formation.

The crew of A/C #42-106998 is as follows:

P	1st Lt	Graeme L. Bow
CP	2nd Lt	Donald Allen
N	2nd Lt	James F. McGee
B	2nd Lt	Richard T. Hibschman
AE	T/Sgt	Chester H. Hall
RO	T/Sgt	John C. Bruggeman
LW	S/Sgt	Chester L. Spurrier
BT	S/Sgt	Robert P. Robinson
TG	S/Sgt	Joseph Navarro

A/C #43-38309 was hit by 20mm fire from E/A in the outer wing near #1 engine. The engine started burning. The A/C peeled out of the formation but leveled out, on a north heading. No more observations were reported as to what happened to the A/C.

The crew of A/C #43-38309 is as follows:

P	2nd Lt	Kenneth E. Guptill
CP	2nd Lt	George H. Keller
NB	2nd Lt	Edmond C. McNamara

CHIN	S/Sgt	Stephen Marklin
AE	S/Sgt	Virgil H. Smollen
RO	S/Sgt	Harry J. Conners
LW	S/Sgt	William E. Rhodes
BT	S/Sgt	Frank A. Kravetz
TG	S/Sgt	Herbert A. Brayman

6 November 1944 – Harburg. The 8th AAF launched over 1,000 heavy bombers, in six forces, and attacked oil and chemical plants. They also attacked M/Ys and T/O in north and northwest Germany.

The 457th put up a 36 A/C box. The target was obscured by cloud cover and was bombed by PFF instruments.

One A/C was lost to unknown reasons, that of Lt. Edward P. McGroarty.

The crew of A/C #43-38904 is as follows:

P	2nd Lt	Edward P. McGroarty
CP	2nd Lt	Robert V. Botwright
NB	F/O	Jack J. Gray
CHIN	Sgt	Henry D. McLeroy
AE	S/Sgt	Angelo Bicamillo
RO	S/Sgt	James R. Reddie
RW	Sgt	Frank T. Mueller
BT	Sgt	Clyde A. Decker
TC	Sgt	Raymond S. Francis

8 November 1944 – Merseburg. The 8th AAF attacked the Merseburg/Luena synthetic oil plant with 250 heavy bombers. The weather was bad and caused the recall of more than 350 bombers briefed to bomb both Merseburg and other targets.

The 457th assembled only 14 aircraft due to bad weather. The mission was recalled; however, one A/C did join another group and bombed the target.

The propellers of another A/C chewed into the fuselage of A/C #42-38064 from the underside. The A/C broke in two pieces, just back of the radio room. The forward part of the A/C went down in a steep glide for about two minutes and then spun and disappeared. The tail section of the A/C also went down in a glide. No parachutes were observed.

The A/C had been rebuilt from two other A/C – one silver, and green – and had been named ARF 'N ARF.

P	1st Lt	Arnet L. Furr
CP	2nd Lt	Sterling R. Book, Jr.
N	2nd Lt	Joseph W. Andrews, Jr.
B	2nd Lt	Leon D. Plagianos
AE	T/Sgt	Gerald D. Brunsvold
RO	T/Sgt	Richard C. Weaver
LW	S/Sgt	Glenn M. Wisdom
BT	S/Sgt	Warren M. Rankin
TG	S/Sgt	Leroy E. Wetzel

30 November 1944 – Bohlen. The 8th AAF launched over 1,200 heavy bombers, some of which bombed synthetic oil plants at Bohler, Zeitz, Merseburg/Luena and Lutzkendorf. Others bombed M/Ys at Neuenkirchen and Homburg/Saar. Twenty-eight heavy bombers were lost.

The 457th B.G. put up 36 A/C, 28 of which bombed the primary target. Two A/Cs were lost to flak. One A/C, #42-107026, "HAMTRAMACK MAMA," piloted by 1st Lt. John W. White, was damaged by flak but crash-landed in France without loss of any crew members.

Another A/C, #42-31505 piloted by 2nd Lt. Joseph C. Frechette, also was damaged over the target but he also crash-landed his A/C in France without injury to the crew.

4 December 1944 – Kassel. The 8th AAF launched over 1,000

457th

Lt. Furr's A/C #42-38064 "ARF 'N ARF" collided with another B-17 and broke into two parts.

heavy bombers which bombed principally M/Ys and some T/Os in Kassel, Soest, Bebra, Giessen, and Mainz. Most of the A/C, 70 bombers and fighters, which did not return to the United Kingdom (U.K.) landed in allied territory on the Continent.

The 457th B.G. put up 36 A/C which bombed a M/Y in Kassel. One A/C did not return to base.

No record was found of the identity of the lost A/C. In fact, the record is conflicting, indicating the loss of an A/C in one report and that all crews returned safely in another.

12 December 1944—Merseburg. The 8th AAF attacked M/Y targets in Dormstadt, Hanau and Aschaffenburg. Also a synthetic oil plant in Merseburg/Luena was attacked by 1,200 heavy bombers.

The 457th B.G. put up 36 A/C, 34 of which bombed the primary target at Merseburg.

One A/C, #43-37567, was lost to unknown reasons.

No flak was reported up to the time A/C #43-37567 dropped its wheels, feathered #4 engine, and dropped out of the formation.

The A/C trailed the formation for a time and then disappeared.

No parachutes were observed.

The crew of A/C #43-37567 is listed hereafter:

P	1st Lt	Montell C. Higgins
CP	2nd Lt	William M. Bell
N	2nd Lt	John C. McCaughan
B	F/O	Harold F. Harstedt
AE	T/Sgt	Francis J. Winder
RO	T/Sgt	Fred E. Lawyer
LW	S/Sgt	Russell A. Perry
BT	S/Sgt	Philip G. Porter
TG	S/Sgt	Bill C. Smigielski

24 December 1944—Koblenz. The 8th AAF dispatched 2,000 bombers to attack A/Fs, Communication Centers, M/Ys, five cities, and over 50 T/Os in the Battle of the Bulge area. Thirteen fighter groups fought with over 200 enemy fighters and claimed 70 destroyed.

The 457th experienced weather problems and because of fog launched only seven A/C.

One A/C #43-38819, piloted by Lt. Carl Sundbaum, crashed on take-off and blew up. One crew member, Sgt. Donald Peacock, was killed.

457th (Bains)

Lt. White's "HAMTRAMACK MAMA" A/C *#42-107026 crash landed in France 30 November 1944.*

The crew of A/C #43-38819 is as follows:

P	2nd Lt	Carl P. Sundbaum
CP	2nd Lt	Galileo F. Basio
N	2nd Lt	Theodore F. Scanlon
B	2nd Lt	Warren W. Nixon
AE	T/Sgt	Julien S. Smith
RO	T/Sgt	John V. Brennan
LW	S/Sgt	Donald R. Peacock
BT	S/Sgt	Edward J. Zeitz
TG	S/Sgt	Brook H. Estes

Sgt. Ralph E. Windell walked over the route with Bernard Bains 39 years later (1983) as they reconstructed the ill-fated takeoff of A/C #43-38819, piloted by Lt. Carl P. Sundbaum.

The A/C were taking off for the mission to Koblenz. Seven or eight of the planes had taken off when fog closed in.

The procedure used by A/C for take-off in the fog was to line the A/C up with the compass heading, the copilot keeping watch for the edge of the runway with the pilot flying on instruments.

In this case Lt. Sundbaum apparently became disoriented and veered to the left of the runway. The runway had recently been repaired and piles of surfacing material remained beside the runway. The left wheel of the A/C struck a pile of the surfacing materials just as the A/C became airborne. The A/C at this point veered sharply to the left. Gun implacements were located around the perimeter of the field between which a telephone line was strung on poles about 14 feet high. The left horizontal stabilizer of the A/C struck one of these poles deflecting the A/C further to the left. As a result of these collisions, the A/C could not maintain flying speed and struck some railroad wagons parked on the nearby siding.

One man, S/Sgt Donald R. Peacock, was killed in the crash. The remainder of the crew survived the crash.

30 December 1944—Kaiserslautern. The 8th AAF launched 1,200 heavy bombers which bombed strategic targets, including 8 M/Ys, 6 bridges, a rail junction and 13 T/Os in West Germany.

The 457th B.G. put up 36 A/C, all of which bombed the secondary target by PFF.

One A/C, Georgia Peach/Remember Me, was lost to weather conditions: A/C #43-37828 piloted by Lt. William R. McCall.

The crew of A/C #43-37828 is listed below.

P	2nd Lt	William R. McCall
CP	2nd Lt	Tommy L. Gregory
N-B	2nd Lt	Arthur M. Livingston
CHIN	S/Sgt	George A. Cooke
AE	T/Sgt	George F. Perry
RO	T/Sgt	Robert J. Haynes
LW	S/Sgt	Linville Wells
BT	S/Sgt	Walter L. Slate
TC	S/Sgt	Larido A. Battisti

13 January 1945—Maximiliansau. The 8th AAF launched over 900 heavy bombers which bombed 7 Rhine bridges, 3 M/Ys, a rail junction and T/Os in battle zone.

The 457th bombed a RR bridge at Maximiliansau with 36 A/C. A direct hit was scored on the bridge from 21,000 feet. One A/C was lost. One witness thought bombs from another A/C had hit the A/C. The cause of the explosion is unknown. No parachutes were observed.

A/C #43-30795, piloted by Lt. Irwin C. Popham, exploded in mid-air at the target where moderate but accurate flak was encountered. The explosion was described by a witness to be one big fire ball.

457th (Bains)

A/C #43-38819, piloted by Lt. Carl Sundbaum, crashed in the fog, while taking off.

457th (Bains)

A/C #43-38819 crashed while taking off in the fog. The aircraft was piloted by Lt. Carl Sundbaum.

The crew of A/C #43-30795 is as follows:

P	2nd Lt	Irwin C. Popham
CP	F/O	Robert H. Dickinson
N-B	2nd Lt	Gus B. Skalski
CHIN	S/Sgt	John F. Kelsey
AE	T/Sgt	Donald D. Shumate
RO	T/Sgt	Keith W. Hill
LW	S/Sgt	Robert W. Hamer
BT	S/Sgt	William A. Marion
TG	S/Sgt	Bruno W. Clifford

22 January 1945—Sterkrade. The 8th AAF launched 200 B-17s to bomb the Sterkrade-Holten synthetic oil plant, a M/Y and T/Os.

The 457th B.G. put up 24 A/C, 18 of which attacked the target. The bombing results were undetermined because of cloud cover.

One A/C, #43-38583 piloted by Lt. Arthur G. Jellinek, was damaged by flak. The pilot of A/C #749 said a piece of the vertical stabilizer of #43-38583 struck his windshield. The A/C dropped

457th (Bains)

Lt. William R. McCall's "Georgia Peach" lost 30 December 1944 A/C #43-37828

out of the formation and when last seen was flying with its wheels down. No parachutes were observed.

The crew of A/C #43-38583 is as follows:

P	1st Lt	Arthur G. Jellinek
CP	2nd Lt	James E. Christy
N-B	2nd Lt	Jack A. Dressler
CHIN	S/Sgt	Joseph W. Farrow
AE	T/Sgt	J. Frank Conti
RO	S/Sgt	Harry J. Jolly, Jr.
BT	S/Sgt	Harley Ernst, Jr.
TG	S/Sgt	Kenneth M. Beattie

28 January 1945—Cologne. The 8th AAF launched 900 heavy bombers which bombed targets including 3 M/Ys, 3 bridges, 4 city areas, and T/Os in West Germany.

The 457th B.G. put up 36 A/C, 35 of which bombed the M/Y in Cologne. One A/C failed to attack the target due to mechanical reasons.

A/C #42-97164 dropped out of the formation about six minutes after bombs away. The aircraft had shown no signs of distress before dropping away. Number two engine however was feathered at the time.

When last seen the A/C was under control. No parachutes were seen.

The crew of A/C #42-97164 is as follows:

P	1st Lt	William P. Boyes, Jr.
CP	1st Lt	Elmer W. Felgenhauer
N	2nd Lt	Kenneth J. Furst
B	2nd Lt	Merritt D. Turner
AE	T/Sgt	Francis J. Horan
RO	T/Sgt	Abraham Feldman
LW	S/Sgt	Frank Thapan
BT	S/Sgt	Roy D. Duftman
TG	S/Sgt	Robert A. Dilley

16 February 1945—Gelsenkirchen. The 8th AAF attacked a synthetic oil plant at Magdeburg, M/Ys at Dresden, Cottbus and Rheine, with 1,000 heavy bombers.

The 457th B.G. put up 12 A/C to bomb industrial works at Gelsenkirchen. The results of the bombing were reported as poor.

A/C #44-6831, piloted by 2nd Lt. Roland H. Brazier, was hit by a flak burst in the vicinity of #3 engine. The right wing broke off, folded up and dropped downward. The A/C rolled over on its back and continued to roll, completing at least two slow rolls. The A/C then went down in a flat spin. When last seen the A/C was burning but had not exploded. No parachutes were seen.

The crew of A/C #44-6831 is as follows:

P	2nd Lt	Roland H. Brazier
CP	2nd Lt	Alvin G. Hazlett
N	2nd Lt	William J. Fiehl
B	2nd Lt	William F. Freeman
AE	T/Sgt	Walter H. Klimoff
RO	T/Sgt	Stanley L. Murray
LW	S/Sgt	Daniel S. Hockberg
BT	S/Sgt	William J. Conner
TG	S/Sgt	Stanley D. Swanson
RW	Sgt	Richard C. Trapp

28 February 1944—Soest. On this mission A/C #44-8255, piloted by Lt. Roy E. Kirk, ditched in the English Channel. #3 engine was on fire and the wing fell off.

Six members of the crew were rescued. Those not rescued included:

2nd Lt.	Roy E. Kirk
T/Sgt	Edward A. Grover
S/Sgt	Williard Krueger

These men are listed on the Madingly Cemetery "Wall of the Missing."

18 March 1945—Berlin. The 8th AAF attacked 2 rail centers, 2 armament plants, several T/Os and M/Ys in Berlin.

The 457th B.G. launched 36 A/C, 35 of which bombed the target, T/O in Berlin. One aircraft was lost to attacks on the formation by jet fighters.

A/C #43-38203, piloted by Lt. John W. Schwikert, was flying in number three slot in the high flight of the low squadron. The squadron was attacked by three Me 262s. The enemy jets attacked the formation from the tail, each attacking one of the B-17s. The B-17s were flying through moderate to heavy accurate flak during the fighter attack.

457th (Bains)

Lt. Braziers A/C #44-6831 was shot down at Gelsenkirchen.

A/C #43-38203 continued to fly in its position for some time after the fighter attack and then engine #2 caught fire. The A/C dropped out of the formation, gradually lost altitude, and when last seen was apparently flying under control.

From six to nine parachutes were reported by observers.

The crew of A/C #43-38203 is as follows:

P	2nd Lt	John W. Schwikert
CP	2nd Lt	Quentin P. Thompson
N	2nd Lt	Reuben C. Everett
B	2nd Lt	Hugh Burton
AE	CPL	Emilie D. Piagini
RO	CPL	Hayford F. Brocks
BW	CPL	Douglas R. Barron
BT	CPL	Irving S. Brod
TG	CPL	James C. Faber

21 March 1945—Hopsten-Achmer. In preparation for the Rhine

River crossing by army units, the 8th AAF bombed 10 A/Fs, a tank factory at Plauen, and a M/Y at Reichenbach all with 1,254 heavy bombers.

The 457th Bomb Group put up 36 A/C, 31 of which bombed the A/F at Hopsten-Achmer, the primary target. The result of the bombing was considered good.

A/C #42-38113, piloted by 1st Lt. Craig P. Creason, was hit by flak a short time before the first dry run over the target. The A/C was hit near #4 engine by a burst of flak, after which fire was seen burning in the engine area. The A/C peeled out of the formation and when last observed was flying under control, with the fire apparently out.

No parachutes were observed.

The crew of A/C #42-38113 is as follows. The crew all evaded capture except T/Sgt Wagner who was taken prisoner.

P	1st Lt	Craig P. Creason
CP	2nd Lt	Ralph L. Gray
N	2nd Lt	Rudolph Haumann
B	2nd Lt	Thomas E. Madigan
AE	T/Sgt	William R. Wagner
RO	S/Sgt	Ralph S. Ingraham
LW	S/Sgt	Garland L. Frost
BT	S/Sgt	Blair Arsenault
TG	S/Sgt	Kenneth L. Hazeltine

24 March 1945—Hopsten. The 8th AAF again bombed A/Fs in northwest Germany in support of army units. One thousand and thirty-three heavy bombers attacked 14 A/Fs in the lower Rhine River area.

The 457th B.G. sent 37 A/C to bomb the A/F at Hopsten. Twenty-eight A/C attacked the target. The bomb results were fair to good. One A/C was lost.

A/C #43-38854, piloted by Lt. Sherrill R. Williams, was hit by flak. The flak at the target was moderate but accurate. One unexploded anti-aircraft shell struck the outer right wing of the A/C. About 9 feet of the wing broke off and fire flashed out at the break.

The A/C peeled out of the formation, turned over on its back and went down out of control. The A/C spun and the fuselage eventually broke apart in the vicinity of the radio room.

One parachute was observed.

The crew of A/C #43-38854 is as follows:

P	2nd Lt	Sherrill R. Williams
CP	2nd Lt	Earl R. Downey, Jr.
N-B	F/O	Benjamin J. Bushey
CHIN	Sgt	Harold R. Rahbe
AE	T/Sgt	Ralph W. Smith
RO	T/Sgt	Eugene P. Bussard
LW	S/Sgt	Burnell L. Scheivert
BT	Sgt	Bernard A. Flimoski
TG	Sgt	Anthony J. Romaro

10 April 1945 – Oranienburg. The 8th AAF bombed 8 A/Fs, 2 M/Ys, and an ordnance plant with 1,224 heavy bombers in north Germany.

The 457th Bomb Group launched 37 bombers, all of which attacked the M/Y in the vicinity of Oranienburg.

Three or four German jet fighters, Me 262s, attacked the group just after bombs away as the group was turning away from the target. The cannon fire from the jets hit the lead ship as well as others in the group.

A/C #44-8368, the lead A/C piloted by Capt. Melvin Fox, was damaged severely, a large hole being blown in the left wing between #1 and #2 engine. Fire and smoke was seen coming from the hole. The A/C pulled away from the formation.

The crew of A/C #44-8368 is as follows:

P	Capt	Melvin M. Fox
AC	Lt Col	Roderick L. Francis
B	Capt	Charles E. Musgrove
N	1st Lt	Beverly C. Robertson
N	2nd Lt	Gerald Zelikofsky
N	2nd Lt	Paul L. Bertinstein
AE	T/Sgt	Lloyd J. Blood
RO	T/Sgt	Adrian A. Belanger
BT	S/Sgt	Alvin P. Prukop
TG	Capt	Monroe J. Hotaling

A/C #43-38606, piloted by Lt. Thomas P. Thompson, was lost to enemy fighter 20mm cannon fire. No parachutes were observed.

P	2nd Lt	Thomas P. Thompson, Jr.
CP	F/O	Sam E. Felder
B-N	F/O	Charlie P. Keith
AE	S/Sgt	Thomas L. Smith
RO	S/Sgt	Keith V. Shinault
CHIN	S/Sgt	Alfred F. Waichwist, Jr.
LW	S/Sgt	William A. Beltoma
BT	S/Sgt	Walter J. Basara
TG	S/Sgt	John V. Lewis

18 April 1945—Freising. The 8th AAF attacked 7 M/Ys, a railroad bridge, and two transformer stations in eastern Germany.

The 457th B.G. launched 30 A/C and 29 bombed the T/T target at Traunstein with good results. One A/C was lost.

Meager inaccurate flak was encountered in the vicinity of the IP. One engine of A/C #44-8557 started smoking, possibly hit by the flak.

(Byers)

Messerschmitt — Me 163B - Komet. The "Komet" was the only rocket-powered A/C to see service in World War II. It was developed too late to make any impact on the defense of Germany. The A/C had a top speed of 596 mph and it could reach 40,000 feet in 3 minutes. However, its range was only 8 minutes which limited its effectiveness. Only about 350 of the A/C were constructed.

While on the bomb run the waist door of A/C #557 was jettisoned and four to six crewmen jumped from the A/C, after which the A/C turned 180 degrees and dropped its bombs. No further reports were made concerning what happened to the A/C.

Lt. Thistle's A/C was the last to be lost to enemy action by the 457th B.G. The crew of A/C #44-8557 is as follows:

P	2nd Lt	William T. Thistle
CP	2nd Lt	Joseph Taylor
B	2nd Lt	Craig S. Winters
N	2nd Lt	Roy M. Truda
AE	S/Sgt	John T. Miller
RO	S/Sgt	Louis E. Domato
LW	Sgt	Luther N. Smith
RW	Sgt	Harvey C. Henkel
BT	Sgt	John M. Taylor
TG	F/O	William W. McIntosh

457th

Lt. Thistle's A/C #44-8557 was shot down on 18 April 1945, only two days before the last mission flown by the 457th B.G., 20 April 1945, the target, Seddin.

Finis

Orders were received at Station 130 on 29 May 1945 for the 457th Bombardment Group to return to the United States. The orders were in the form of a letter from headquarters, European Theatre of Operations, United States Army, 370.5 Op.G.C. Subject: Movement Orders Shipment 10034.

Departure from the base by the flying echelon of the 457th B.G. began on 1 June 1945. They flew from England to Bradley Field, Connecticut, over the same North Atlantic route which many of the echelon had flown 18 months previously. The movement was supervised by the Air Transport Command. Seventy-two A/C were flown to the United States by crew members of the 457th B.G.

The ground echelon departed Station 130 on the 21st and 22nd of June with destination to be Holme, England, Port of Embarcation. The troops were loaded on H.M.S. Queen Elizabeth, joining the 15,000 other troops to be transported to the United States. The Queen Elizabeth arrived in New York City four and a half days after embarking from Greenock, Scotland.

The troops were transported from New York harbor to Camp Kilmer, New Jersey, for processing. There orders were issued for transfer of all personnel to Sioux Falls AAB, Sioux Falls, South Dakota. Advance units were sent to Sioux Falls AAB; however, most of the personnel were issued leave orders for a much-deserved 30-day vacation in the United States.

The troops reassembled at Sioux Falls AAB on or about the middle of July 1945 to learn that the 457th Bombardment Group (H) had been essentially disbanded. All personnel were reassigned on 5 August 1945 to Squadron X, 211 Army Air Force Base Unit, Sioux Falls AAB, Sioux Falls, South Dakota.

The command and staff personnel of the 457th B.G. were reassigned to other units as were eventually all flight and support personnel.

So ended the short but valorous life of one of the best Heavy Bomber Groups to fight in the skies over Europe. Those of us who were fortunate enough to live through the fierce aerial battles and return to civilian life unscathed, now in later life recall the days and search for a romantic attachment to the agency, the 457th Bombardment Group, which caused us so much grief so many years ago.

We recall with reverence those who gave their lives for their country. To them we have dedicated a monument that, while not auspicious, stands as a symbol of our thanks and appreciation for their patriotic dedication to a principle to which we all adhere — Freedom.

There will always be needed the professional soldier, men like Col. James Rhea Luper, Col. Harris E. Rogner, Lt. Col. William F. Smith, Jr., Lt. Col. Wilbur D. Snow, Lt. Col. Leroy Watson, Jr., men who are needed by this nation to mold into a fighting unit the relatively undisciplined civilian from the highways, the streets, the farms, the forests, the mines, the offices, the stores, the colleges, the factories, and from throughout this vast and wonderful nation. Men who desire peace but who must be willing to fight for preservation of their rights and freedom.

There will always be needed to win the peace the civilian soldier, men like, but limited to: Lt. Col. J. McGavock Dickinson, Major Edward B. Dozier, Capt. Clarence E. Schuchmann, Lt. Robert M. Krumm, Lt. Leo R. Green, Capt. Thomas A. Goff, Major Norman A. Kriehn, Lt. William J. P. Meng, Lt. Harry G. Vaal, Capt. Alfred W. Fischer, Lt. Clayton E. Bejot, Lt. Robert C. Dvorak, M/Sgt. Sumner Marshall, M/Sgt. Harold W. Wiseman, Lt. Col. Theodore C. Hoffman, Lt. Col. Roderick L. Francis, Lt. Col. Fred A. Spencer, Major Raymond Syptak, Sgt. Ralph E. Windell, Lt. Clyde B. Knipfer, Lt. Jerome Silverman, Capt. Donald L. Seesenguth, Lt. Robert G. Horn, Lt. Ralph D. Stutzman, Lt. Charles E. Newmeyer, and Lt. Charles R. Blackwell.

Epilogue

The SAC (Strategic Air Command) KC135 cleared the runway at Fairchild Air Force Base and climbed swiftly eastward to an altitude of 33,000 feet with destination Mildenhall RAF Base in East Anglia, United Kingdom.

The crew of the SAC KC135, pilot Capt. Jerry Moore of Spraggs, Pennsylvania, co-pilot Lt. Steve Schuch of South Plainfield, New Jersey, navigator Capt. Timothy Feeley of Phoenix, Arizona, and boom operator S/Sgt Perry Sauro of San Jose, California, had been very cordial to an old soldier who was returning , space available, to England for the first time after 40 years.

The flight to England was very interesting even though Capt. Feeley never did ask me for help in navigating the North Atlantic. I had even taken my old warped E-6-B computer with me just in case I was needed for consultation. He had so many gadgets with which to navigate he was kept busy the entire trip and had little time for conversation. He could punch a button and the latitude and longitute of our position would appear in lights! Sure beat the "seat of the pants" navigation we used 40 years ago.

When we arrived in England I contacted Bernard Bains of Peterborough, a historian of the 457th B.G., and he picked me up and drove to his home where I stayed for three days with him and his wife Sadie.

One of our first visits was to Station 130 Glatton AAF Base. I had wanted to see the base even though I knew there would be very few buildings or places I would identify after 40 years. To tell the truth, if Bernard Bains hadn't been there to tell me I was at Glatton I would not have identified anything except the Church—Connington Tower. The Quonset huts and hangers had long since been torn down and only the runways remained—one runway was currently used by a small flight service company. I did recognize some civilian houses that were located next to our living area, as well as the farm that was located in the middle of the air base. Forty years erases a lot of memories.

On this day, however, the nascent green fields of East Anglia were splashed with the warmth of the pale spring sun, an April sun which seemed uncharacteristic, as I seemed to recall only the miserable weather that had been the cause of so many "scrubbed" missions, and was the nemesis of many a B-17 bomber crew.

We walked over to the Connington Churchyard in which is located the new, yet-to-be dedicated, memorial to the men of the 457th who had given their lives for their country. I stood with cap in hand and looked out over the pastoral countryside which once had been a bustling air base over which the memorial surveyed and tried to visualize and recall the activity that had once occurred.

I imagined the staccato sound of a newly repaired protesting R-1820-97 Wright Cyclone engine being run up for the first time, a sound which soon gave way to the synchronous hum that comes from the caring and experienced hands of a veteran crew chief.

Later as the bomb laden bombers queued up for take-off the air was filled with the synchronous sound of the engines straining to provide the aircraft with speed sufficient to defy gravity and lift the silver wings from the earth and into the sky.

Then came the quietness, the long hours during which the maintenance crews and the ground personnel awaited the return of the valiant air crewmen—knowing that some would not, but hoping that all would, return to base. Then in the distance could be heard the roar of airplanes flying homeward, flying in loose formation—there had been 18 planes sent out this morning. The ground crew counted only 15 in the formation—what had happened to the others? Then, flying in low—with only three engines running and one propeller feathered—the radio operator shooting red flares—comes a badly damaged B-17. The plane was given preference in landing. The fire trucks and the ambulance raced down the runway in pursuit of the damaged airplane. There were wounded aboard.

On that day two aircraft did not return to base—victims of the Luftwaffe fighters over Germany. The interrogators at debriefing asked the questions as to who had seen the airplanes go down.

Recalling such instances was vivid—while geographical features now eluded my memory.

There were two other places I wanted to visit, one of which was the crash site of A/C 152—Miss Ida—April 5, 1945.

The crash had occurred soon after I had completed my second

tour and had returned to the United States. I had wanted to see for my own eyes where the crash had occurred. Ed Dozier had been a good friend. He and I had bunked together for almost half a year—a long time when you're fighting a war. Bill Meng, who had survived the crash, had been my replacement as Squadron Navigator of the 748th Squadron.

The crash site showed no evidence that many years ago, 40 almost to a day, nine men had given their lives for freedom at this place. The lush green hay field had erased all the physical evidence but not the heartaches and misery for many people.

Our next stop was to Maddingly Cemetery near Cambridge. Located on 30.5 acres of land donated by Cambridge University, it is where so many American servicemen are interred, including Edward Dozier, my friend, and many other men.

The SAC KC135 roared down the runway at Mildenhall Air Base, this time heading west. Another crew, Capt. Randy Panisello of West Nyack, New York, Lt. Harry Bolton of Meadow Vista, California, Lt. Kent Johnson of Floresville, Texas, and S/Sgt. Clyde Loumas of Bossier City, Louisiana, were taking me back, space available, to the United States.

After only a week, the long thought-about and yearned for trip back to the green spot in the fens of East Anglia was over. I would probably never return there again. Memories sometimes are best left undisturbed.

457th (Zemper)

"Queen Bea" on fire.

Appendix I

LIST OF MISSIONS - 457TH BOMBARDMENT GROUP

The Mission Board lists all missions flown by crews of the 457th Bombardment Group.

No.	Name	Date	A/C Flown	A/C Losses	Bombing Results*
1	Guttersloh/Lippstadt	2-21-44	36	1	T/O
2	Oscherleben	2-22-44	3	0	P
3	Schweinfurt	2-24-44	18	1	F
4	Augsburg	2-25-44	27	2	E
5	Frankfurt	3-2-44	18	0	U
6	Berlin	3-3-44	21	0	None
7	Berlin	3-4-44	24	0	None
8	Berlin	3-6-44	18	2	P
9	Berlin	3-8-44	19	0	F
10	Berlin	3-9-44	18	0	U
11	Munster	3-11-44	19	0	U
12	No Ball	3-13-44	21	0	U
13	Augsburg	3-16-44	18	0	U
14	Landsberg	3-18-44	18	1	P
15	No Ball	3-19-44	24	0	F
16	Frankfurt	3-20-44	17	0	None
17	Berlin	3-22-44	19	0	U
18	Lippstadt	3-23-44	27	0	F
19	Schweinfurt	3-24-44	17	0	U
20	No Ball	3-26-44	18	0	P
21	Tours	3-27-44	24	0	P
22	Brunswick	3-29-44	18	1	U
23	Gdynia	4-9-44	24	3	E

*GE = gross error; P = poor; F = fair; E = excellence; U = unobserved; T/O = target of opportunity.

No.	Name	Date	A/C Flown	A/C Losses	Bombing Results
24	Brussels	4-10-44	18	0	E
25	Sorau	4-11-44	23	0	U
26	Schweinfurt	4-13-44	18	0	P
27	Oranienburg	4-18-44	18	0	T/O
28	Eschwege	4-19-44	17	0	GE
29	No Ball	4-20-44	24	1	A-GE
30	Hamm	4-22-44	18	0	T/O
31	Erding	4-24-44	18	0	P
32	Nancy-Essey	4-25-44	19	1	None
33	Brunswick	4-26-44	18	1	U
34	No Ball	4-27-44	18	0	GE
35	Nancy-Essey	4-27-44	18	0	Lost in smoke
36	Berlin	4-29-44	17	0	U
37	Lyon	4-30-44	18	0	E
38	No Ball	5-1-44	18	0	T/O-F
39	Bergen Airfield	5-4-44	20	0	T/O
40	Berlin	5-7-44	18	0	U
41	Berlin	5-8-44	28	0	U
42	Luxembourg	5-9-44	18	0	GE
43	Luxembourg	5-11-44	18	0	P
44	Lutzkendorf	5-12-44	36	1	F-GE
45	Stettin	5-13-44	18	0	U
46	Berlin	5-19-44	35	1	U
47	Villa Coublay	5-20-44	12	0	G
48	Kiel	5-22-44	10	0	U
49	Epinal	5-23-44	24	0	U
50	Berlin	5-24-44	16	0	U
51	Metz	5-25-44	23	0	G-G
52	Ludwigshafen	5-27-44	36	3	T/O
53	Dessau	5-28-44	16	3	F
54	Sorau	5-29-44	18	0	E
55	Oschersleben	5-30-44	18	0	P
56	Luxeuil	5-31-44	12	0	E
57	Hardelot	6-2-44	17	0	U
58	Dannes – Nesles	6-3-44	37	0	U
59	Paris	6-4-44	34	0	G
60	Le Havre Area	6-6-44	39	0	U
61	Falaise	6-7-44	17	0	U
62	Etampes	6-8-44	37	0	None
63	Gael	6-10-44	17	0	U

No.	Name	Date	A/C Flown	A/C Losses	Bombing Results
64	Bernay St. Martin	6-11-44	18	0	U
65	Vitry-en-Artois	6-12-44	36	0	E
66	Lemun Airdrome	6-14-44	50	5	F
67	Angouleme	6-15-44	35	0	E
68	Monchy-Breton	6-17-44	18	0	U
69	Hamburg	6-18-44	35	0	U
70	Landes de Bussac	6-19-44	35	0	VG-P
71	Hamburg	6-20-44	34	1	E
72	Watten	6-20-44	12	0	T/O
73	Berlin	6-21-44	37	2	T/O
74	Rouen	6-22-44	23	0	E-G
75	No Ball	6-23-44	17	0	U
76	Holque	6-24-44	13	0	E
77	Montbartier	6-25-44	35	0	E
78	Laon-Cauvron	6-28-44	23	0	VG-GE
79	Leipzig	6-29-44	22	0	U-T/O
80	Saumur	7-4-44	24	0	None
81	Bertreville-St. Ouen	7-6-44	33	0	T/O
82	Reenesgure	7-6-44	11	0	E
83	Leipzig	7-7-44	34	0	G
84	No Ball	7-8-44	24	0	None-T/O
85	No Ball	7-9-44	22	0	None
86	Munich	7-11-44	34	0	U
87	Allach-Munich	7-12-44	33	2	U
88	Munich	7-13-44	19	0	U
89	Munich	7-18-44	34	0	U
90	Peenemunde	7-18-44	36	0	U
91	Augsburg	7-19-44	34	0	P
92	Leipzig	7-20-44	23	0	GE
93	Schweinfurt	7-21-44	24	1	G
94	St. Lo Area	7-24-44	45	0	Frags
95	St. Lo Area	7-25-44	49	0	Frags
96	Merseburg	7-28-44	32	0	U
97	Merseburg	7-29-44	34	0	U
98	Allach-Munich	7-31-44	34	1	U
99	Chateudun	8-1-44	36	0	E-G-E
100	Strasbourg	8-3-44	36	0	E
101	Anklam	8-4-44	12	0	E
102	Coubronne Fiefs	8-4-44	25	0	T/O-None
103	Nienburg	8-5-44	35	0	G

No.	Name	Date	A/C Flown	A/C Losses	Bombing Results
104	Genshagen	8-6-44	34	1	E-F-E
105	Nanteiul Bridge	8-7-44	36	0	E
106	Elsenborn	8-9-44	23	0	T/O
107	Brest	8-11-44	33	0	E
108	Brionne Area	8-13-44	36	0	E-G-G
109	Stuttgart	8-14-44	35	0	P-U
110	Schkeuditz	8-16-44	34	0	E-E-Frags
111	Huy	8-18-44	36	0	E-F-E
112	Weimar	8-24-44	34	2	F-P-F
113	Peenemunde	8-25-44	34	1	E-F-E
114	Henin Lie Tard	8-25-44	12	0	E-G
115	Berlin	8-27-44	34	0	None
116	Kiel	8-30-44	35	0	U
117	Ludwigshafen	9-3-44	36	0	U
118	Ludwigshafen	9-8-44	36	0	U
119	Mannheim	9-9-44	36	0	U
120	Gaggenau-Karlsrhu	9-10-44	34	3	G-F-P
121	Lauta	9-12-44	36	2	G-G-P
122	Lutzkendorf-Giessen	9-13-44	36	0	P-G-P
123	Nijmegen	9-17-44	48	1	Frags
124	Soest	9-19-44	36	0	E-U-U
125	Frankfurt	9-25-44	36	0	U
126	Osnabruck	9-26-44	35	1	G-T/O
127	Cologne	9-27-44	36	0	U
128	Magdesburg	9-28-44	35	6	U
129	Munster	9-30-44	36	1	U
130	Kassel	10-2-44	35	0	F
131	Cologne	10-5-44	36	0	U
132	Stargard	10-6-44	36	0	VG-P
133	Politz	10-7-44	48	5	G-P-U
134	Cologne	10-14-44	36	0	U
135	Cologne	10-15-44	36	0	U
136	Cologne	10-17-44	36	1	U
137	Mannheim	10-19-44	36	0	U
138	Hannover	10-22-44	36	0	U
139	Hamburg	10-25-44	36	1	U
140	Bielefeld	10-26-44	36	0	U
141	Munster	10-28-44	36	0	U
142	Munster	10-30-44	34	0	U
143	Bernburg	11-2-44	36	9	U

No.	Name	Date	A/C Flown	A/C Losses	Bombing Results
144	Frankfurt	11-5-44	35	0	P
145	Harburg	11-6-44	36	1	U
146	Merseburg	11-8-44	14	1	U
147	Metz	11-9-44	35	0	U
148	Eschweiler	11-16-44	36	0	Frags
149	Friedberg	11-21-44	36	0	T/O
150	Gelsenkirchen	11-23-44	36	0	U
151	Merseburg	11-25-44	36	0	U
152	Misburg	11-26-44	36	0	U
153	Misburg	11-29-44	48	0	U
154	Bohlen	11-30-44	36	2	P
155	Kassel	12-4-44	36	0	U
156	Merseburg	12-8-44	36	0	U
157	Boblingen	12-9-44	36	0	F
158	Frankfurt	12-11-44	36	0	U
159	Merseburg	12-12-44	36	1	U
160	Kassel	12-15-44	36	0	U
161	Gemund	12-19-44	30	0	U
162	Coblenz	12-24-44	44	0	U
163	Gerolestein	12-27-44	36	0	GE
164	Bingen	12-20-44	36	0	VG-VG-E
165	Kaiserlautern	12-30-44	36	0	U
166	Krefeld	12-31-44	36	0	U
167	Kassel	1-1-45	34	0	T/O-G
168	Mayen	1-2-45	37	0	E-E-G
169	Cologne, H.K.	1-3-45	36	0	U
170	Kempenick	1-6-45	36	0	U
171	Bitburg	1-7-45	36	0	U
172	Euskirchen	1-10-45	34	0	U
173	Maximiliansau	1-13-45	36	1	E-E-E
174	Cologne	1-14-45	12	0	UTA
175	Paderborn	1-17-45	36	0	U
176	Rheine	1-20-45	34	0	U
177	Aschaffenburg	1-21-45	36	0	U
178	Sterkrade	1-22-45	24	1	UTA
179	Cologne	1-28-45	35	1	U
180	Siegen	1-29-45	36	0	U
181	Ludwigshafen	2-1-45	35	0	U
182	Berlin	2-3-45	36	0	G-P-P
183	Schmalkalden	2-8-45	38	0	T/O

No.	Name	Date	A/C Flown	A/C Losses	Bombing Results
184	Lutzkendorf	2-9-45	36	0	E-P-U
185	Dulmen	2-10-45	35	0	U
186	Dresden	2-14-45	36	0	U
187	Dresden	2-15-45	24	0	U
188	Gelsenkirchen	2-18-45	24	0	U
189	Gelsenkirchen	2-19-45	36	0	U
190	Nuremburg	2-20-45	36	0	U
191	Nuremburg	2-21-45	36	0	U
192	Salzwedel	2-22-45	36	0	GE-E-T/O
193	Ellingen	2-23-45	37	0	T/O
194	Harburg	2-24-45	35	0	U
195	Munich	2-25-45	36	0	GE-E-P
196	Berlin	2-26-45	35	0	U
197	Leipzig	2-27-45	36	0	U
198	Soest	2-28-45	34	0	U
199	Goppingen	3-1-45	34	0	U
200	Chemnitz	3-2-45	36	0	U
201	Chemnitz	3-3-45	36	0	U
202	Chemnitz	3-5-45	35	0	U
203	Siegen	3-7-45	34	0	U
204	Bottrop	3-8-45	36	0	U
205	Kassel	3-9-45	35	0	F-U-UTA
206	Hamm	3-10-45	33	0	U
207	Bremen	3-11-45	36	0	U
208	Swinemunde	3-12-45	37	0	U
209	Lohne	3-14-45	37	0	E-E
210	Zossen	3-15-45	37	0	U
211	Altenberg	3-17-45	37	0	U
212	Berlin	3-18-45	36	2	U
213	Fulda	3-19-45	37	0	E-P-U
214	Hopstein-Achmer	3-21-45	36	1	G
215	Barmingholten	3-22-45	37	0	G-G-GE
216	Recklinghausen	3-23-45	36	0	G
217	Hopsten	3-24-45	37	1	GE
218	Twente-Enschere	3-24-45	12	0	GE
219	Plauen	3-26-45	35	0	Failure
220	Berlin	3-28-45	32	0	U
221	Bremen	3-30-45	36	0	G
222	Halle	3-31-45	36	0	U
223	Rottenburg	4-4-45	37	0	U

No.	Name	Date	A/C Flown	A/C Losses	Bombing Results
224	Ingolstadt	4-5-45	35	0	F
225	Luneburg	4-7-45	37	0	P-P-E
226	Halberstadt	4-8-45	37	0	F
227	Furstenfeldbruck	4-9-45	33	0	VG
228	Oranienburg	4-10-45	36	2	G
229	Freiham	4-11-45	37	0	VG
230	Royan	4-14-45	37	0	GE
231	Pointe de Grave	4-15-45	37	0	E
232	Regensberg	4-16-45	36	0	E
233	Dresden	4-17-45	31	0	G
234	Freising	4-18-45	30	1	E
235	Falkenberg	4-19-45	29	0	E
236	Seddin	4-20-45	29	0	E

Administration

Group Commanders

Col. Herbert E. Rice	24 July 1943
Lt. Col. Hugh D. Wallace	3 Sept 1943
Col. James Rhea Luper	4 Jan. 1944
Col. Harris E. Rogner	11 Aug. 1944 (Aug. '45)

Deputy Group Commanders

Lt. Col. Hugh D. Wallace	24 July 1943
Major Jack A. Mandrell	3 Sept. 1943
Lt. Col. Henry B. Wilson	4 Jan. 1944
Lt. Col. Roderick L. Francis	5 July 1944
Lt. Col. William F. Smith, Jr.	10 Apr. 1945

748th Squadron Commanders

Capt. Edward P. Clark	24 July 1943
Capt. Leroy H. Watson, Jr.	24 Dec. 1943
Major George C. Hozier	7 Mar. 1944
Major J. McGavock Dickinson	17 Sept. 1944
Lt. Col. Wilbur D. Snow	27 Oct. 1944
Major Edward Dozier	19 Mar. 1945
Major James A. McGuire	5 Apr. 1945

749th Squadrom Commanders

Lt. Col. Theodore G. Hoffman	24 July 1943
Lt. Col. Wilbur D. Snow	1 Sept. 1944
Major Raymond Syptak	27 Oct. 1944
Lt. Col. Leon Stann	10 Apr. 1945

750th Squadron Commanders

Lt. Col. Roderick L. Francis	24 July 1943
Lt. Col. William F. Smith, Jr.	25 Apr. 1944
Capt. William K. Doherty	2 Dec. 1944
Major James M. Havey	7 Feb. 1945

751st Squadron Commanders

Lt. Col. Fred A. Spencer	24 July 1943
Major Raymond Syptak	14 Aug. 1944
Lt. Col. Fred A. Spencer	2 Oct. 1944
Lt. Col. Eugene Peresich, Jr.	2 Jan. 1945

The 457th Bombardment Group was credited with participation in the following campaigns:

Campaign

Air Offensive Europe
Normany
Northern France
Rhineland
Ardennes-Alsace
Central Europe

Campaigns in a treatre of operations are displayed by a star worn on the campaign ribbon for that Theatre.

457th

A/C #42-32051 "LADY LUCK" was not so lucky when someone accidentally released the wheels up switch. 1 November 1944.

457th

Lead crew of mission to NUREMBURG 21 Feb. 1945. Lt. Col. Fred A. Spencer C.O. 751 Squadron C.O. flew as Air Commander. Capt. Donald Seesenguth was lead pilot, Author completed a second tour after one more mission.

Left to right: Cpl. Allen Ladd and wife, Aerial Gunner in 457th Bomb. Group 750th Squadron; Capt. and Mrs. Musgrove on right.

457th

"Little Friend" P47 "Thunderbolt" U.S. Fighter nicknamed "JUG."

457th

A/C #43-38534 — Lt. Cornelius Woolf's "Wolf Pack" (High Rear). A/C #43-39200 — "Rattlesnake Daddy" (High). A/C #44-8157 A "Mickey" (H_2X) equipped lead ship (Forward).

457th

June 22, 1944, A/C 620 and 056 collided.

457th

A/C #42-97162 crash landing, Erding Mission, 24 April 1944.

457th

A/C #42-106985 crash landing, Hamm Mission, 22 April 1944.

457th

WHEELS UP LANDING A/C 118, 28 August 1944.

457th

A/C #43-38540 "MYSTERIOUS WITCH."

457th

Flying formation "Tucked in Tight."

457th

A/C #43-37694 "Patty Ann" piloted by Lt. Gordon E. Gallagher landed without hydraulic pressure. The A/C hit a weapons carrier, veered off and ran into the ordinance hut. 18 Aug. 1944.

457th

Lt. Americo Procopio home safe in A/C #42-31615 albeit "A little worse for wear." Epinal Mission, 23 May 1944.

Appendix II

Key officer personnel assigned to the 457th Bomb. Group (H) Headquarters Unit on or about 1 October 1943 included:

Group Commander	Lt. Colonel Hugh D. Wallace
Deputy Group Commander	Major Jack A. Mandell
Group Executive Officer	Major Raymond M. Schuler
Group Adjutant	Major Frank B. Conselman
Group Flight Surgeon	Major Gordon H. Haggard
Group Intelligence Officer	Captain Charles P. Nelson
Group Operations Officer	Captain John S. Chalfant
Group Communications Officer	Captain Richard N. Herbert
Commanding Officers:	
748th Bomb Squadron	Captain Edward P. Clark
749th Bomb Squadron	Captain Theodore C. Hoffman
750th Bomb Squadron	Captain Roderick L. Francis
751st Bomb Squadron	Captain Fred A. Spencer
Group Chaplain	(Unknown)
Group Navigation Officer	Captain Robert D. Newcomb
Group Armament Officer	Captain Paul H. Sayer
Group Material Officer	1st Lieut. Richard C. Taylor
Group Bombardier Officer	1st. Lieut. James C. Mattison
Group Dental Officer	1st Lieut. Carlos A. Salinas
Group Photo Interpreter	1st Lieut. Larry D. McDonald
Group Aerial Photographer	2nd. Lieut. Wilbur W. Allen, Jr.
Group Statistical Officer	2nd. Lieut. Gerald H. Galligan
Group Special Services Officer	2nd. Lieut. Carl E. Walker
Group Weather Officer	2nd. Lieut. Charles D. Weber

748th SQUADRON

Captain Edward P. Clark was designated commanding officer of the 748th Squadron. Other key personnel assigned to the 748th Squadron included:

Executive Officer	Major Frederick W. Hutchinson
Adjutant	Captain William H. Rethke
Squadron Flight Surgeon	Captain Shelby G. Bale
Intelligence Officer	1st. Lieut. Kenneth R. Luck
Operations Officer	1st. Lieut. Wilbur D. Snow
Armament Officer	2nd. Lieut. Samuel S. Evans, Jr.
Communications Officer	2nd. Lieut. George E. Harf
Engineering Officer	2nd. Lieut. William P. Roach
Navigation Officer	2nd. Lieut. Earl E. Woodard

ORIGINAL CREW

One original crew was received at Camp Rapid, Rapid City, South Dakota, on 27 July 1943, under provisions of Special Order number 206, paragraph number 1, dated 25 July 1943, Army Air Base, Ephrata, Washington.

The status of crews in the 748th Bombardment Squadron as of 1 October 1943:

Original Crews

Pilot	1st. Lieut. Jacob M. Dickinson
Co-pilot	2nd. Lieut. Charles R. Blackwell
Bombardier	1st. Lieut. Carl M. Nainon
Navigator	2nd. Lieut. Earl E. Woodard
Aerial Engineer Gunner	S/Sgt. James L. Free
Armorer Gunner	S/Sgt. Thomas G. Leahy
Radio Operator Gunner	S/Sgt. Laymon N. Mahan
Aerial Engineer Gunner	S/Sgt. John P. Sarico
Armorer Gunner	S/Sgt. Charles O. Webber
Aerial Engineer Gunner	S/Sgt. Michael (NMI) Woyurka

749th SQUADRON

Captain Theodore C. Hoffman was designated commanding officer of the 749th Squadron. Other key personnel assigned to the 749th Squadron included:

Executive Officer	Captain John B. Roberts
Squadron Flight Surgeon	Captain Richard D. Crow
Intelligence Officer	1st. Lieut. Frank (NMI) Taylor

Operations Officer	1st. Lieut. William F. Smith, Jr.
Adjutant	2nd. Lieut. Herschel V. Kennedy,Jr.
Armament Officer	2nd. Lieut. Saul (NMI) Tobias
Communications Officer	2nd. Lieut. Joseph H. Beach
Engineering Officer	2nd. Lieut. Guy E. Sturdevant, Jr.
Navigation Officer	2nd. Lieut. Clarence R. McRae

ORIGINAL CREW

One original crew was received at Camp Rapid, Rapid City, South Dakota, on 27 July 1943, under provisions of Special Order number 180, paragraph number 2, dated 24 July 1943, Army Air Base, Moses Lake, Washington.

The status of crews in the 749th Bombardment Squadron as of 1 October 1943:

Original Crews

Pilot	2nd. Lieut. Hugh R. Ashby
Co-pilot	2nd. Lieut. Marvin J. Bible
Navigator	2nd. Lieut. Clarence R. McRae
Bombardier	2nd. Lieut. John W. Newman
Aerial Engineer Gunner	T/Sgt. Joseph (NMI) Barboza
Aerial Engineer Gunner	S/Sgt. Bryon F. Cook, Jr.
Radio Operator Gunner	T/Sgt. Neil D. Buck
Radio Operator Gunner	S/Sgt. Ernest E. Hunt
Armorer Gunner	S/Sgt. Gordon D. Hobson
Armorer Gunner	S/Sgt. Robert A. Timmons

750TH SQUADRON

Captain Roderick L. Francis was designated commanding officer of the 750th Squadron. Other key personnel assigned to the 750th Squadron included:

Executive Officer	Major Robert R. Love
Squadron Flight Surgeon	Captain Arthur J. Fischer
Operations Officer	1st. Lieut. Thomas J. Hanley, III
Adjutant	2nd. Lieut. Clifford J. Craven
Intelligence Officer	2nd. Lieut. John E. Dineen
Armament Officer	2nd. Lieut. Harold E. Nelson

Communications Officer	2nd. Lieut. Robert A. Drives
Engineering Officer	2nd. Lieut. Roy E. Kerr
Supply Officer	2nd. Lieut. Donald C. Forrey

ORIGINAL CREW

One original crew was received at Camp Rapid, Rapid City, South Dakota, on 7 September 1943, under provisions of Special Order number 246, paragraph number 4, dated 3 September 1943, Army Air Base, Walla Walla, Washington.

The status of crews in the 750th Bombardment Squadron as of 1 October 1943:

Original Crews

Pilot	1st. Lieut. Thomas J. Hanley III
Co-pilot	2nd. Lieut. William F. Rogers
Navigator	2nd. Lieut. Wilbert J. Collard
Bombardier	2nd. Lieut. Dino H. Tonelli
Aerial Engineer Gunner	T/Sgt. Joshua D. Lane, Jr.
Radio Operator Gunner	T/Sgt. John (NMI) Chumas
Radio Operator Gunner	S/Sgt. William C. Young
Armorer Gunner	S/Sgt. David H. Quick
Armorer Gunner	S/Sgt. Ray (NMI) Jones
Aerial Engineer Gunner	Sgt. Orion H. Shumway

751st SQUADRON

Captain Fred A. Spencer was designated commanding officer of the 751st Squadron. Other key personnel assigned to the 751st Squadron included:

Executive Officer	Major Charles D. Vinson
Adjutant	Captain Tom O. Moore
Squadron Flight Surgeon	1st Lieut. Walter W. Crawford
Intelligence Officer	1st. Lieut. Edwin R. Roberts
Operations Officer	1st. Lieut. George C. Hozier
Armament Officer	2nd. Lieut. Andrew J. Arvish
Communications Officer	2nd. Lieut. Archille F. Rischiotto
Engineering Officer	2nd. Lieut. Whitby K. Maddern
Navigation Officer	2nd. Lieut. Arthur W. Hoffman

ORIGINAL CREW

One original crew was received at Camp Rapid, Rapid City, South Dakota, on 26 July 1943, under provisions of Special Order number 205, paragraph number 4, dated 24 July 1943, Army Air Base, Walla Walla, Washington.

The status of crews in the 751st Bombardment Squadron as of 1 October 1943:

Original Crews

Pilot	2nd. Lieut. Vinton H. Mays
Co-pilot	2nd. Lieut. Douglas L. Crawford
Bombardier	2nd. Lieut. Lloyd T. Belanger
Navigator	2nd. Lieut. John D. English
Aerial Engineer Gunner	T/Sgt. Stanley H. Krohn
Radio Operator Gunner	T/Sgt. Jack E. Berry
Radio Operator Gunner	S/Sgt. Cecil D. Burroughs
Armorer Gunner	S/Sgt. Albert F. Rothbauer
Armorer Gunner	S/Sgt. Jack D. Bush
Armorer Gunner	S/Sgt. James V. Ambrose

The following crews transferred from Moses Lake AAB and joined the 457th B.G. on 28 October 1943.

Crew 16 S-10

2LT	Adrian W. Seabock	P
2LT	Lloyd E. Igenogle	CP
2LT	William H. Dupont	N
2LT	William G. Smith	B
Sgt	Louis M. Gastelucci	AEG
S Sgt	Francis E. Cornue	AAG
Sgt	Frank T. Ingersoll	AAEG
Sgt	Prosser Jeffreys	AG
Sgt	Leslie B. Reid, Jr.	AROG
Sgt	William B. Woodell	ROG

Crew 16-S134

2LT	Leonard P. Soenke	P
2LT	Howard B. Collins	CP
2LT	Curtis J. Overdahl	N
2LT	Albert L. Thompson	B
Sgt	Aaron L. Barriss	AAG
Sgt	James R. Cavett	AROG
Sgt	Walter A. Ginter	ROG
Sgt	Arthur J. Kimball	AAEG
Sgt	Joseph J. Lukkasik	AEG
Sgt	Harold M. Moberg	AG

Crew 16 S-1

2LT	Charles D. Brannan	P
2LT	Harry P. Polensky	CP
2LT	James H. Kincaid	N
2LT	George A. Sipp	B
Cpl	Joseph M. Colechia	ROG
Sgt	Prentis A. Pooler	AROG
Sgt	Edward M. Hardin	AAEG
Sgt	Milton Lowenstein	AAG
S Sgt	John T. Matovina	AEG
Sgt	Charles R. Vandeventer	AG

Crew 16 S-8

2LT	Cornelius R. Woolf	P
2LT	Kinney Hellums	CP
2LT	Charles W. Mitchell	N
2LT	Kenneth B. Taylor	B
Sgt	John L. Batts	AAEG
Sgt	Ernest R. Campen	AAG
Sgt	Samuel I. Craft, Jr.	AG
S Sgt	Gerard J. Hyink	AEG
Cpl	Alden B. Orr	AG
Sgt	Roman A. Zelazo	ROG

Crew 16 S-6

2LT	Edward J. Reppa	P
2LT	Aaron J. Ayres	CP
2LT	Robert E. Jackson	N
2LT	George H. Stateman	B
Sgt	Francis A. Boyson	AROG
Sgt	Stephen F. Billisits	AEG
S Sgt	Irving Feldman	AAEG
Sgt	John Harmke	AG
Sgt	Charles W. Mehring	AAG
Pfc	Ivan W. Browning	ROG

Crew 16 S-135

2LT	Mervin J. Christensen	P
2LT	Fred H. Kleppe	CP
2LT	Paul J. King	N
2LT	Karl K. Weiman	B
Sgt	Anthony D. Coluccio	AROG
Sgt	Robert W. Flagg	AEG
Sgt	Juan C. Lopez	AAG
Sgt	Irvin L. Maleh	AAEG
Sgt	Paul L. Nalbach	AG
Sgt	Marion D. Spivey	ROG

Crew 15 S-10

2LT	Robert L. Wetherald	P
F/O	Francis G. Bogle	CP
2LT	Thomas W. Burns	N
2LT	Alex W. Fisher	B
S Sgt	Gleo F. Corder	AEG
Sgt	John J. Arazewm	AAEG
S Sgt	George Stiller	ROG
Sgt	Secondo P. Pentacolne	AROG
Sgt	Onnie B. Baskette Jr.	AG
Sgt	Frank R. Machak	AAG

Crew 16 S-5

2LT	Rudolph M. Stohl	P
2LT	David W. Schellenger	CP
2LT	John O. Millham	N
2LT	James E. Thomas	B
M Sgt	Robert C. Kreite	AEG
Sgt	William F. Bemus	AAEG
Sgt	John R. Billington	ROG
Cpl	Sheldon J. Moore	AROG
Sgt	Erwin A. Welling	AG
Sgt	Francis J. Lape	AAG

Crew 16 S-20

2LT	Jesse L. Smith	P
2LT	Ennis E. Brown	CP
2LT	Kenneth Galyean	N
2LT	William G. Party	B
S Sgt	Randall N. White	AEG
Sgt	Milton B. Davison	AAEG
Pvt	Clarence A. Ray	ROG
Sgt	Steve Vargo	AROG
Sgt	Ethan A. Schaeffer	AG
Sgt	Raymond L. Osborn	AAG

Crew 1-0-15

2LT	David P. Parks	P
2LT	Floyd O. Grove	CP
2LT	William C. Ellerbusch	N
2LT	Harold W. Dershimer	B
Sgt	Donald J. Kesselmayer	AEG
Pvt	Cosmo J. Fazzio	AAEG
Sgt	Ruben H. Halverson	ROG
Sgt	Charles M. Kerr	AROG
Sgt	Anthony My. Pasce	AG
Sgt	George H. Grebe	AAG

Crew 16 S-12

2LT	Donald E. Lady	P
2LT	Wade E. Knudson	CP
2LT	Judson Krueger	N
2LT	David B. Jones	B
S Sgt	Bernard L. Baker	AEG
Sgt	William G. Arterburn	AAEG
S Sgt	Marvin H. Sloan	ROG
Sgt	Walter F. Palmer	AROG
Sgt	Carl W. Ostlind	AG
Sgt	Ross Pogue	AAG

Crew 16 S-106

2LT	Benny M. Flowers	P
2LT	Harry E. Cameron	CP
2LT	Roy A. Hoegh, Jr.	N
2LT	Frank H. Pearman	B
Sgt	William L. Finley	AEG
Sgt	Andrew H. Bouchard	AAEG
Sgt	William Zamecnik	ROG
Sgt	Charles O. Lay	AROG
Pvt	Virgil G. Maier	AG
Sgt	Victor U. Meador	AAG

Crew 16 S-16

2LT	Marsden W. Mattatall	P
2LT	John L. Fowler	CP
2LT	Manford Markowitz	N
2LT	Ralph C. Jordan	B
Sgt	Joseph Wesziersc z	AEG
Sgt	Axel R. Olson	AAEG
Sgt	Milton P. Rudd	ROG
S Sgt	Gilbert C. Goode	AROG
Cpl	Anthony J. Nunes	AG
T Sgt	James P. Sullivan	AG

Crew 457S-1

1LT	Edward M. Bender	P
2LT	Charles R. Blackwell	CP
2LT	Earl E. Woodard	N
2LT	Edwin K. Fuller	B
S Sgt	James L. Free	AEG
S Sgt	John P. Sarico	AAEG
S Sgt	Laymon M. Mahan	ROG
S Sgt	Charles O. Webber	AROG
S Sgt	Thomas G. Leahy	AG
S Sgt	Michael Woyurka	AAG

Crew 16 S-17

2LT	Edward B. Dozier	P
2LT	Charles E. Newmeyer	CP
2LT	Alexis P. Umoff	N
2LT	Charles L. Hilton	B
S Sgt	Dwight M. Anderson	AEG
Sgt	Hyman Kalb	AAEG
Sgt	Seymour C. Pliss	ROG
Pfc	Frederick L. Exley	AROG
Sgt	Gerald E. Poston	AG
Sgt	Frank L. Ridenhour	AAG

Crew 16 S-7

1LT	Russell M. Selwyn	P
2LT	William M. Hammersley	CP
2LT	William H. Bowman, Jr.	N
2LT	Warren H. Suddath	B
S Sgt	Arvele Mizell	AEG
Sgt	Truman H. Simley	AAEG
Sgt	Harold B. Rhodes	ROG
Sgt	Oscar C. Hightower	AROG
Sgt	Wayland R. Keefover	AG
Sgt	Clifton H. Harrel	AAG

Crew 16 S-119

2LT	Tracy E. Geiger	P
2LT	Theodore R. Baskette	CP
2LT	Irving R. Meyers	N
2LT	Verne M. Boone	B
T Sgt	Thomas W. Howard	AEG
Pvt	Morgan J. Newman	AAEG
T Sgt	Edward Nabozny	ROG
Sgt	Billy L. Dalton	AROG
S Sgt	Francis W. McCall	AG
Sgt	Sylvester C. Kuraszkiewicz	AAG

Crew 16 S-129

2LT	Alfred W. Fischer	P
2LT	Joseph W. Kell	CP
2LT	John W. McDonnell	N
2LT	Ralph D. Stutzman	B
S Sgt	Robert M. Jensen	AEG
Sgt	Andrew E. Jasso	AAEG
Sgt	James E. Pickle	ROG
Sgt	Leo McHatton	AROG
S Sgt	Thomas N. Norton	AG
Sgt	James H. Long	AAG

Crew 457S-51

2LT	William F. Rogers	P
2LT	Stanley J. Wolczanski	CP
2LT	Wilbert J. Colard	N
2LT	Dino H. Tonelli	B
T Sgt	Joshua D. Lane	AEG
Sgt	Orion H. Shumway	AAEG
T Sgt	John Chumas	ROG
S Sgt	William C. Young	AROG
S Sgt	David H. Quick	AG
S Sgt	Ray Jones	AAG

Crew 16 S-121

2LT	Max R. Morrow	P
2LT	Thomas G. Davis	CP
2LT	Daren A. McIntyre	N
2LT	John B. Blachley	B
S Sgt	George B. Lee	AEG
Sgt	Everett M. Tyler	AAEG
Sgt	David E. Wallace	ROG
Sgt	Bernard E. Harris	AROG
Sgt	Italo Stella	AG
Sgt	Merton R. Cattanach	AAG

Crew 16 S-19

2LT	Clarence E. Schuchmann	P
2LT	Franklin J. Marra	CP
2LT	Thomas A. Goff	N
2LT	Charles S. Gelber	B
S Sgt	Joseph L. Hibbs	AEG
Sgt	Lorne G. Smith	AAEG
Sgt	H. R. Pike	ROG
Sgt	Sanford P. Thorpe	AROG
Sgt	Edgar D. Lanzoni	AG
Sgt	Regis J. McMullen	AAG

Crew 16 S-2

2LT	Americo Procopio	P
2LT	Robert Discoll	CP
2LT	Bernard B. Owingberg	N
2LT	Edward P. Palika	B
S Sgt	John T. Clements	AEG
Sgt	E. L. Angell	AAEG
Sgt	Russell H. Babel	ROG
Sgt	Thaddeus F. Lubej	AROG
Sgt	James R. Norman	AC
Sgt	Walter W. Megin	AAG

Crew 16 S-122

2LT	Francis L. Shaw	P
2LT	William R. Cole	CP
F/O	Carl F. Hansen	N
2LT	Alfred L. Autrey	B
S Sgt	Richard W. Macomber	AEG
Sgt	Carl K. Seagren	AAEG
Sgt	Kenneth A. Terroux	ROG
Sgt	John L. Hurd	AROG
Sgt	Robert T. Gordon	AG
Sgt	Howard S. Kneese	AAG

Crew 16 S-9

1LT	Edwin A. Post	P
2LT	Vincent L. Ledray	CP
2LT	Lionel J. Cusson	N
2LT	Joe C. Wilmeth	B
T Sgt	Emanuel L. Romano	AEG
Sgt	Alva L. Bunger	AAEG
S Sgt	Charles F. Casner	ROG
Sgt	Lawrence F. Brennan	AROG
S Sgt	William G. Cameron	AG
S	Walter F. Thompson, Jr.	AAG

Crew 16 S-14

2LT	Green B. Poore	P
2LT	James F. Oldenhage	CP
2LT	George L. Brice	N
F/O	Frank J. Rowe	B
Sgt	Frederick A. Smith	AEG
Sgt	Oren E. Hobbs	AAEG
S Sgt	John F. Nechak	ROG
Sgt	Lynn W. Rice	AROG
Sgt	George T. Murphy	AG
Sgt	Ralph R. Stowe, Jr.	AAG

Crew 16 S-18

1LT	Milton M. Jaraslow	P
2LT	Joseph S. Norman	CP
2LT	Bert (NMI) Graham	N
2LT	Russell H. Auten	B
Sgt	Charles T. Darnell	AEG
Sgt	Robert L. Jackson	AAEG
Sgt	Nicholas F. Bendino	ROG
Sgt	William L. Stringer	AROC
Sgt	Sidney Vanook	AG
S Sgt	Joseph A. Toth	AAG

Crew 16 S-145

2LT	Kenneth L. Anderson	P
2LT	Kaspar O. O. Lamvik	CP
2LT	Thomas F. Monaghan	N
2LT	Robert J. Larson	B
Sgt	Laurel W. Phillips	AEG
Sgt	Carl F. Gravez	AAEG
Sgt	Raymond J. Daly	ROG
Sgt	Dean K. Adams	AROG
Sgt	Donald J. Doughwright	AAG
Sgt	John W. Brown	AROG

Crew 16 S-4

2LT	Richard T. Bennett	P
2LT	Charles E. Robb	CP
2LT	Charles R. Hunnicutt	N
2LT	Robert F. Lotz	B
Sgt	Deward D. Dunn	AEG
Sgt	Eugene M. Beamer	AAEG
Sgt	George Ribeiro	ROG
Sgt	Robert R. Fowlkes	AROG
S Sgt	Donald J. Lighthizer	AG
S Sgt	Charles L. Campbell	AAG

Crew 16 S-15

2LT	Albert L. Sikkenga	P
2LT	Carl E. Gamblin	CP
2LT	Clifton J. Chandler	N
2LT	Edward C. Cannon	B
Sgt	Jerome A. Fogleman	AEG
Sgt	Helner Beck	AAEG
T Sgt	Lyle W. Johnson	ROG
Sgt	Alton A. Schaffner	AROG
S Sgt	Ralph L. Haldiman	AG
Sgt	George H. Davis	AAG

Crew 1-C-27

2LT	Richard W. Davis	P
2LT	John A. Cooper	CP
2LT	Kenneth S. Perlitch	N
2LT	Leroy A. Coy	B
Sgt	George C. Miller	AEG
Sgt	Glenn A. Fredenburg	AAEG
Sgt	William E. Patton	AROG
Sgt	Donald L. Enslow	AROG
Sgt	William A. Good, Jr.	AG
Sgt	Robert H. Cheathem	AAG

The 36 crews of the Hutchison Provisional Group included the following and they joined the 457th at Wendover Field Utah on 4 December 1943:

Crew s 1

P	2nd Lt	Thomas E. Lee, Jr.
CP	2nd Lt	John M. Bristow
N	2nd Lt	John C. Sherwin
B	2nd Lt	Regis J. Creehan
AEG	S/Sgt	Clayton L. Betterton
ROG	S/Sgt	John R. Barber
AAEG	Sgt	Jasper (NMI) Stewart
AAEG	Sgt	Irvin V. Gerlich
AG	Sgt	Ralph R. Zagorski
AAG	Sgt	John A. Robinson

Crew s 2

P	2nd Lt	Kenneth R. Johnston
CP	2nd Lt	Kenneth W. Brucker
N	F/O	Herbert N. Webb
B	2nd Lt	Harry G. Vaal
AEG	Sgt	Daniel A. Malcom
ROG	Sgt	Nolan V. Claxton
AAEG	Sgt	Francis F. Friedel
AROG	Cpl	Paul O. Connor
AG	Sgt	Gilbert (NMI) Slocum
AAG	Sgt	Edwin D. Waggoner

Crew s 3

P	2nd Lt	Roy E. Graves
CP	2nd Lt	Wayne G. McLeod
N	2nd Lt	James (NMI) Salay
B	2nd Lt	Herbert W. Witte
AEG	S/Sgt	Horace J. Gillespie
ROG	Cpl	Weldon F. Brown
AAEG	Sgt	Donald L. Lillehaug
AROG	Sgt	Robert R. Kent
AG	Sgt	Eldon A. C. Williams
AAG	Cpl	Shirley (NMI) Marx

Crew s 4

P	2nd Lt	James R. Chinn
CP	2nd Lt	R. F. Cooper
N	2nd Lt	Frank J. McNichol
B	2nd Lt	John C. Vollmuth
AEG	S/Sgt	Vito (NMI) Peragine
ROG	Cpl	Robert J. Mullins
AAEG	Sgt	Marion D. Ross
AROG	Cpl	William J. Sullivan, Jr.
AG	Sgt	Dillard V. Engdahl
AAG	Sgt	Jeremiah B. Rolison

Crew s 5

P	2nd Lt	Mark R. Belcher, Jr.
CP	2nd Lt	Bernard V. Conner
N	2nd Lt	Clement H. Marsden
B	F/O	Robert (NMI) Shan
AEG	S/Sgt	Frank W. Aylstock
ROG	Cpl	Edward J. Brazinski
AAEG	Sgt	Carl W. Lewis
AROG	Sgt	James A. McCamey
AG	Sgt	Hal H. Willett
AAG	Sgt	Leo L. Lange

Crew s 6

P	2nd Lt	Roger W. Birkman
CP	2nd Lt	Robert L. Cole
N	2nd Lt	Michael M. Stanko
B	2nd Lt	James M. Cochran, Jr.
AEG	S/Sgt	Raymond (NMI) Koch
ROG	Cpl	Andrew (NMI) Kafka
AAEG	Cpl	John L. Toney
AROG	Sgt	James C. Jones
AG	Sgt	Errol (NMI) Bailey
AAG	Sgt	John (NMI) Buchel

Crew s 7

P	2nd Lt	Kenneth W. Burkhart
CP	2nd Lt	Noble L. Webster, Jr.
N	2nd Lt	William B. Wescott
B	2nd Lt	Julius (NMI) Venerofsky
AEG	Sgt	Earl L. Shaner
ROG	Pfc	Samuel B. Goff, Jr.
AAEG	Sgt	Paul (NMI) Lizura
AROG	S/Sgt	Charles L. Stewart
AG	Sgt	Howard W. Barrier
AAG	Sgt	Sidney N. Erickson

Crew s 8

P	2nd Lt	Frank O. Kuhl
CP	2nd Lt	Edward J. Czupryk
N	2nd Lt	Armand M. Sussman
B	2nd Lt	William C. Urry
AEG	S/Sgt	Charles E. Robbins
ROG	Cpl	Edward (NMI) Shaw, Jr.
AAEG	Sgt	Ray P. Dziadzia
AROG	Sgt	John W. Cole
AG	Cpl	Kenneth A. Rister
AAG	Sgt	Robert D. Funk

Crew s 9

P	2nd Lt	Paul V. Chapman
CP	2nd Lt	James E. Oscher
N	2nd Lt	William C. Albro
B	2nd Lt	George R. Walker
AEG	S/Sgt	Kenneth E. Myers
ROG	Cpl	Richard T. Trundy
AAEG	Sgt	Robert S. Wood
AROG	Sgt	Anthony (NMI) Marrone
AG	Sgt	Waldron S. McGibbon
AAG	Cpl	Mendell L. Segesman

Crew s 10

CP	F/O	Francis G. Bogle
N	2nd Lt	Thomas W. Burns
B	2nd Lt	Alex W. Fisher
AEG	S/Sgt	Cleo F. Corder
ROG	Cpl	George (NMI) Stiller
AAEG	Sgt	John J. Brazem
AROG	Sgt	Onnie B. Baskette, Jr.
AG	Cpl	Secondo T. Tentacalone
AAG	Sgt	Frank R. Machak

Crew s 11

P	2nd Lt	Donald G. Karr
CP	2nd Lt	John E. Height
N	2nd Lt	Richard M. Condon
B	2nd Lt	Joel H. Appel
AEG	S/Sgt	Kenneth M. Krise
ROG	S/Sgt	Morris J. Woodell
AAEG	Sgt	Philip (NMI) Finkelstein
AROG	Sgt	Eugene H. Paprota
AG	Sgt	Paul M. Rogers
AAG	Cpl	Charles L. Edwards

Crew s 12

P	2nd Lt	Clyde R. Weid
CP	2nd Lt	Billy B. Blackman
N	2nd Lt	Earl W. Klatte
B	2nd Lt	Ralph S. Combs
AEG	Cpl	George E. Lynn
ROG	Cpl	Blair L. Holmes
AAEG	Sgt	Edward F. Beers
AROG	Sgt	Raymond L. Moore
AG	Sgt	Henry F. Smith
AAG	Cpl	Emil (NMI) Anderson, Jr.

Crew s 13

P	2nd Lt	Frank A. Huntley
CP	2nd Lt	James V. Elduff
NB	2nd Lt	Reed Bryant
B	2nd Lt	Ras M. Clausen
AEG	S/Sgt	Gilbert C. Goode
ROG	Cpl	Patrick J. Fusci
AAEG	Sgt	Norbert A. Meeuwsen
AROG	S/Sgt	Mildredge C. Dean
AG	Sgt	Clifford F. Duell
AAG	Sgt	Charles R. Carlisle

Crew s 14

P	2nd Lt	Lewis W. Lennartson
CP	2nd Lt	Everett L. Keesee, Jr.
N	2nd Lt	Marsh (NMI) Hovey
B	2nd Lt	Patrick A. Walls
AEG	Sgt	Thomas B. Haag
ROG	Sgt	William T. Graham
AAEG	Sgt	Thomas J. Head
AROG	Sgt	Clyde E. Garnhart
AG	Sgt	Omer (NMI) Fontaine
AAG	Sgt	James E. Blackwell

Crew s 15

P	2nd Lt	Archie F. Bower, Jr.
CP	2nd Lt	William R. Baxendale
N	2nd Lt	Lee E. Hoskins
B	2nd Lt	Richard W. Cooke
AEG	S/Sgt	Frank S. Giordano
ROG	Sgt	Joseph M. Snyder
AAEG	S/Sgt	John W. Popowitz
AROG	Sgt	Jesse J. Hirschberg
AG	Sgt	John J. Waskovich
AAG	Sgt	Wesley W. Schneider, Jr.

Crew s 16

P	2nd Lt	Richard J. Dudek
CP	2nd Lt	Russell M. Debyns
N	2nd Lt	John F. Moore
B	2nd Lt	James H. Coonrod
AEG	Sgt	John J. Connell
ROG	Sgt	John (NMI) Kessock
AAEG	Cpl	Alfred A. Sapory
AROG	Sgt	Henri A. Bouley
AG	Sgt	Harold D. McFarland
AAG	Sgt	Robert E. Bergeron

Crew s 17

P	2nd Lt	Malcom E. Johnson
CP	2nd Lt	Morris H. Shuff
N	2nd Lt	Lewis S. Jaffe
B	2nd Lt	George (NMI) Cahelo
AEG	Sgt	Joseph (NMI) Barbett
AAEG	Sgt	Francis B. Fieseler
AROG	Sgt	Glen W. Barnes
AG	S/Sgt	Leonard A. Smith
AAG	Cpl	Wallace C. Nicholson

Crew s 18

P	2nd Lt	William L. Gibbons
CP	2nd Lt	George J. Bennett
N	2nd Lt	William J. Brandt
B	2nd Lt	Robert K. Creed
AEG	S/Sgt	Harold G. Beams
ROG	Sgt	John R. Graham
AAEG	Sgt	Paul A. Birchem
AROG	Sgt	Jasper L. Smith
AAG	Sgt	Reginald W. Buxton

Crew s 19

P	2nd Lt	Amos W. Shepard
CP	2nd Lt	Ralph O. Hammerstrom
N	2nd Lt	Harley O. Honeberger
B	2nd Lt	Herbert W. Spaulding
AEG	S/Sgt	Joseph E. Fasone
ROG	Sgt	Jon (NMI) Roberts
AAEG	Sgt	Amos T. Bunch
AROG	Sgt	Arnold E. Kaufman
AG	Sgt	William H. Good
AAG	Sgt	Harold E. Smith

Crew s 20

P	2nd Lt	Eugene H. Whalen
CO	2nd Lt	James R. Cawley
N	2nd Lt	George S. McPeake, Jr.
B	2nd Lt	Robert J. Kuncl
AEG	S/Sgt	Robert J. Vaughan
ROG	Cpl	Jerome J. Hartings
AAEG	Sgt	Virgil L. French
AROG	Sgt	John C. McVey
AG	S/Sgt	John F. Tierney
AAG	Sgt	Alphus D. Maddox

Crew s 21

P	2nd Lt	Robert M. Krumm
CP	2nd Lt	Leo R. Green
N	2nd Lt	Roland O. Byers
B	2nd Lt	Robert G. Horn
AEG	S/Sgt	Lawrence J. Walsh
ROG	Cpl	Billy E. Hightower
AAEG	Sgt	Charles J. Hrubos
AROG	Cpl	Anthony W. Vitale
AG	Sgt	John D. Barrett
AAG	Pvt	Anthony J. Tozzi

Crew s 22

P	2nd Lt	Llewellyn G. Bredeson
CP	2nd Lt	George M. Barnes
N	2nd Lt	Robert A. Whitby
B	2nd Lt	Samuel L. Kalman
AEG	S/Sgt	Howard R. Collins
ROG	Cpl	Leonard V. Luchonok
AAEG	Sgt	Louis P. Rigaud
AROG	Sgt	John F. Lewis
AG	Cpl	William H. Schemkel
AAG	Sgt	Walter J. Jutze

Crew s 23

P	2nd Lt	Dana M. Lenkeit
CP	2nd Lt	James R. Irwin
N	2nd Lt	Myrick J. Whiting
B	2nd Lt	Dene C. Gober
AEG	S/Sgt	Morris C. Harp
ROG	Cpl	James E. Fahnestock
AAEG	Sgt	Stephen F. Kleiber
AROG	S/Sgt	Daylia C. Gregory
AG	Cpl	Victor P. Street
AAG	Sgt	Arnold H. Carpenter

Crew s 24

P	2nd Lt	Dan C. Knight
CP	2nd Lt	William B. Huegin
N	2nd Lt	Lawrence T. Cummings
B	2nd Lt	Edward C. Chambers
AEG	S/Sgt	William D. Starter
ROG	Cpl	Charles B. Atcher
AAEG	Sgt	Charles L. Paceley
AROG	Sgt	Frederick L. Cope
AG	Sgt	Charles J. Wilson
AAG	Sgt	William E. Mackowiak

Crew s 25

P	2nd Lt	Robert D. Lane
CP	2nd Lt	Howard E. James
N	2nd Lt	Robert C. Dvorak
B	2nd Lt	Thomas C. Guest
AEG	S/Sgt	Winfred C. Kincaid
ROG	Cpl	John E. Misener
AAEG	Sgt	Joe D. McCall
AROG	Sgt	George J. Shukaitis
AG	S/Sgt	Garvin E. McBride
AAG	Sgt	James O. Vaughan

Crew s 26

P	2nd Lt	Garland M. Hutson
CP	2nd Lt	Edwin S. Jones
N	2nd Lt	Elmer W. Engelhardt
B	2nd Lt	Clifford D. Hughes
AEG	Sgt	Charles O. Coffman
ROG	Pfc	Harold E. Reader
AAEG	Sgt	Howard C. Layton
AROG	Sgt	Solomon W. Brackman
AG	S/Sgt	Jachin M. Forbes
AAG	Sgt	George A. Pfeifer

Crew s 27

P	2nd Lt	Stephen J. Lozinski
CP	2nd Lt	Eldon R. Child
N	F/O	Louis S. Rush
B	2nd Lt	Harold E. Hughes
AEG	S/Sgt	Michael J. Mercurio
ROG	Cpl	Bernard J. Weber
AAEG	Sgt	Kenneth E. Brock
AROG	Sgt	Irwin I. Friedman
AG	Sgt	John A. Williams
AAG	Sgt	James F. Keller

Crew s 28

P	2nd Lt	Claude M. Kolb
CP	2nd Lt	Milton F. Maloney
N	2nd Lt	Raph R. Emdel
B	2nd Lt	Edward C. Jones
AEG	S/Sgt	Fred H. Webb
ROG	Cpl	Edward (NMI) Wallach
AAEG	Sgt	Clarence S. Conerty
AROG	Sgt	Luther A. Raymer
AG	Sgt	Leo A. Podlasck
AAG	Sgt	Frank R. Lutzi

Crew s 29

P	2nd Lt	Emanuel (NMI) Hauf
CP	2nd Lt	Donald V. Swain
N	2nd Lt	William R. Hawley
B	2nd Lt	Richard E. Jaqua
AEG	S/Sgt	Willis H. Johnson
ROG	Cpl	James J. Kilroy
AAEG	Sgt	Percy H. Davis
AROG	Sgt	Joseph S. Reid
AG	Sgt	Donald A. Lawrence
AAG	Sgt	Louis F. Boske

Crew s 30

P	2nd Lt	Jerome E. Godfrey
CP	2nd Lt	John E. Grimes
N	2nd Lt	Charles E. Graf
B	2nd Lt	Houston L. Levers
AEG	Sgt	Alfred E. Calhoun
ROG	Sgt	Donald W. Blackwell
AAEG	Sgt	Leroy W. Heibert
AROG	Sgt	James E. Doerr, Jr.
AG	Sgt	Carl A. Robbie
AAG	Sgt	George T. Gulywasz

Crew s 31

P	2nd Lt	John W. Fay
CP	2nd Lt	James E. Carels
N	2nd Lt	Bernard N. H. Hirsch
B	2nd Lt	James V. Walsh
AEG	Sgt	Edward T. Sawyer
ROG	Pfc	George H. Staudt
AAEG	Sgt	William A. Spoerner
AROG	Sgt	Richard M. Bassett
AG	Sgt	Frederick G. Wagner
AAG	Sgt	Hugh C. Arant

Crew s 32

P	2nd Lt	Louis O. Auld
CP	2nd Lt	Jack (NMI) Gumm
N	2nd Lt	Jerome (NMI) Silverman
B	2nd Lt	Alden N. Rittman
AEG	S/Sgt	Carl D. Siebrands
ROG	Cpl	Lloyd C. Walton
AROG	Sgt	Nicholas P. Weber
AG	Sgt	Joseph (NMI) Bryan, Jr.
AAG	Sgt	William H. Murry

Crew s 33

P	1st Lt	Leroy S. Lassegard
CP	2nd Lt	Seymour E. Diamond
N	2nd Lt	Charles R. Hunnicut
B	2nd Lt	Russell H. Auten
AEG	Cpl	Joseph F. Faughn
ROG	Cpl	Donald L. Enslow
AAEG	Sgt	Paul R. Moore
AROC	Sgt	John W. Brown
AG	Sgt	Richard (NMI) Mellott
AAG	Sgt	Robert H. Cheathem

Crew s 34

P	2nd Lt	Stuart H. James
CP	2nd Lt	Martin W. Biehn
N	2nd Lt	Charles C. Canon
B	2nd Lt	John J. Cides
AEG	Sgt	Ora W. Murch
ROG	Cpl	Patrick C. Toomey
AAEG	Sgt	Angelo J. Ruscito
AROG	Sgt	Eugene G. Goslee
AG	Sgt	Carl N. Davis
AAG	Sgt	Dale L. Vance

Crew s 35

P	2nd Lt	Clyde R. Knipfer
CP	2nd Lt	Richard A. Bruha
N	2nd Lt	George R. Derdzinski
B	2nd Lt	Stanley V. Gray
AEG	Sgt	Stephen T. Voit
ROG	Cpl	Harvey M. Conover
AAEG	Sgt	Harvey C. Cottrell
AROG	Sgt	Nicholas W. Furrie
AG	Sgt	Joshua (NMI) Goldstein
AAG	Sgt	Percy (NMI) Waltho

Crew s 36

P	2nd Lt	Douglas V. Hickerson
CP	2nd Lt	J. B. Latham
N	2nd Lt	Frank S. Jackson
B	2nd Lt	Marlin D. Greenawalt
AEG	S/Sgt	Lionel W. Havlas
ROG	Cpl	David M. Gerber
AAEG	Sgt	Kneeland I. Parshley
AROG	Sgt	Leland E. Mills
AG	Sgt	Joseph J. Maer
AAG	Sgt	Frank L. Croft, Jr.